# THE OLDEST PROFESSION

Emma Procter, English prostitute. Anonymous photo, *c* 1860

# THE OLDEST PROFESSION

## AN ILLUSTRATED HISTORY OF PROSTITUTION

HILARY EVANS

with the Mary Evans Picture Library

DAVID & CHARLES
Newton Abbot London

**British Library Cataloguing in Publication Data**

Evans, Hilary
The oldest profession
1. Prostitution—History
I. Title II. Mary Evans Picture Library
301.41'54'09 HQ111

ISBN 0-7153-7792-2



Typeset by ABM Typographics Limited, Hull
and printed in Great Britain
by Redwood Burn Limited Trowbridge and Esher
for David & Charles (Publishers) Limited
Brunel House Newton Abbot Devon

# *CONTENTS*

The men, I have no feelings about. I'm just lucky they feel about sex the way they do and are willing to pay for it.

Betty B., call-girl

If there were no customers, there certainly would be no whorehouses.

Polly Adler, brothel proprietor

There are times when I think the prostitute today needs to be half a psycho-analyst.

Sheila Cousins, streetwalker

If they don't like the brothels, they needn't go to them.

Charles II, King of England

# *PREFACE*

An unmarried mother in a squalid apartment in Greenwich Village—or Bayswater—or Saint Germain-des-Prés—offers access to her diseased body to earn the price of milk for her baby and drugs for herself. The social worker who has to deal with her case has the right to ask, what the hell good can it do to learn about the temple prostitutes of ancient Babylon, the rantings of the early Christian fathers, the child prostitutes of Victorian London, the splendours and miseries of the French courtesans?

Agreed, reading this history is unlikely to help that particular girl in that particular predicament. But it may help to prevent such a predicament recurring. An enormous proportion of the confused thinking and writing on the subject of prostitution—including that still being produced today—would be avoided if the historical background were properly studied. Even a dedicated reformer like Josephine Butler, whose courage and sincerity are beyond question, would have made a more useful contribution if she could have seen her subject in a wider perspective. A broad view of the errors and misconceptions of the past is the surest way to avoid similar pitfalls in the future.

But though our history takes the broad view, it is not our aim to stand so far back from the subject as to become clinical and detached. Far from it; as far as possible, we have derived our material from the views and comments of prostitutes and customers themselves. This history is about one of the most universally popular of human activities, in one of its most widespread and enduring manifestations. Even though it is anything but a sensational book, you will not read it with the same detachment with which you would read a motorcycle handbook or a cookbook, a military history or a book of political argument. You will almost certainly already have your own views on the subject, and they probably do not wholly correspond with our own.

No matter; the important thing is that you are ready to give the subject thought, thus distinguishing yourself from the large proportion of mankind who, even in these enlightened days, would prefer not to acknowledge the prostitute's existence or concern themselves with the problems her existence creates. For ultimately it is ignorance which underlies the bigotry and prejudice that still bedevil the subject; in this historical record, it is ignorance we hope to help to dispel.

## MALE AND FEMALE CREATED HE THEM?

Just as heterosexuality is more widespread than homosexuality, so the prostitution of women to men has always been more widespread than that of men to men or women to women; the prostitution of men to women is on a smaller scale still, for social and biological reasons which we shall touch on later. Nevertheless male homosexual prostitution has existed for as long as female prostitution, throughout every period and in virtually every society.

Unfortunately the taboo respecting male prostitution is very much stricter even than that respecting female prostitution. The institution itself has always had to be more clandestine and, even when it has been practised relatively openly, it has not been written or spoken about openly. Public attitudes to homosexuality have always involved responses of extraordinary virulence, for which psychologists no doubt have their explanations; but one consequence is that, with the best will in the world, the historian cannot treat the subject with the thoroughness it deserves. The materials are simply not there. What is clear, however, and what we ask the reader to assume throughout this history, is that in every age, every society, homosexuals were provided for by social institutions, and that in most cases male prostitution was flourishing on a scale not much below that of the heterosexual version.

For social reasons—chiefly the simple fact that in most societies and most periods women have been compelled to be more stay-at-home than men—female homosexuality has not often taken the form of female-to-female prostitution; though not entirely non-existent, it has never become the organised institution that heterosexual, and to some extent male homosexual, prostitution have become.

Because a prostitute may be either male or female, we would not wish to give offence to those who are striving for sex equality by suggesting otherwise; but even the most dedicated anti-sexist would grow restive if, every time a prostitute is referred to—that is, several times on each page—we were conscientiously to spell out 'she or he'. So, since female prostitutes preponderate numerically over their brothers, we have used the word 'she' wherever a prostitute *per se* is intended. We would ask the reader to accept this as standing for 'she or he'—just as, when he or she uses the word 'mankind', he or she understands this to refer to both sexes alike.

### SOURCES

The material for this book has been drawn from a vast number of sources; if we were to indicate this in every instance, the text would be overloaded with footnotes and references. As this history is intended for the general reader rather than the scholar, we have thought it sufficient to indicate specific sources only when that information is relevant—for instance, when quoting the views of a particular authority—and, for the rest, to list at the end of the book the most important of our sources, giving the reader our assurance that every fact and every figure has the backing of some authority.

### ILLUSTRATIONS

All the illustrations are from the Mary Evans Picture Library, with the following exceptions:

Bibliothèque Nationale, Paris: 165
Chicago Historical Society: 204
Werner Forman, London: 176
Marvin Newman, New York: 226, 227
Preussischer Kulturbesitz: 52, 54, 60, 194, 199
Rex Features, London: 211, 218
Sven Simon, Bonn: 244
State Historical Society of Wisconsin: 209

# 1
# THE OLDEST PROFESSION

What school-leaver, consulting her career guidance officer, has it suggested to her that she might consider becoming a prostitute rather than a nurse or a computer programmer? What bookshops stock instruction manuals on How to Succeed as a Prostitute? The work is relatively well paid, demands a minimum of training, and can be seen as performing a socially beneficial function. Yet only in very restricted sections of society is it regarded as a viable career option to become a prostitute.

Nevertheless this has been the way of life chosen by a substantial proportion of working women, as well as a sizeable number of men, in almost every culture, every country, every period. In the year Jesus was born, there were 36,000 of their kind registered in Rome, besides innumerable unlisted amateurs. In 1170 the Abbot of San Pelayo, Spain, kept seventy for his personal use. In 1189 the French Crusaders took a shipload of 300 to cater for their needs, maybe fearing that the Holy Land might live up to its name. In 1501 Pope Alessandro VI invited fifty to a party, had them strip and dance naked, then watched the young men of his establishment compete to fuck the greatest number. In Paris in the 1760s, while the philosopher Diderot was writing his *Encyclopédie* in which the prostitute rates a three-and-a-half line mention, there was one of her trade among every eight marriageable females; a century later, and on the other side of the globe in Amoy, China, she numbered one in ten of the female population. In Birmingham, England, in 1844, she plied her trade in 797 houses, competing with countless others who worked in the streets; in New York during the same decade there was one to satisfy the needs of every seven men. In times of peace, men have paid hundreds of pounds for a few hours of her services; in times of war,

'That? That's my Higher Certificate!' J. L. Forain in *Le Journal*, 1893

they have stood in line for hours in anticipation of two or three short and brutish minutes with her at the cost of a few shillings. In the USA in 1948 more than two out of three white males admitted having used her services on at least one occasion. And yet it is more than likely that in any account of any society during any period she will not be mentioned.

The prostitute's trade is by tradition the oldest profession. It is also, as this random selection of statistics shows, quite simply the largest and the most widespread. On a purely quantitative basis, the prostitute plays a substantial role in the fabric of society. Why, then, the silence?

Of course we know why. The prostitute follows a way of life which is in conscious defiance of a universal taboo on sexual promiscuity. But answering that question only leaves an underlying one to be answered. That taboo has existed in virtually every culture, and yet, in spite of it, prostitution too has existed in virtually every culture. Why, given the taboo, has prostitution been permitted to exist? Alternatively, given the persistence of prostitution, how has the taboo retained its force?

Prostitution came into being because marriage, which in some form or other is the fundamental unit of almost every social structure, is inadequate to meet all of society's sexual needs. To take just one example, there is the inconvenient biological fact that humans reach puberty before they attain social responsibility. Do you marry them off while they are still psychologically too immature to cope with the demands of married life—or do you hold down the lid on their sexual urges until they are old enough to be married? Prostitution offers a way out of the dilemma.

Another awkward biological fact: most men and women would like to enjoy more frequent and more rewarding sexual experiences than most social structures can allow. Consciously or subconsciously, almost every woman would like to play the whore, at least occasionally, just as almost every man, at least occasionally, would like to consort with a

The taboo creates hypocrisy: a German *Ladenbordellhaus*—a brothel disguised as a milliners' workshop—in the 1830s. From a drawing by Johann Erdmann Hummel

Victorian sportsmen and 'sporting ladies' meet on Boat Race night in a public house in the West End of London. From *The Day's Doings*, 1871

Confused thinking: in times of war, public opinion rounds on the prostitute. During the Franco-Prussian War of 1870, the street girls were rounded up and packed into prison. Similarly, in 1941, the Americans enforced the laws against prostitution as never before. From *L'Illustration*, 1870

variety of women. But sexual promiscuity is socially disruptive, so it must be prevented; and, because ordinary rules are not strong enough to restrain man's most powerful urge, it must be controlled by extraordinary means. So a frontier of respectability is set up. Different cultures set it closer or farther, permitting less or more freedom; but, strict or slack, the taboo-line is there, and those who cross it must expect to be treated as a class apart—tolerated, perhaps, but ostracised none the less.

The situation that results is, of course, a paradox, and to live with both prostitution and the taboo against prostitution requires one to be either a hypocrite or a cynic. Throughout history, except in the rare instances where the taboo itself has not existed or has been disregarded, public attitudes to prostitution have swung uneasily between cynicism and hypocrisy. Today, in Western Europe, a few societies have come closer to a true acceptance of the prostitute than ever before in history. But the paradox will never be entirely resolved until we have dispensed with the taboo, and that will not happen till we have learnt to see the prostitute both as a social component and as an individual, recognising what we want from her and also why she is willing to supply what we want.

The Roman writer Ulpianus defined the prostitute as a woman who openly abandons her body to a number of men, unselectively and for money; in the twenty centuries which have followed, it has not proved easy to take his definition much farther. Havelock Ellis, the outstanding sexologist of the early twentieth century, suggested that she is a person who makes it a profession to gratify the lust of several persons. Kinsey, closer to our time, defines her as an individual who indiscriminately provides sexual relations in return for money payments. But these, like all the thousands of other attempted definitions we refrain from quoting, are too limiting. It is incorrect to limit the definition to women only. It is incorrect to use the word 'profession' when many prostitutes are moonlighting amateurs. It is incorrect to call her indiscriminate; a high-class Paris brothel or New York call-girl are as exclusive as a three-star Paris restaurant or fashionable New York analyst. Perhaps it is best to say simply that a prostitute is a person who exchanges sexual intimacy with herself for material reward, as opposed to granting it as a no-strings-attached gift out of love, lust, pity, for career advancement or domestic tranquillity. Or, of course, in order to become a parent.

The favours themselves remain fundamentally the same, in most cases (though by no means all) comprising the bringing to orgasm of the customer in one or more of the limited number of available ways, in return for a payment usually in cash. One might suppose, therefore, that the transaction would be straightforward enough—a preliminary negotiation of terms, followed by the fulfilment of the contract. Yet so complex are the psychological, emotional and sociological factors involved, that the basically simple act, designed by nature (who recognised that while engaged in copulation the participants would be highly vulnerable to their enemies) to be completable in two or three minutes, is executed in a dazzling variety of forms ranging from simple fun to the perverse and the downright pathological. Man the Artificer, always ready to demonstrate his superiority to nature by improving on her efforts, has evolved innumerable sophistications, till in the hands of a truly skilled performer the act of sex is raised to a work of art just as raw foodstuffs are caused by a master chef to transcend their basic nature.

Specialised establishments are created where the act may be more effectively or enjoyably performed. Special apparatus is devised to enhance that provided by nature. All this inevitably calls for financial outlay, often on a very lavish scale, until an act that can be performed for a few pence in a hurried cut-and-thrust against an alley wall will, when conducted in a luxuriously furnished establishment with a carefully trained partner armed with an arsenal of sophisticated weaponry, cost a thousand times as much.

And even this is not all. Because there are powerful social forces involved, the participants are liable to all manner of pressures which in turn affect what is done and where and how. Often the entire operation has to be clandestine; nearly always it has to be discreet. Thus an opportunity for criminal exploitation is created, and with it the need for police surveillance and legal safeguards, until society ends up protecting activities of which it nominally disapproves. So, while the prostitute and her client are busy with their brief exchange, all sorts of third parties are involved: the prostitute's pimp, ponce or procurer; the madam and the staff of the premises where she works; the madam's financial backers and 'protectors'; lawyers who try to maintain a semblance of control even when the act itself is illegal; police who may or may not seek to enforce the law; the medical authorities and the social workers with their respective interests; and the moralists and preachers who conceive it their business to tell the prostitute and her customer that they shouldn't be doing it anyway.

Well, should they or shouldn't they? Before we try to answer that, we ought first to consider why it is that, since the dawn of time, the prostitute and her customer have obstinately challenged the taboo, defied the moralists, the preachers and the lawyers, submitted to the madams, the blackmailers and the pimps.

The act of prostitution, by any definition, requires—like any other sales transaction—a minimum cast of two. A self-evident fact? You'd think so, yet an astonishing number of those who have tried to analyse the nature of prostitution have concentrated their efforts on the supplier and disregarded the purchaser. Clearly, though, as the American madam Polly Adler puts it with her customary lucidity, 'If there were no customers, there would certainly be no whorehouses.' For the primary causes of prostitution, we must look first to the customer.

We may start with the fact that, on a purely social level, in many cultures the prevailing moral codes do not allow men access, outside marriage, to women of their own cultural and social level. When unmarried men are prevented from having sexual relations with unmarried women of their own class, a prostitute is often the only alternative. Even today, most Latin/Catholic countries provide examples of this, where young men traditionally get their first experience of sex in brothels. In such circumstances the professional prostitute is preferred because there is less danger of contracting disease; knowing that her trade would be impaired by any infection, she is more likely to look after her health, and will know how to do so more effectively, than the housewife earning pocket-money on the side or the party-girl who is simply doing it for kicks.

Moreover, in most societies a man must invest considerable time and effort in acquiring sufficient familiarity with a respectable girl to get her to grant him sexual favours. Even if a man is prepared to make the effort, often he hasn't the time, particularly if a temporary relationship is all he's after anyway. Paradoxically, too, the cost of seducing a girl—the dinners, theatre tickets, flowers and chocolates—can easily outweigh that of frequenting a professional prostitute.

Many men are denied the opportunity for normal sexual relations by some physical deformity, some psychological hang-up acquired during upbringing, or simply because they are downright ugly. For such a customer the only solution may be the prostitute with her lower threshold of tolerance, the incentive of reward, and the comforting knowledge that the connection will be only a temporary one. Anne Salva, a French prostitute forced out of work when the brothels in her country were closed in 1946, wrote in her memoirs:

> The majority of our customers, most of them middle class, were unbalanced, obsessed or vicious. According to my own experience and that of my colleagues, at least 40 per cent of brothel clients are sexually abnormal. When our place closed we asked one another, with malicious amusement, to which of those respectable ladies who had voted to close the brothels, the various sadists, flagellants, chain-maniacs and ludicrous masochists, who had formerly come to us, would now turn? While we were packing, we kept thinking of the incest-oriented clients whom we had always to remember to call 'Dad' unless they happened to be characters who called us 'Mother' or by the name of one of their sisters, not to mention the frequent visitors who, not daring to approach boys, forced us women to play Adonis to them . . . All those prosperous citizens, respectfully saluted throughout the neighbourhood, tender husbands and affectionate fathers, arrogant lawyers, eminent doctors and eloquent politicians, were in truth mentally sick. For the most part their wives had no idea of the nature and degree of their aberrations. It was only to us that they dared make their appalling demands.
>
> (*Je n'en rougis pas*)

Today we acknowledge that certain types of sexual behaviour, formerly stigmatised as 'abnormal', should be seen rather as minority needs, which should be gratified both to preserve the emotional equilibrium of the individual and to protect society from the consequences if he were repressed. But it isn't easy to win a wife's or girl-friend's co-operation when (as in one of Havelock Ellis's case histories) you can achieve orgasm only at the sight of a pigeon having its neck wrung by a naked girl. Even so widespread a deviation as fellatio, which the American psychologist Greenwald estimates is requested by nineteen out of twenty prostitutes' clients, is (literally) not to the taste of many legitimate sexual partners. The man with such urges will generally prefer to avoid embarrassment and patronise a professional for whom such activities are part of the daily round, one who will not feel—or at least will try not to show—any repulsion.

Throughout history and in all parts of the world it has been accepted as a basic human characteristic that the male is more likely than the female to want sexual relations with a variety of partners. Of recent years and particularly among feminists this inequitous state of affairs has been questioned; but evidence continues to support it, and the American sexologist Kinsey comments:

The effects of a peepshow. Reznicek, *c* 1908

> The capacity of many males to respond to *any* type of female is a demonstration of the fact that psychologic conditioning, rather than the physical or the psychologic stimuli that are immediately present, is a chief source of his erotic response. As far as his psychologic responses are concerned, the male in many instances may not be having coitus with the immediate sexual partner, but with all the other girls with whom he has ever had coitus, and with the entire genus Female with whom he would like to have coitus.
>
> (*Sexual Behavior in the Human Male*, 1948)

Havelock Ellis, in more human terms, states:

> Even men who are happily married to women in all chief respects fitted to them, are apt to feel, after some years of married life, a mysterious craving for variety. They are not tired of their wives, they have not the least wish or intention to abandon them, they will not, if they can help it, give them the slightest pain. But from time to time they are led by an almost irresistible and involuntary impulse to seek a temporary intimacy with women to whom nothing would persuade them to join themselves permanently.
>
> (*The Psychology of Sex*, 1910)

He goes on to describe the appeal the prostitute has for many men, particularly in sophisticated cultures:

> The prostitute appeals by her fresh and natural coarseness, her frank familiarity with the crudest facts of life; and so lifts her customer for a moment out of the withering atmosphere of artificial thought and unreal sentiment in which so many civilised persons are compelled to spend the greater part of their lives.

Even to the man who wouldn't dream of deserting his cultural and social level permanently, the company of a blatant tart can be as welcome as a visit to a music-hall for a person whose more lasting theatrical preference is for Verdi or Racine.

The ultimate reason for patronising a prostitute can be, quite simply, *because* she is a prostitute. Not merely because she is more likely to give him sexual satisfaction, but because the transaction is openly commercial. The very reason which repels some is precisely that which appeals to others. The customer has paid for the prostitute's services, a bargain has been struck; now he feels relaxed, under no further obligation.

Many of these motivations emerged when the French writer Marguerite Duras interviewed an unnamed prostitute, who told her:

To us, all customers are pretty much alike. Always the same categories. The one who talks too much—he's a bore and a time-waster; what he really needs is a girl-friend, only he hasn't got one . . . The client who's having trouble with his love-life, though he's not a very common type . . . The client who doesn't want to saddle himself with a mistress . . . The one who's married, who's got a mistress, who's got a girl-friend as well, and who comes just to shoot off a quick round; he doesn't give a damn about us, but he's the best kind, quick off the mark and no mucking about . . . There's the client who grows amorous—it happens to every whore; they write verses—I've got a whole packet from one affectionate customer . . . The show-off, who insists on telling you about his yacht—and like as not leaves you with a lousy fiver . . . The idiot who reckons *he's* giving *us* a thrill . . .

Not every man would find Black Sarah to his taste, but she was a popular character on the Ratcliffe Highway, in London's East End, in the 1830s. From *The Town*, 1837

And the vicious clients; but you don't meet them when you're working the street, they go to the houses where they can ask Madame for just what they've got in mind. I'm sorry for them, but once they've done their business, they're alright. With us, they're no trouble. That's what we're here for.

(*France-Observateur*, 1963)

Whether its basis is sociological or psychological, there is evidently a clear demand for the prostitute's services. But it is a demand which comes for the most part from the less attractive members of the community; the working conditions are seldom congenial; disapproval is the least hostile attitude she can expect from society as a whole, and she may have to struggle to overcome her own personal feelings. Nevertheless, despite these discouragements, there has seldom been a shortage of prostitutes; supply has nearly always been more than enough to meet the demand. What inducements and incentives attract a girl into this trade?

The prostitute as victim: a girl fresh from the country falls into the hands of a procuress in eighteenth-century London. The first scene from Hogarth's *The Harlot's Progress*

The traditional cause is familiar enough:

> She was poor, but she was honest,
> Victim of another's whim.
> First he loved her, then he left her,
> And she lost her honest name.

Seduction indeed accounts for a number of recruits to prostitution, especially when it results in pregnancy which, in the traditional stories, it statistic-defyingly did. The kindly officers of the Salvation Army, as described in General Booth's *Darkest England*, were ready to believe the seduced-and-abandoned story no matter how often they heard it, but more sceptical investigators found that not every clergyman's daughter was as naive as she seemed.

The simple fact that a girl can earn far more than in any other way, and earn it far more easily, by lying on her back and spreading her legs, is evident to every female. Faced with a choice between starvation on the one hand, and overcoming an instinctive reluctance on the other, it is hardly surprising that women in desperate situations have at all times turned to prostitution as the way out. This is particularly evident when moral obstacles have been eroded by a general breakdown in morale, as in Germany in the 1920s or Italy during the latter phases of World War II. More often it is not out-and-out necessity that compels the hesitating recruit but the chance of rapidly and dramatically improving her standard of living. The French prostitute Marie-Thérèse wrote in 1964:

> Before, most of them worked in humble and poorly-paid occupations. It's a rare girl who, once she's taken that first step, will have either the strength or the will to retrace that step. She's got into the habit of having banknotes in her handbag, visiting her hairdresser every week, taking a cab wherever she goes, living in a hotel where she doesn't have to bother with housekeeping, working just when it suits her. She's not lightly going to trade all this in for a 'normal' way of life.
>
> (*Histoire d'une prostituée*)

Nor is the work necessarily so uncongenial, especially compared with the alternatives. Moralists who mock at phrases like 'woman of pleasure' and '*fille de joie*', as though the only pleasure in the prostitute's life is what she gives her clients, are judging by their own standards. No doubt ladies of taste feel little attraction to a series of temporary relationships with strange men perhaps of low social status and frequently drunk; but for

THE GREAT SOCIAL EVIL.

TIME:—Midnight. A Sketch not a Hundred Miles from the Haymarket.

*Bella.* "AH! FANNY! HOW LONG HAVE YOU BEEN *GAY*?"

'The Great Social Evil'. Prostitutes in the Haymarket, London. John Leech in *Punch*, 1857. It is alleged that this unique appearance by prostitutes in the ultra-respectable *Punch* of the Victorian era was secretly managed while the editor was on holiday girls from a less refined background this is not so unattractive a prospect. A career offering a continual succession of relationships with members of the opposite sex possesses a variety and piquancy which other life-styles lack. The sociologist Meyrick Booth gave this account of girls working in a London department store in 1929:

> In a large hostel 80 girls live together, 3 in each bedroom, the average wage being about £2 per week. The hours are from about 9 till 6.30. The life is one of unutterable monotony. There is no social life: the girls do not even possess a social room in the hostel; and the worst day of the week is felt to be Sunday. Small wonder that no small proportion of those girls find that the only way open to them of bringing some life into the drab round of their existence is by way of the 'kind young gentlemen' whom they meet as they stroll along the streets.
>
> (*Women and Society*)

By contrast, many descriptions of life in a well-conducted brothel show it to be a comfortable, easy-going existence, of friendly camaraderie during the day and with a non-stop party every night of the week. Of course, it isn't always like that—as we shall see—and, even if it were, it wouldn't be every woman's idea of a well-spent life; but there are less attractive fates.

In a celebrated passage, the Victorian moral historian Lecky wrote of the prostitute:

> The supreme type of vice, she is ultimately the most efficient guardian of virtue. But for her, the unchallenged purity of countless happy homes would be polluted, and not a few who, in the pride of their untempted chastity, think of her with an indignant shudder, would have known the agony of remorse and despair. On that one degraded and ignoble form are concentrated the passions which might have filled the world with shame. She remains, while creeds and civilisations rise and fall, the eternal priestess of humanity, blasted for the sins of the people.
>
> (*History of European Morals*, 1869)

His sentiments have been echoed by many prostitutes, though more usually in some such formulation as 'It's the likes of us what saves your sisters from getting raped!' Briefly and temporarily, the prostitute is *wanted* by her customers, and in a fierce and exciting way. This psychological fact can be a source of self-confidence and reassurance to a girl who otherwise receives no indication from society that she is anything

'I wonder why they call us *filles de joie*?' Th.Th. Heine in *Simplicissimus*, 1906

but an outcast. Though this sense of fulfilling a social role is not likely to provide a reason for becoming a prostitute in the first instance—few welfare workers will take their philanthropy quite so far—it can be a reason for staying in the business. Here is Polly Adler again:

> If I could think of myself as fulfilling a need, as one in a long line which stretched back to the beginning of civilisation, then, no matter what stigma was attached to my calling, at least I was not 'anti-social'. I had a job to do, and I could find satisfaction in doing it the very best way I knew how.
>
> (*A House is Not a Home*, 1953)

Does it take a woman of a particular temperament to feel the force of these incentives? In Britain the Wolfenden Committee on Homosexual Offences and Prostitution reported in 1957:

> The great majority of prostitutes are women whose psychological make-up is such that they choose this life because they find in it a style of living which

> is to them easier, freer, and more profitable than would be provided by any other occupation.

The suggestion of an inherent difference in character or temperament is guaranteed to have contemporary sociologists and feminists up in arms. Yet this is what a prostitute herself has to say on the matter:

> If you ask a prostitute how she got there, you can be pretty sure her answer will be a superficial one—maybe because she doesn't choose to give you her true reason, maybe because she can't, because the roots of her reason are the roots of her life itself. I don't for a moment imagine it would be true to say that it's the same reason for every one of us. It could be a certain feebleness of character which we all share, which made each of us give way before circumstances or yield to influences which had led us to the point where we had to choose between being a prostitute or not, but this word feebleness is an umbrella word, which covers a wide range of human fallibility. But one thing is certain, that feebleness of character alone isn't enough to bring a girl onto the pavement.
>
> (XXX, *My Life as a Prostitute*, 1960)

Such, briefly sketched, are some of the reasons why men need prostitutes and why women are willing to become prostitutes. (It is understood that, with the appropriate transpositions, the same applies to homosexual prostitution and to traffic in which the male prostitutes himself to the female.) The history of the trade that has grown up in consequence—the subject matter of this book—is the story, sometimes tragic and sometimes comic, of how people in different societies and cultures, in different parts of the world at different times, have tried to control supply and demand, and to live with an institution which in principle they deplore.

# 2
# *HOMAGE TO APHRODITE*

You have gone on business to a strange town. Being a religious man, you visit the cathedral—and, as a mark of respect, you pick out one of the girls who work there, and have sex with her. She thanks you for the offering you subsequently make to the cathedral restoration fund, and you go on your way with the satisfaction of having performed a pious deed.

Barbaric, you think? Yet such customs were widespread over many centuries in countries which, from their works of art and codes of law and other relics, we know to have reached a high degree of cultural and social development.

We cannot be sure which came first, religious or secular prostitution, but both existed as far back as any social records survive. The legal codes of Assyria, for example, dated about 1100 BC, contain explicit regulations about prostitution which clearly distinguish between religious and secular prostitutes. A prostitute plays a vital role in one of the earliest of all literary works, the Assyrian *Epic of Gilgamesh*, probably composed about 2000 BC. The ruler Gilgamesh is anxious to subdue the wild hero Enkidu, who lives in the desert with his flocks; Gilgamesh sends a prostitute to reduce his enemy's strength:

> The whore untied her loin-cloth and spread her legs,
> and he took possession of her beauty.
> For six days and seven nights
> Enkidu came to the harlot and lay with her.
> When he had had enough of her charms
> he once again turned his face towards his prey,
> but now the gazelles fled before him,
> and when Enkidu tried to pursue them
> his knees failed him. He had become feeble,
> and his strength was not as it had been.

Though any reconstruction of the development of religious prostitution must be largely conjectural, it is not difficult to discern its origins. In primitive communities, every aspect of life is governed by religious checks and sanctions, and this is particularly true of sexual behaviour, which if uncontrolled can cause so much social disruption. So the everyday management of sex is subject to strict regulation which seeks to establish a workable balance between what people want to do as individuals and what they can be allowed to do as members of the community. This is dramatically evident in two of the countless ways in which sex was involved in the life of the community: fertility and defloration.

> For four days before they committed the seed to the earth, the Pipiles of Central America kept apart from their wives in order that on the night before planting they might indulge their passions to the fullest extent: certain persons are even said to have been appointed to perform the sexual act at the very moment when the first seeds are deposited in the ground.
>
> (Sir J. G. Frazer, *The Golden Bough*, 1922)

Taking out an insurance policy on next year's harvest has always been a vital function in community life, and customs designed to effect it are found in every culture. They invariably have a sexual character; here are two more of Frazer's examples:

> In some parts of Java, at the season when the bloom will soon be on the rice, the husbandman and his wife visit their fields by night and there engage in sexual intercourse for the purpose of promoting the growth . . .
>
> In some parts of Germany at harvest the men and women who have reaped the corn roll together on the field. This is probably a mitigation of an older and ruder custom.

By what seems to be a natural process, the observances would as time went on become more formalised. Rites which had formerly been performed in the harvest field would be transferred to sacred groves, and then to temples built on sacred sites. The rites themselves would come to be performed not by the community as a whole but by chosen representatives. So, from rolling around in the cornfield and copulating at seedtime, our ancestors progressed to a state of affairs in which certain appointed persons performed sexual acts on specific occasions in honour of a fertility deity.

Whether she was named Ishtar, Astarte, Ashtoreth, Isis, Aphrodite or Venus, this deity was worshipped in much the same way:

> We may conclude that a great Mother Goddess, the personification of all the reproductive energies of nature, was worshipped under different names but with a substantial similarity of myth and ritual by many peoples of Western Asia—that associated with her was a lover, or rather series of lovers, divine yet mortal, with whom she mated year by year, their commerce being deemed essential to the propagation of animals and plants; and that the fabulous union of the divine pair was simulated by the real though temporary union of the human sexes at the sanctuary of the goddess.
>
> (Frazer)

Fertility rites are communal functions in which individual acts are harnessed for the common good. Defloration, on the contrary, is an event in individual life which in primitive cultures is considered so critical that the community rallies round to support the individual. So crucial and irreversible is the act of deflowering a virgin that the responsibility is more than the bridegroom can bear, so ways are found to spread the burden. Among certain Marquesan islanders of the Pacific, for example, it was customary until quite recently for the virgin bride to be laid on a platform of stones while the men of the tribe formed a line, singing and dancing, each in turn copulating with her and so accepting a share of the 'blame'.

The *droit de seigneur*, whereby local landowners claimed the right to sleep with every newly-wed bride in their domain, is often misinterpreted as an instance of feudal tyranny. In fact it is quite the opposite: a survival of the old defloration custom which reflects nothing but credit on the ruler; being divinely anointed, he is strong enough to bear the full weight of the responsibility on his shoulders and so spare his subjects entirely. So we can understand the respect given to Conchabar, king of Ulster in Ireland's legendary past, who pierced the maidenhead of every virgin in his kingdom; it was not for his sexual prowess but for his sheer courage that he was praised.

Then an even better solution was found. Why risk your fellow tribesmen, why endanger your king, when you can persuade some complete stranger to do the job? Since he is not subject to your gods, he may hope to escape unscathed from the ordeal; in any case, being a foreigner, his fate is no concern of yours. So the stranger is made welcome in the virgin's bed; this is what lies behind the readiness—so often misconstrued by people from other cultures—of primitive peoples to allow their guests access to their womenfolk. Marco Polo was astonished by the thirteenth-century Tibetans:

> The people of these parts are disinclined to marry young women as long as they are left in their virgin state, but on the contrary require that they should have had commerce with many of the opposite sex; this, they claim, is pleasing to their deities, and they regard a woman who has not had the company of men as worthless. So, when a caravan of merchants arrives, as soon as they have pitched tent for the night, the mothers of marriageable daughters bring them to the place and entreat the strangers to accept their daughters and enjoy their society so long as they remain in the district. The merchants are expected to give them presents—trinkets, rings or other tokens. When later they are designed for marriage, they wear these ornaments about the neck or other part of the body, and she who exhibits the greatest number is considered to have attracted the greatest number of men, and is on that account esteemed highest by the young men looking for a wife.

We can see sex as religious rite and defloration by strangers combined in many of the practices intended to honour the Mother Goddess. In Cyprus all women were obliged to give themselves before marriage to strangers in the sanctuary. At Baalbek in Syria every virgin had to give herself to a stranger at the Temple of Astarte. Herodotus has described how the ceremony was conducted in Babylon in the fifth century BC:

> Every woman is obliged, once in her life, to sit down openly in the Temple of Venus and prostitute herself to some stranger. Yet because the most wealthy disdain to expose themselves in public among the rest, many come in covered chariots to the gates of the temple, and make that their station, with a numerous train of servants attending at a distance. But the far greater part enter into the temple, and sit down crowned with garlands. When a woman has seated herself, she must not return home, till some stranger throws a piece of silver into her lap, and lie with her at some distance from the temple, using this form as he gives her the money, I beseech the goddess Mylitta to favour thee; for the Assyrians call Venus by that name. The law forbids any woman to refuse this present, how small soever, and commands her to follow the first that offers it, without rejecting any man. Those women who excel in beauty and shape are soon dismissed, but the deformed are sometimes necessitated to wait three or four years before they can satisfy the law.

Lucian, in his *De Dea Syria*, describes similar practices in Lebanon seven centuries later; here, women were supposed to go into mourning annually for the death of Adonis: 'Those who refuse to shave off their hair are obliged to prostitute themselves on a certain day. To this market only strangers are admitted, and the proceeds are given to the Temple.'

From this point the next step would be the adoption of a selective procedure; instead of every virgin in the community being required to give herself, selected ones would serve on behalf of the remainder, just as the priests performed their functions as representatives of the community as a whole. Girls might be recruited on a permanent basis, becoming brides of the deity and renouncing earthly husbands; they were the precursors of Rome's vestal virgins and Christianity's nuns. Records show that these temple prostitutes could be of either sex, but which gender did what to which remains open to conjecture. By this point, of course, the virginity would have become purely symbolic.

A different kind of development is that whereby girls become temple prostitutes in order to earn their marriage dowries, a quaint blending of religious with practical motives. Customs of this sort have been recorded from the ancient Etruscans to the Mfiote of West Africa. Until very recent times marriageable girls of this tribe would pass through the village, singing, dancing, and calling out the sum for which they would permit a man to take their virginity.

It is not possible to pinpoint precisely the moment when customs of this kind were transformed into prostitution as we recognise it; we can only register the fact that, sooner or later, virtually every community reached that point. The Finnish anthropologist Westermarck, in his *History of Human Marriage* (1891), noted that among the Line Islanders of the Pacific a woman was free to accept as many men as would take her, so long as they paid her for the privilege; he cited similar practices from places as far apart as Uganda, Greenland and Central America. So, while it would be unscientific to presume its existence except where it has been positively identified, it would seem that some form of prostitution is to be found at some stage in the development of every primitive society.

A somewhat ambiguous sentence in Herodotus suggests that the Egyptians were the first people to abolish religious prostitution. Certainly all the references to prostitution in ancient Egypt are to professional courtesans: the famous Rhodope, a Greek slave who caught the fancy of the Pharaoh Amasis, or Archidice for whom many wealthy Egyptians are said to have ruined themselves. It was of Archidice that the story was told of a would-be client who was refused because he couldn't afford her costly favours, whereupon he had a dream in which he enjoyed them. Archidice, hearing of this, insisted that she was entitled to her customary fee, and took him to court. The lawyers agreed that she had a true claim; but, since her client had only *dreamed* of enjoying her, she should *dream* that she had been paid.

No such colourful tales are told of the prostitutes of Israel. As any teacher of religious instruction knows to his discomfort, the Bible is rich in references to whores and harlots, the nature of whose trade has either to be boldly tackled or discreetly skirted. The American sexologist Sanger noted that 'prostitution is constantly assumed as an existing fact in Biblical history', but the prostitute is always an outcast and the references always derogatory:

> Do not prostitute thy daughter, to cause her to be a whore: lest the land fall to whoredom, and the land become full of wickedness.
>
> (Leviticus XIX, 29)

However, the frequency of reference shows that the people of Israel had no more intention of listening to their preachers than any other nation. Since the priests could not stamp it out altogether, their fiercest exhortations were directed against participation by Jewish women; so here, as so often elsewhere, the prostitute's trade was conducted very largely by foreigners. Moses himself is described as taking an Ethiopian concubine, and Jesus's encounter with the woman of Samaria again links the profession with outsiders.

Some of the appearances made by prostitutes in the Bible are curious, to say the least. The Book of Judges tells of a certain Levite whose concubine cheats on him and then goes home to mother. He goes to fetch her back again; on their return journey, lodging in a strange town, they are troubled by a gang of local toughs. To keep them happy, he sends his girl out to them, 'and they knew her, and abused her all the night until the morning, and when the day began to spring they let her go'. Her master then took her home where 'he took a knife, and divided her, together with her bones, into twelve pieces, and sent her into all the coasts of Israel'. 'In those days', the writer adds, 'there was no King in Israel; every man did that which was right in his own eyes.' The justice of the Levite's actions escapes us, but presumably it seemed right also in the eyes of his countrymen, for it sparked off yet another of those inter-tribal wars which characterise the early history of that afflicted land.

The few Jewish prostitutes we know by name—Rahab of Jericho who sheltered Joshua's spies; Delilah who delivered Samson to his enemies—were identified only because they played a part in some male biography. There were none to match the Rhodopes and Archidices to the south, even fewer to equal the career of Theodora, to the north in Byzantium. In this history we shall encounter a number—perhaps, for the moralist, a dismayingly large number—of prostitutes who made good; but none did better for herself than Theodora, who began her career by masturbating slaves in the lowest taverns and ended upon the imperial throne.

According to Procopius of Caesarea—not the most reliable of historians, but in this instance his story is confirmed by others—young Theodora followed her sister Comito into the prostitute's trade. While still too young for intercourse, she was taught to do what she could with her hands, and then by 'intercourse of the male kind', generally serving slaves accompanying their masters to the theatre. When old enough, she displayed what amounted to a natural vocation for her chosen profession, 'plying her trade with almost every part of her body . . . forever trying out new ideas in intercourse . . . she won the hearts of the licentious for she did not wait for the man to make the advances, but she herself, with obscene jokes and waggling her hips like a clown, would seduce all comers, particularly unbearded youths'.

One youthful heart she won was that of a young man who happened to be heir to the imperial throne. She became Justinian's mistress; then, as her hold over him increased, she persuaded him to change the law which forbade marriage with a prostitute. The law was changed and she married him; and when Justinian became emperor, she became empress. Procopius, who was not at all prejudiced in her favour, admits that she was as adept in her new career as in her former trade. She was by no means the last of her kind to demonstrate that knowledge of men acquired in the brothel can be put to good use if given a chance to operate in a wider sphere.

> Man has the *hetairae* for erotic enjoyment; concubines for daily use; and wives of his own rank to bring up children and to be faithful housewives.
>
> (Demosthenes)

The ancient Greek attitude to sex was almost wholly permissive. No bigotry distorted their dealings, or required them to cloak what they did with hypocrisy. They were restrained only by a sense of social responsibility which ensured that as little offence as possible was given to other members of the community. Sex was still intimately linked to religious worship—the positive side of religion—and so free from the associations of guilt—religion's negative side—with which the Jews, and still more,

Greek courtesan and companion

soon, the Christians, invested it. The Greeks saw the prostitute as inferior, true, but as socially, not morally inferior; she was not an outcast in Athens as she was in Jerusalem. Like a Victorian kitchenmaid, her lowly status was a simple fact of life.

Classical Greek culture still contained much of that widespread worship of the Mother Goddess; like the multifarious Ishtars and Astartes of neighbouring peoples, the Greek Aphrodite was a fertility deity, feted at orgiastic seasonal festivals and honoured by temple prostitution. Even during the classical period it was customary for prostitutes to devote all they earned on the fourth day of the month—sacred to Aphrodite—as a temple offering. The goddess herself—like Mary in the Christian religion—was given a variety of descriptive sobriquets; but Aphrodite's nicknames were nearly always sexual: Aphrodite who writhes, Aphrodite of the Night, Aphrodite of the Beautiful Buttocks. In Abydos, when the city had been delivered from certain enemies by the concerted efforts of the prostitute population—how, we can only conjecture—a temple was dedicated to Aphrodite the Courtesan, a frank and unequivocal linking of prostitution with religion.

Religious sanction did not mean, however, that sex was not enjoyed for its own sake. The Greek antiquary Athenaeus of Naucratis, writing in the second century AD, says of the Tyrrhenians:

> Tyrrhenian women take the greatest care of their bodies, often practising gymnastic exercises either among themselves or with men. When Tyrrhenians are with friends or relatives, and have had enough of drinking and are ready for bed, it is the custom for servants to bring in to them courtesans, beautiful boys or women, while the lamps are still burning. When they have enjoyed themselves sufficiently with these, they fetch young men in their prime, and let them enjoy themselves with these courtesans, boys or women. They pay homage to love and sexual intercourse, sometimes looking on at one another, but generally letting down curtains from poles fastened on the beds. They are very fond of women, but find more pleasure with boys and young men.

The sexual latitude allowed to men by Greek public opinion was virtually unrestricted; women, on the other hand, were divided into two distinct classes—the respectable and the others. Wives and mothers were respected and honoured, assured of their rights and protected by law; they lived dull, dutiful lives of unremembered domesticity, mistresses of their homes but in all public or cultural spheres nonentities. For the statesman Alcibiades, his wife Hipparete was a convenient person to bear and raise his children; but it was in the arms of the courtesan Nemea that he chose to have his portrait painted.

It could as well have been in the company of a graceful youth. Homosexuality was so fundamental to the Greek social structure that it was seldom referred to specifically; it was simply taken for granted. A poem may be addressed to a girl-friend or a boy-friend; a man is wretched because his lover has treated him unkindly, and only the name will tell us if the lover is a he or a she. Relationships between men and youths—in which the older man played the roles of teacher, protector, friend and lover with varying emphasis according to each individual case—were as normal as heterosexual relationships in our own society. But with this vital difference: the Greeks were equally fond of female company; theirs was a genuinely bisexual society. For most of us today, a preference for one sex implies no sexual relations with the other; but the Greeks, men and women alike, found it practicable and rewarding to enjoy both.

Just as boy-friends existed as an alternative to girl-friends, so professional prostitutes had their place in Greek society as an alternative to non-commercial companions. The first brothel was introduced into Athens, as a piece of deliberate state policy, by Solon, the wise lawgiver of the sixth century BC. He purchased a suitable building, furnished it with trained girls imported from Asia Minor, and kept the prices deliberately low to encourage patronage; his aim was, quite simply, to distract men from adulterous affairs which could only lead to trouble. Athenaeus compared Solon's brothel girls favourably with the clandestine alternative:

> With breasts bare beneath thin dresses of gauze, they flaunt themselves in the sunlight. You pick whichever takes your fancy—slim or well-covered, lanky or well-rounded, upright or crooked, young or mature . . . You don't have to sneak in with a ladder, or climb through a window or smuggle yourself in beneath a load of straw. Quite the contrary: the girls themselves drag you into the house by force, calling you 'Daddy' if you are getting on in years, 'Little Brother' or 'Little Boy' if you're still young . . .

No free citizen of Athens was permitted to prostitute herself, so the brothels were recruited from the slave market. Once she had been registered, the prostitute's activities were supervised by state officials whose first concern was for public decency. She was not allowed to leave the brothel except in the evenings, and she had to wear distinctive dress—most notably a blonde wig. Her price was officially regulated, and she was liable for tax. The house where she worked was open night and day, but curtained off from vulgar curiosity. Clients passed a porter into a courtyard where the girls, scantily dressed, sat at the entrances to their rooms. The brothel was respected as a sanctuary where the law might not intrude; debtors could not be pursued here, nor relatives hunt their errant kinsfolk. When business was slack, the girls might join the streetwalkers outside. The shoe of one of these girls has been preserved; it has a pattern of nails on the sole which, as she walked, left imprinted in the dust the Greek equivalent of 'Follow me'! Equally forthright was the sign which indicated the brothel's trade: a carving of an erect phallus.

Superior to the brothel girls were the entertainers—flute-players and dancers who performed at festivals and at private functions; their lightly dressed if not actually naked performances generally led to an orgy for guests and entertainers alike. One of the most celebrated of all Greek courtesans, Lamia, began her career as a flute-player; she rose to the bed and favour of Demetrius Poliorcetes who ruled Macedon around the close of the third century BC and proved herself, like Theodora, a lady of real accomplishment.

But the most distinctive class of prostitute in ancient Greece came into being in consequence of Greek ideas on marriage. When his wife was regarded simply as a housekeeper and a breeder of heirs, the husband looked elsewhere not only for sexual pleasure—a concubine or a brothel girl could give him that—but also for deeper female companionship. So there grew up a class of prostitute at the courtesan level, the *hetairae*.

So much has been written about these women, with so little solid fact to go on, that it is hard to know how much is exaggeration. We may certainly doubt that every hetaira was beautiful, witty, elegant, charming and accomplished; most were surely good-class call-girls doing a sound professional job. Yet a few do seem to have been very exceptional creatures, for not only do we have an extensive literature in their praise but also the testimony of witnesses whose word should carry weight. The philosopher Socrates, no fool and certainly no respecter of persons, was unstinting in his admiration for Aspasia, mistress and subsequently wife of the ruler Pericles. Lais—whose beautiful breasts, glimpsed at the public well, inspired the painter Apelles to purchase her freedom—must have had brains as well as beauty if the philosopher Aristippus could tolerate her company for the two months of every year they spent together on the island of Aegina.

After Pericles' death, Aspasia married a flour-merchant and gave lectures on philosophy. Another admirer of culture was Phryne, who refused more than £2,000 offered by the statesman Demosthenes for her favours, yet gave them freely to the penniless philosopher Diogenes. (I suspect that particular anecdote was invented by a philosopher *pour encourager les autres.*) Phryne was so sought-after that she had no need to display herself naked, as others did, to bring in business; but, as a concession to widespread curiosity, she made an exception for the annual religious festivals. To honour the sea-god Poseidon, she enacted the role of Aphrodite emerging from the sea, performing a pious strip-tease at the water's edge which must have been one of the high spots of the Athenian religious calendar. The fame she won by such exhibitions inspired a deplorable jealousy among her rivals, one of whom lodged a formal complaint that her performance profaned the sacred mysteries—a capital offence. When her case was almost lost, her defence counsel Hyperides tore off her veil to reveal her naked beauty to the judges. How, he demanded, could a festival in honour of the gods be desecrated by beauty which the gods themselves had bestowed? The point was incontestable, the evidence overwhelming, the case dismissed.

Fact or fiction, such anecdotes leave no doubt that the hetairae played an important and respected part in Greek social life. They were portrayed

Phryne strips in honour of Poseidon. Anonymous French engraving in *Le Journal Illustré*, c 1890

on stage, and books were written whose authorship was credited to them; they became legends in their own lifetime and death only heightened their mystique. The fact that they were prostitutes, blatant and mercenary, was not held against them in the slightest degree.

With boys it was otherwise. Prostitution was a role that a woman could play without betraying her nature, but when the commercial element intruded into relationships between males it seemed a profanation of a cherished ideal. Inevitably, though, some of the pretty boys saw how they could turn their charm to good account; one of the characters of the philosopher Straton laments:

> What are you crying for, my boy? You hold out your hollowed hand again—are you begging for payment? Who taught you that trick? You're no longer satisfied with cakes, nuts or sweet sesame seeds: your mind is set on gain. A curse on whoever taught you, for he has ruined my boy.

A man might take such a boy to live with him on the same footing as a mistress, or enjoy a momentary encounter, picking him up at a barber's shop or perfumer's. Available youth haunted particular districts, easily recognisable with their long hair, depilated bodies, coquettish manners and eye-catching make-up. There were male brothels where a choice was constantly available, and also houses where boys and girls could be hired together to provide maximum variety. Perhaps the best known of all Greek male prostitutes is Phaedo, to whom Plato addressed some of his finest dialogues; a prisoner of war, he was bought by an Athenian brothel-keeper before Socrates persuaded a friend to purchase his liberty.

Here, as with all aspects of prostitution in classical Greece, we find ourselves on ground that is half familiar, half strange. The information is so scattered, and often presented so obliquely, that we can never be sure we have the picture quite right. This brief account has been built up from literally hundreds of references and allusions, any one of which may be exaggerated, distorted or simply invented; yet together they create a coherent and convincing impression of a society which faced the social problems of sex and worked out viable solutions to them. Greek society, despite its presumption of female inferiority, found a formula which worked tolerably well, and applied it without hypocrisy, conflict, bitterness or bigotry. No subsequent society was to manage half so well.

Every schoolchild knows that Rome was founded by Romulus and Remus, two baby heroes who were accidentally found and suckled by a kindly she-wolf—*lupa* in Latin. Older scholars know that *lupa* is also one of the many Latin words for prostitute; this has suggested to the less reverent that what really happened was that two stray children were taken in and fostered by a whore with the traditional heart of gold. Some accounts even identify the lady as Acca Laurentia, wife of the shepherd Faustulus, known as 'Lupa' for her generosity with her favours, and whose house, the Wolf's Lair or *Lupercal*, became the archetype of later Roman brothels. She prudently invested her substantial savings in real estate and was eventually able to pass on to her foster-children as their inheritance the site of the future city of Rome.

Fact or fiction, there's a nice irony in the suggestion that the city whose excesses of debauchery were to be the scandal of the world and whose state church was to be labelled 'the Scarlet Woman' should have its origins in a prostitute's bed. And it is fitting that for centuries some of the most notable events in the Roman calendar should be those licentious religious festivals which, deriving from traditional fertility ceremonies, were developed by the spectacle-loving Romans into elaborate municipal occasions. The *Lupercalia* and the *Ludi Floreales*, though they each culminated in what was little more than a massive public orgy, were blessed both by the city fathers and by the priests as therapeutic outlets for excess sex.

The *Lupercalia*, held annually on 15 February, originally commemorated the death of Acca Laurentia herself. Later Romans felt that so vulgar a tale was incompatible with Rome's growing dignity, so the festival was transferred to the patronage of the god Faunus, the Roman Pan, no ascetic but less directly associated with sex. However, changing the name didn't alter the product; the occasion lost none of its sexual character. It was the same with the *Ludi Floreales*, inaugurated in honour of the prostitute Flora who bestowed the accumulated savings of a successful career to benefit the people of Rome; for this in 238 BC the Senate decreed a perpetual feast day in her memory. Later the real-life Flora was metamorphosed into a goddess of spring, honoured through six days of non-stop merrymaking from 28 April to 3 May each year. The high spot took place in the Circus, where the gathered prostitutes of Rome stripped and performed dances of growing lasciviousness until a crowd of naked young men came whooping into the arena and performed as you might expect while the crowd applauded their efforts.

Thus extra-marital sex was woven into the fabric of Roman life from

Roman brothel. From Rabutaux, *La Prostitution en l'Europe*, 1865

the outset, and co-existed even with the austerities of the early republican days when Rome was fighting hard to establish its supremacy and all forms of luxury were condemned. Such high-minded Romans as existed during the later imperial epoch were apt to look back with regret to the austere morals of the republic. That had been the time when Rome had been laying the foundations of her mighty empire; what had made her strong, they claimed, had been the self-discipline and sexual restraint of their ancestors.

What these later critics forgot was that the high moral tone of the earlier republic had been sustained by a pragmatic attitude which not only condoned the *Lupercalia* and the *Ludi Floreales* but also permitted the establishment of brothels catering for those who required relief more than twice a year. Even if that she-wolf story is nonsense, we know that prostitution existed almost from the date of Rome's foundation. The historian Livy tells how in 501 BC a group of Sabine youths kidnapped a bevy of Roman prostitutes—perhaps in retaliation for the celebrated rape of the Sabine women by the Romans? The early Romans had the sense to see that regulated prostitution makes for higher, not lower moral standards. In one of his *Satires*, Horace quotes the views of Cato, a statesman renowned for his moral severity:

Seeing emerge a man he knew,
'That's the proper thing to do!'
was Cato's well-considered view.
'When your veins swell with brutal lust,
the brothel is the place to trust.
Girls await your pleasure there—
so other people's wives you'll spare.'

The poet Propertius explains a similar preference:

The woman I prefer is she
who walks the pavement bold and free;
who shuffles up the Sacred Way
in slippers soiled with mud and clay;
who wears no veil upon her head
and has no concierge to dread.
She will not, should a man accost,
suffer a moment to be lost.
No assignation will she break,
nor be importunate to take
sums that a father would lament,
good thrifty soul, his son had spent.
Nor say 'I'm frightened, get up, pray,
my man is coming back today!'
Clandestine, shamefaced love I'll make
no longer, but my pleasure take
with girls the Syrian pimps export
and those from Babylonia brought.

Just as the history of Rome itself is fundamentally one of steady growth from warring city-state to imperial super-power, so its moral history is of a steady swing from austerity to indulgence. Successful wars of conquest gave Romans a chance to sample other races' more permissive ways; they tasted Eastern hedonism and liked it. Slaves and captives, brought back to Rome with other loot, included girls trained in the arts of love, a refinement new to the matter-of-fact Romans. The cult of Isis, imported from Egypt with the Roman's readiness to add other peoples' gods to his pantheon—you never knew when they might come in handy—provided the excuse for yet more licentious festivals, for Isis was the Egyptian

The *aedile* Hostilius Mancinus driven off by Mamilia and her companions, *c* 180 BC. Castelli, in Dufour's *Histoire de la Prostitution*, *c* 1860

equivalent of Venus and worshipped in the same appropriate fashion.

As early as the fifth century BC the city fathers appointed censors to watch over Rome's morals, but not until 180 BC did they feel it necessary to appoint officials to inspect and control prostitutes in this city which had grown from a small township to a world power. These *aediles* had authority to enter prostitutes' houses and brothels; it is on record how the *aedile* Hostilius Mancinus one night tried to force his way into the house of the courtesan Mamilia. Driven off by a barrage of stones, he complained to the authorities that his official rights had been defied. It came out, however, that he had been on his way home from a party at the time and was more than a little drunk; it was deduced that his call was more in the line of Mamilia's business than his own, and Hostilius Mancinus lost his case.

The aediles introduced a system of registration for prostitutes. It was a voluntary step, which though it denied a girl certain privileges also ensured her official protection. It was irrevocable; once a prostitute, always a prostitute. The new recruit told the *aediles* how much she intended to charge, and this became a fixed sum which could not be changed without their consent. Registered prostitutes were generally either slaves or widows who needed the money; but as time went on, the practice of amateur prostitution grew among wives who wished for more pocket-money or who relished the excitement. Tacitus in his *Annals* tells how voluntary prostitution of well-born ladies was limited by, of all people, that supremely debauched emperor Tiberius:

> That same year (AD 19) the lubricity of women was restrained by the Senate, who decreed that no woman could become venal if her father, grandfather or husband were Roman knights. This was because Vistilia, a lady born of a Pretorian family, had published herself a prostitute before the *aediles*, according to custom.

Other discouraging measures were passed at intervals, even during the most profligate periods of Roman history. The Emperor Domitian (who seduced his niece and liked to share his bath with a clutch of prostitutes) revived the old laws against homosexuals. Vespasian (who once gave 4,000 gold pieces to a woman who asked him to seduce her) ordered cutbacks in court luxury. Macrinus condemned adulterers to be tied together and burnt alive. Hadrian banned mixed bathing. But these sporadic attempts to inculcate higher moral standards were doomed to failure so long as such flagrant examples were set by the highest in the land. We may take with a pinch of salt some of the excesses attributed to the Caesars by Suetonius, but there seems no reason to question the penchant for amateur prostitution displayed by Messalina, wife of the Emperor Claudius, who once issued a challenge to the Guild of Prostitutes that she could exhaust more men in a night than the most skilful professional. She won. The satirist Juvenal described her activities:

The good old sluggard but began to snore
when from his side up rose the Imperial whore.
To the known brothel-house she takes her way,
and for a nasty room gives double pay—
that room in which the rankest harlot lay.
Prepared for fight, expectantly she lies,
with heaving breast and with desiring eyes.
Still as one drops, another takes his place,
and baffled still succeeds to like disgrace.
At length, when friendly darkness is expired,
and every strumpet from her cell retired,
all filth without, and all a fire within,
tired with the toil, unsated with the sin,
old Caesar's bed the modest matron seeks,
the steam of lamps still hanging on her cheeks.
(Dryden's translation)

While the upper classes enjoyed such excesses, the more regular prostitutes conducted their business with well-organised efficiency. There were several grades, headed by the *famosa*, the woman of good family who, like Messalina, took to prostitution for her own reasons. The *famosa* and the *delicata*—who lacked her family background but possessed accomplishments like the Greek *hetaira*—were not required to wear distinctive dress or submit to the *aedile*'s supervision as were the lower grades.

These included the *dorides* who stood naked in their doorways to attract passers-by; the *bustiariae* who did their business in graveyards, perhaps catering for the recently bereaved as well as necrophiliacs; the *lupae* (our she-wolves again) who used a wolf-like cry to attract—though it sounds more calculated to repel—their customers; the *blitidae* who took their name from the cheap wine sold in the taverns where they plied for custom; and the *gallinae* (hens) who had a name for robbing on the job.

Favourite haunts of prostitutes were the theatres and circuses, where customers might be caught in a compliant mood. Ovid in his *Ars Amoris* advises a would-be client:

But above all the playhouse is the place—
there's choice of quarry in that narrow chase.
There take thy stand, and sharply looking out
soon mayest thou find a mistress in the rout,
for length of time, or for a single bout.

Roman street woman. From Rabutaux, *La Prostitution en l'Europe*

Short-time prostitutes would often take their customers to the *cellae fornicae*, the arches beneath the public buildings, hence our word fornication.

Other favoured places were the Via Sacra by day and the Via Appia by night, where high-class whores were carried in litters, trading like modern taxi girls. The public baths were so notorious that *bagnio* has come to be synonymous with brothel. At first the baths had simply been places where men and women, girls and boys could mingle naked; but these conditions, so propitious for mutual inspection, were found equally apt for mutual enjoyment. The dim lighting encouraged intimacy, and soon thoughtful managements were providing cubicles for their patrons' convenience. Massage was provided by youths and girls attached to the establishment, and *fellatrices* were available if required; children in particular were taught the simple skills needed for the satisfactory exercise of this trade.

All these various practitioners were competing directly with the more regular brothels, of which Rome was said to contain forty-six in the top category alone under the empire. Since there were 36,000 registered prostitutes at the time, only a small proportion can have been working in these more select establishments.

While some girls lived on the premises, the majority were *meretrices*, who left their own homes after the evening meal and made their way to the brothel as to any other place of work. Unlike the Greeks who allowed the brothels to remain open all day, the practical Romans required that they should be closed during working hours so as not to lure customers away from more important matters. So the brothels opened at 4 pm and closed again at daybreak.

The premises comprised a row of cells round a courtyard: on each door was the girl's name and her price, and a sign to indicate if she was occupied. Unoccupied girls sat outside their doors in the lamplight. The house employed women to attend the girls and keep them looking attractive from one session to the next; boys brought washing-water to the cell afterwards, and an *aquarius* would fetch wine and food when called for. As everywhere, prices varied according to the quality of the service and the attractions of the girl who provided it. A special value was placed on a virgin, and the occasion when she received her first customer called for celebration. The house was decorated, and the customer—who had paid handsomely for the privilege—was garlanded with a victor's laurel wreath. This may sound unpleasantly cynical to us, but it demonstrates why we must never lose sight of the connection, still strong in Roman days, between religion and sex. This custom, similar to that which applied to newly married couples, was a survival of the traditional defloration rituals. The job that had once been entrusted to a stranger was now performed by the brothel client; and, though he had paid for the privilege instead of being rewarded with the thanks of the tribe, he was nevertheless performing the same ritual role.

We know very little about male prostitution in Rome, but some historians assert that there were if anything more male prostitutes than female. For the Romans homosexuality owed little to the example of the Greeks, whom they despised; there was little or none of that many-sided and open relationship which the Greeks valued so highly. With the Romans it was simply a matter of physical preference, in many cases no doubt induced by habits acquired during those long military campaigns which formed so large a part of their lives. We are told that a slave who was of age to be a prostitute was valued at ten times the standard rate, and that male prostitutes wore their togas after the female fashion.

There were also animal brothels; Juvenal refers to the unique talents of the donkey, which apparently came in very useful at the all-female *Bona Dea* festival in the absence of other equipment.

Fundamentally, the prostitute was not respected in Rome—partly, paradoxically, because on the whole women were rated more highly by the Romans than by the Greeks. Whereas in Greece the dowdy respectable wife had suffered by comparison with the captivating hetaira, in Rome she enjoyed greater freedom, wider legal rights, more respect within the family—and the prostitute suffered in consequence.

But even in imperial Rome the situation of the prostitute was fortunate compared with that of those who plied her trade in the following centuries. Despite our fragmentary knowledge, it is clear that throughout the pre-Christian world the prostitute had generally been accepted into the social structure without overmuch embarrassment or awkwardness. In some cultures, this fact-facing acceptance was able to continue; but things were to change dramatically in those societies which chose henceforth to follow Jesus of Nazareth rather than pay homage to Aphrodite.

# 3
# *DOGMA AND DOUBLETHINK*

> Christianity taught, as a religious dogma, invariable, inflexible, and independent of all utilitarian calculations, that all forms of intercourse of the sexes, other than life-long unions, were criminal. By teaching men to regard this doctrine as axiomatic, and therefore inflicting severe social penalties and deep degradation on transient connections, it has profoundly modified even their utilitarian aspect and has rendered them in most countries furtive and disguised. There is probably no other branch of ethics which has been so largely determined by special dogmatic theology.
>
> (W. E. H. Lecky, *The History of European Morals*, 1869)

Not even the most high-minded citizen of republican Rome had suggested there was any virtue in, say, a man remaining a virgin till he married. The Emperor Alexander Severus, who vehemently opposed vice throughout his career, insisted that his unmarried provincial governors should be furnished with concubines, on the simple grounds that it was unimaginable they could manage without, and that official permission was preferable to unofficial subterfuge.

But well before the end of the pre-Christian era, a growing number of new creeds and philosophies had sprung up in Western Asia, advocating a more ascetic, less indulgent way of life. The Stoic philosopher Musonius Rufus insisted that no union of the sexes, outside the marriage bond, was tolerable. The philosopher Dion Chrysostom urged the authorities to abolish prostitution on ethical grounds. The Pythagorean mystic Apollonius of Tyana held that even marriage was tainted, and should be avoided; to show it could be done, he himself lived a celibate. Zenobia, Queen of Palmyra, though recognising the necessity of a limited amount of sexual activity to maintain the race, refused to lie with her husband any more than was essential to provide an heir to the throne.

None of these were Christians; and Christianity, when it came, was only one of many creeds advocating in one form or another the virtues of restraint. The reasons why Christianity gained such a lead over its rivals have been the subject of scholarly debate for two thousand years. It is less a question of finding explanations than of choosing between them. Even to those reluctant to accept that divine intervention may have been involved, it is evident that the ethical package presented by Jesus of Nazareth had a very broad basis of appeal. It was rigorous—but not unduly so. It was just—without being bigoted. It was tough on hypocrites—but tolerant towards the feeble. The message was flexible enough to appeal on all intellectual levels; it has a superb 'story' and its protagonist possessed a unique charisma.

It may have been shrewd thinking on the part of the first exponents of Christianity to lay particular stress on the sexual aspect of morals; but, when they found people were ready to listen to such exhortations, it is hardly surprising that the early fathers continued to exploit the vein. The more they exploited it, the more authority they gained; and the more their authority was buttressed by the guilt they aroused in their flocks, the greater the moral demands they were able to make, provoking ever greater paroxysms of guilt, ever wilder hysteria. Sex, for the Christian, became an evil in itself. Not just adultery, or masturbation, or sodomy, or prostitution, but sex itself. Paul admitted it was better to marry than to burn, but reserved his highest praise for the man who managed to do neither. The virulence displayed by the early fathers against sex is hard to account for except by attributing it to a kind of religious mania.

We shall never know to what extent these extreme views were accepted by the congregations. The fact that Christianity continued to win converts indicates a general acceptance of its teachings; but the fact that the fathers had to go on thundering, century after century, indicates a reluctance on the part of their hearers to do more than listen. Christian dogma won approval but not obedience; the gap was bridged with hypocrisy.

The extent of this teaching is evident in the pious legends which sprang up around the early heroes and heroines of the growing church; a resolute stand in some sexual matter, preferably accompanied by sacrifice, was the surest way to canonisation. From countless examples, here are three relating specifically to prostitution:

Saint Gregory Thaumaturgus was accused by a courtesan, in the second century, of having been her lover, and of bilking her of her fee. Though denying the accusation, he nevertheless paid her the sum she claimed, whereupon she was immediately possessed by a demon.

Saint Mary the Egyptian, at the age of twelve, entered an Alexandrian brothel and worked there for seventeen years before hearing from customers about Christianity. She was at once inspired to make the pilgrimage to Jerusalem, paying for her passage by sleeping with the ship's crew. After visiting the Holy Places she was again inspired, this time to become a hermit in the desert, taking with her three loaves of bread which sufficed to sustain her for forty-seven years until her death in 422.

Another twelve-year-old, Saint Agnes, convicted of Christianity under the Diocletian persecutions, was ordered by Sempronius, Prefect of Rome, to work in a brothel. No sooner was she stripped, than a miraculous growth of hair sprouted to conceal her private parts. This instant puberty scared off all her would-be customers except one, the prefect's own son; luckily providence again came to Agnes' aid, striking the deflowerer with a thunderbolt before he could make any headway.

Behind such legends was an attitude of mind which has tainted human relations for centuries—an attitude, moreover, which was a gross

The false concubine and the priest. Anonymous fifteenth-century German woodcut from *Die Unehrlichkeit der Pfaffenhuren* (The wickedness of the priests)

misrepresentation of the teachings of the man who was nominally the founder of the Church and the author of its doctrines. The end-result of such distortions was not to make men give up sex nor to turn them away from women; what it did was to make men feel guilty about their impulses. And, such is human nature, they looked for a scapegoat on which to unload their guilt. The Church fathers had given them a lead by tracing all human ills to the misbehaviour of Eve and her descendants; the subordinate sex became the despised sex, and most despised of all were the ones who openly flaunted their femininity. So the prostitute became the vicarious victim of man's theology-induced self-reproach, the receptacle of his loathing as well as his lust, condemned to be alternately cursed and caressed so long as the Church's teaching had effect.

A few Church teachers were willing to concede that the prostitute could serve some kind of purpose. In 383 Augustine of Hippo compared her to an executioner—the activities of both were distasteful, but society would suffer if it tried to do without them. Two centuries later Thomas Aquinas compared the prostitute to a sewer in a palace—take away the drains, and the whole place will start to stink. But even these concessions sprang from a totally negative approach; moreover, they led to awkward theological questions. If the prostitute followed a trade that was socially beneficial, but damned herself in the process, should the Church seek to discourage her? If the prostitute was a drain to carry off effluent, it was surely logical to start by eliminating the waste at its source? At various ecclesiastical councils in places like Aix or Elvira where learned men gathered to try and puzzle out what Jesus really meant, the question was raised whether a man should regard his visits to prostitutes as a sin when he made his weekly confession.

Whatever the Church said or didn't say, medieval Europe was in practice generally tolerant about sexual behaviour. It expected everyone to have sex, for the simple reason that everyone needs it, and so sex was provided for those to whom it was not regularly available. The brothel was part of the everyday scene, whether in town or country, in taverns and roadside inns, in palaces and abbeys. When armies marched—and throughout the medieval period armies were continually marching this way or that—they were accompanied by a horde of camp-followers who lived off the soldiers, providing them with food, drink and sex. The rich man in his castle had a seraglio for himself and his fellow knights. The poor man at his gate took his sex as he found it; if there were no village girls to give him what he wanted, he'd find one at the tavern who would provide it for a modest fee.

Brothel outside a medieval German city. They were customarily located outside the walls. Anonymous fifteenth-century print

In the towns, matters were not quite so simple; with people packed close together, careful regulation was needed if social life was to run smoothly. So, increasingly as the medieval period went by, the urban prostitute found herself being hedged in by legal constraints. This was not necessarily a disadvantage, for it implied official recognition of her existence and a limited degree of protection. The history of medieval prostitution is of a gradually evolving balance struck between the prostitute and the rest of the community—toleration in return for good conduct. On that basis, society was prepared to make a deal.

There had been a brothel at Toulouse for as long as anyone could remember. An *ordonance* issued by Louis XI in the fifteenth century specifies:

> From the earliest times it has been customary in our Land of Languedoc, and particularly in our towns, to maintain an house and dwelling, outside those towns, for the habitation and residence of public women.

The Toulouse brothel was already well established in 1201; in that year it had to shift to Grant l'Abbaye, outside the city walls, where new buildings had been financed jointly by the city and the university in expectation of a steady source of income. The arrangement apparently continued without incident until 1389, when rioting broke out in Toulouse—presumably part of the social unrest caused by the war against England, then part-way through its hundred-year span. Brothels are traditionally among the first, being one of the easiest, targets against which mobs turn their violence. The rioting had a deplorable effect on business, and the shareholders faced the prospect of a dismaying drop in dividends. So the city fathers appealed to the King, who issued an order requiring people not to smash the windows of the brothel; he went so far as to affix his *fleur-de-lys* device at the entrance. Unfortunately the King's authority didn't count for much in France at that period, least of all in traditionally insubordinate Languedoc; his deterrent failed to deter, so the ladies were moved back within the walls.

Two hundred years later, in 1557, Toulouse was afflicted with the plague. As was customary, the prostitutes were required to keep to their houses and trade fell off sharply because they were regarded as potential carriers of the disease. Many decided to flee the city, relishing neither the confinement nor the loss of trade. But others remained and, in 1559, four of them were caught inside the monastery of Les Grands Augustins. Three were hanged at the monastery gate, while a monk was sent in irons to explain matters to his bishop as best he could. The punishments failed to deter, and the following year three more girls were caught, this time in the monastery of Les Beguins. They too were hanged, and the authorities threatened to close the brothel altogether; they do not seem to have considered closing the monastery, nor is any punishment of the monks recorded.

Despite the defection of those who fled the city's physical bounds or the execution of those who crossed the Church's spiritual ones, the girls of Toulouse were soon once again up to strength. But by now the moral climate was being affected by the ideas of the Reformation, and the authorities were embarrassed by taunts that the robes on their backs were paid for by what the public girls earned on theirs. The brothel revenues were thereupon donated to the city hospital; after six years, however, the hospital returned the gift, not caring for the condition that it should, in return, provide free treatment for ailments contracted by the brothel girls.

In 1587 Toulouse was again visited by plague, and again the girls left town in large numbers. Profiting by their absence, a zealous councillor,

The *accabussade* at Toulouse. From Dufour, *Histoire de la Prostitution*

inspired by the new spirit of ascetism which was spreading as a result of Protestantism, seized the opportunity to close the brothel once and for all. When the girls began to drift back, he set them to work cleaning the streets. But his experiment in occupational re-education was short-lived; the sexual amenities of Toulouse were soon operating as busily as ever.

Occasionally a girl would make a public nuisance of herself while drunk, or a madam would refuse to toe the official line. On such occasions the authorities had recourse to the *accabussade*, the city's traditional penalty for sex offenders. The sinner was taken to the *hôtel de ville;* her hands were tied and a sugar-loaf hat with feathers was placed on her head. She was led in procession to the river Garonne and then ferried to a rock in mid-stream where she was forced to enter a small cage; the girl and the cage were then ducked three times, being submerged just so long—a period of time established, presumably, by trial and error—that she did not suffocate. If she survived, she was confined to the municipal hospital for the rest of her life.

The most complete records of prostitution in medieval Europe come from France; this does not imply that there was more prostitution there than elsewhere, it is simply that the French are more given to keeping records. The great historian of prostitution, Dufour, who in the 1860s published his eight-volume fact-crammed survey of the subject, declared that it would be possible to reconstruct a comprehensive pornography of France by working steadily through the records of every community. But, for all his dedication, he jibbed at the task; he excused himself by affirming that the resulting data would only duplicate the facts he had already collected and would put no additional flesh on to the dry bones of legal reports and municipal proceedings.

Trivial details, however, help to fill out our picture of medieval prostitution. Street names reveal how each town had its prescribed district where prostitutes might ply their trade—Blois, for example, has a rue Rebrousse-Penil and a rue Pousse-Penil, impossible of translation but perhaps the equivalent of Hairycock Lane or Pushprick Alley. That another favoured place of assignation was the public bath is indicated by a law passed in Dijon in 1409 forbidding mixed bathing, and by another in Avignon in 1441 when the clergy were banned from the public baths.

Avignon was one of the places where prostitution was most effectively regulated. On 8 August 1347 'our good Queen Jeanne' (who by a quirk of political circumstance was in fact Queen Joanna of Naples, one of the most notoriously lascivious ladies ever to occupy a throne) decreed that a brothel should be officially recognised there with regular medical inspection and a uniform for the girls. There were to be no visits on religious feast days and Jews were not admitted—this we know, because in 1408 a client named Doupedo, who had been recognised as a Jew, received a public flogging.

Such records of punishment often provide picturesque details. When a prostitute named Isabelle la Boulangère gave her favours to a friend called

Georges on Easter Sunday 1414, she was fined 10 sous because sin is doubly sinful when committed on a holy day. At Beaucaire the 'Abbess' of the officially tolerated house was not permitted to spend two consecutive nights with a customer; but a certain Marguerite so caught the fancy of one Anequin that she infringed the rule on no less than six occasions—and was fined a sou for each offence. The fiercest punishments were meted out to procurers; in 1478 Belut Cantine of Abbeville had her hair burnt off for procuring a girl named Jeannette for a soldier from the local garrison.

Though, in general, French society was willing to live with the prostitute, hers was nevertheless considered an ignoble trade. In Berri a woman accused by another of being a prostitute could, if the accuser failed to prove her charge, require the slanderer to walk through the town wearing only a chemise in which she carried a boulder named The Stone of Scandal; the victim walked behind her, pricking her thighs with a pointed stick.

A few moralists, with the vision to see that abolitionary legislation would never achieve anything, started at the other end of the problem by offering the girls a way out of their profession. But there is a drawback to such schemes, as Jean Simon, Bishop of Paris, discovered in 1492 when he founded his home for repentant prostitutes. He made it as attractive as possible in order to entice the girls from their ways of wickedness; unfortunately he overdid it, and honest women began to prostitute themselves in order to qualify for admission.

If prostitution was prevalent throughout medieval France, it was particularly so in Paris. In his thirteenth-century *Historia Occidentalis*, Jacques de Vitry wrote thus of the Parisian scene:

> Public women wander everywhere in the streets and squares, accosting respectable men and dragging them forcibly into the brothels: if they refuse, the women shout ribald insults after them. You find buildings which house a college upstairs and a brothel downstairs; on the ground floor professors are lecturing while below them the prostitutes exercise their shameful trade.

None tried harder to reform the morals of the Parisians than Louis IX, though it was zeal for the Crusades, not his fight for morality, that earned him his sainthood. In 1254 he made a valiant bid to eradicate prostitution from Paris; all prostitutes were to leave the brothels, and their goods were to be confiscated. What followed was what always follows: open prostitution became clandestine prostitution, unsupervised and uncontrolled. Respectable women suffered because now there was no way to tell the virtuous from the vicious. After two chaotic years the government capitulated; the revised code of 1255 aimed to do no more than contain prostitution within certain bounds.

For thirteen years this semi-tolerant official stance was maintained. Then, just before leaving for the Crusades and perhaps inspired by the solemnity of the occasion, Louis ordered the brothels to be closed; he then set sail without waiting to see what effect his laws had.

As early as 1189, when previous French crusaders had set forth, they had taken with them a shipload of whores, refusing to embark upon the holy enterprise without their companionship. Soon the Saracens were finding that some of their allies were demanding the same aids to morale; however, the Arab chroniclers inform us that the true believers continued to trust Mahomet who assured them that God would provide an endless supply of houris to the Moslem who died fighting the Christian invader.

Now the hapless Louis found that his fighting companions were no more willing to dispense with female company. He had to order them to remove a house of debauchery which they had set up within a stone's throw of his royal pavilion. When an officer was discovered in a house of ill-fame, Louis offered him a choice: he could either be led round the camp at a rope's end by the girl he'd been caught with, or forfeit his horse, armour and harness, and quit the army. This was a delicate point of honour for a nobly born Frenchman; history records that he opted for the second alternative.

While references to heterosexual prostitution are frequent enough in the French records, the homosexual variety is seldom mentioned; but this is only because it was carried on less openly. In fact, so widespread was homosexuality in medieval France that one twelfth-century gentleman, who simply kept a brace of female concubines, was complimented as a model of respectability because he did not also have male companions. Three centuries later the conduct of the bisexual Henri III was so blatantly scandalous that he was publicly caricatured with his '*mignons*'.

While no other nation recorded its history so fully as France, it is evident that prostitution took much the same form throughout Western Europe. The Germans, characteristically, adopted a more consistently practical approach; in their cities a prostitute was apt to be treated more or less as a civil servant—tolerated, protected and sometimes actually employed by the authorities. The Italians, by contrast, set up severe prohibitions

German *Frauenhaus* of the fifteenth century. Anonymous engraving

which were unenforceable and consequently seldom regarded. Rome was notorious for its depravity, which often took its lead from the papal palace; on one occasion Pope Clement VII required the city's brothels to donate half their income to the maintenance of the convent of Santa Maria della Penitenza.

But it was, extraordinarily, in England that the earliest European laws aimed at regulation rather than suppression were formulated. The regulations passed by Henry II's parliament in 1161 to control conduct in the stews of London's Bankside are a key document in the history of the subject. The chronicler John Stow tells us:

> On this bank was sometimes the Bordello, or Stewes, a place so called of certain stew-houses privileged there, for the repair of incontinent men to the like women; of the which privilege I have read thus:
> In a parliament holden at Westminster, the 8th of Henry II, it was ordained by the commons, and confirmed by the king and lords, that divers constitutions for ever should be kept within that lordship or franchise, according to the old customs that had been there used time out of mind: among the which these following were some, viz.
> That no stew-holder or his wife should let or stay any single woman, to go

> and come freely at all times when they listed. No stew-holder to keep any woman to board, but she to board abroad at her pleasure. To take no more for the women's chamber in the week than fourteen pence.
>
> Not to keep open his doors upon the holidays. Not to keep any single woman in his house on the holidays, but the bailiff to see them voided out of the lordship.
>
> No single woman to be kept against her will that would leave her sin. No stew-holder to receive any woman of religion, or any man's wife.
>
> No single woman to take money to lie with any man, but she lie with him all night until the morrow. No man to be drawn or enticed into any stew-house. The constables, bailiff and others, every week to search every stew-house.
>
> No stew-holder to keep any woman that hath the perilous infirmity of burning.

It is clear that these rules were intended to be fair to all parties, and particularly to protect the girls from exploitation. It is interesting that they were expected to live elsewhere and come to the stews only to work; also that short-term visits were discouraged, it was to be all night or nothing, a surprisingly civilised requirement. Indeed the entire document seems a typically British combination of the practical with the humane.

Brothels were also to be found in other parts of medieval London; as in France, street names provide a clue. Unfortunately some of the more picturesque have been amended over the years; you will look in vain today for Gropecuntlane. It was still known by this name in 1276, but records of 1349 show that the 'Grope' had become 'Grape', the lane a street, the cunt forgotten. Later still 'Grape' became 'Grub', and the phrase 'Grub Street' became a synonym for hack writing—so that, despite everything, the street remained dedicated to prostitution of one sort if not another.

However, the Southwark stews continued to be London's leading brothel area. The word 'stews' signifies hot baths, and it is likely that the brothels had grown up on the site of baths built in Roman Londinium, just south of the Thames crossing; here, as in Rome, the baths may have been used for more exciting purposes than washing. By 1380 the stews had become the property of a leading businessman, William Walworth, Mayor of London; he leased them to Flemish women who at this time were prominent in the brothel trade. When, in the following year, the peasants revolted against the injustices of the day, one of their first acts when they marched on London was, like their opposite numbers in Toulouse, to attack the brothels. But these houses were soon back in business and prospering; by the end of the fifteenth century there were eighteen—named 'The Castle', 'The Bell', 'The Cardinal's Hat' and so on, as though they were inns. In 1506 they were officially closed down by the aging Henry VII who, past it himself, was perhaps determined to save his subjects from sin; but he died shortly afterwards, and the brothels quickly opened again. His debauched son, Henry VIII, acted in exactly the same way; a chronicle of 1546 records:

> This year at Easter the stewes was put down by the King's proclamation made there with a trumpet and a herald at arms. Those householders as do inhabit those houses white and painted with signs on the front for a token of the said houses shall avoid with bag and baggage before the feast of Easter.

Mother Holland's Leaguer, Paris Gardens. From the *Roxburghe Ballads*, early seventeenth century

But in the following year Henry died, and his sickly son became Edward VI. Too young to know what lechery was all about, he had to listen while Bishop Latimer thundered against the prevalent debauchery:

> I say that there is now more whoredom in London than ever there was on the Bancke . . . You have put down the stewes, but I pray you, how is the matter amended? What avayleth it that you have but changed the place and not taken the whoredom away?

The colourful reign of Elizabeth saw the Bankside stews back in business, alongside the bear-baiting and the theatres. Sometime around 1603 a lady trading under the name of Donna Britannica Hollandia, but more generally known as Mother Holland, took over the Manor House of Paris Gardens, and opened it as a brothel of a higher class than any previously seen in the district. Its proprietress aimed at attracting the patronage of the highest in the land, and was soon boasting of numbering among her clientele both King James and his favourite, the Duke of Buckingham. Hand-picked girls catered for their needs; good food, fine drink and elegant entertainment were provided. But the standard was not maintained; in 1630 the writer Daniel Lupton was commenting 'this may better be termed a foule denne than a faire garden: here-at foul beasts come to it and as bad or worse keep it'. A year later a troop of soldiers was sent to close down Holland's Leaguer. The aging madam showed a flash of her old spirit; the moment the soldiers set foot on the drawbridge, it was abruptly lowered, plunging them into the water where the girls emptied chamberpots on to their heads. But authority triumphed in the end; by the following year the brothel had been closed and the Manor House reverted to more respectable use.

We do not know precisely why the authorities took action against Mother Holland, but it is more likely to have been on some particular point of dispute than with any intention of closing her establishment simply because it was what it was. For by now the general trend was towards finding a more rational solution to the problem of prostitution—containment rather than confrontation. Two factors encouraged this trend, one in the mind, the other very much in the body.

How many clients must a lady entertain before she qualifies as a prostitute? The question resembles those disputed by medieval theologians, but was in fact posed with a very practical intention by fifteenth-century Italian jurists. It was among the thousand-and-one details which must be settled before the precise status of the prostitute in society could be legally established.

Such legal niceties were part of the process of humanism which was the mainspring of the Renaissance in Europe: the growing realisation that society should be seen, not as an undifferentiated mass, not as a simple pyramid of inferiors below and superiors above, but as a complex structure—as complex as the human body itself—in which even the lowliest members had a part to play. What the prostitute did remained the same as ever, and so did the way she did it. But how what she did affected others became an issue in a way it never had before.

Such abstract considerations might have remained a matter for scholars and academics alone, had there not been a second and more tangible reason which made the problem of prostitution one of immediate public concern—syphilis. There are references to venereal disease throughout the history of sex, but syphilis was something new. From its first recorded incidence on 19 January 1496, four years after Columbus landed in the West Indies, the disease scourged Europe on a terrifying scale. The French armies of Charles VIII, ravaging Italy and its women, picked it up at second-hand from the Genoese sailors and carried it home to France with the rest of their loot. Thence it spread to Britain, Germany and Holland, and eastward as far as China where, as in Europe, it had hitherto not been known. From this time on, the problem of the prostitute could never be dissociated from that of disease; henceforward she represented a sanitary as well as a moral problem.

---

The Renaissance/humanist rediscovery of the individual is appropriately symbolised by the *cortegiane*, Italian courtesans who were the closest latter-day equivalent to the *hetairae* of that earlier golden age of the individual, classical Greece. As the rulers of Europe improved in refinement and culture, so did the women with whom they surrounded themselves; the royal whores and mistresses formed an essential part of establishments where the nominal queen was generally a foreigner, chosen for political and dynastic reasons, maintaining her own entourage and seldom sharing her husband's private life.

Several of the *cortegiane* became famous in their own right: Imperia Cognata, whose apartments were so magnificent that a Spanish guest, looking for somewhere to spit, chose the face of a manservant as the only ugly thing in the room: after modelling for Raphael she died at the age of

Thomas Coryate and a Venetian *cortegiana*. From *Coryat's Crudities*, 1611 edition

thirty-one, despite the efforts of Rome's finest doctors and the blessing of Pope Giulio II; Tullia d'Aragona, a cardinal's daughter who, between professional duties, wrote verses sufficiently skilful to win the patronage of Cosimo de Medici; and Veronica Franco, who successfully roused the more-homosexual-than-otherwise Henri III of France when he came to visit her as a tourist attraction and was persuaded to stay for the complete performance.

We are fortunate to have a detailed account of the Venetian courtesans from the traveller Thomas Coryate, son of the rector of Odcombe in Somerset, whose description of his visit to Venice, in his *Coryats Crudities* of 1611, deserves to be quoted at length:

> The name of a Cortezan of Venice is famoused all over Christendom. It is thought there are of them at the least twenty thousand, whereof many are esteemed so loose, that they are said to open their quivers to every arrow. Methinks the Venetians should be daily afraid lest their winking at such uncleanliness should be an occasion to draw down upon them God's curses and vengeance from Heaven and to consume their city with fire and brimstone.
>
> But they not fearing any such thing do grant large dispensation and indulgence unto them, and that for these two causes. First, they think that the chastity of their wives would be the sooner assaulted, and so consequently they should be capricornised* (which of all the indignities in the world the Venetian cannot patiently endure) were it not for these places of evacuation. The second cause is for that the revenues which they pay unto the Senate for their toleration do maintain a dozen of their galleys and so save them a great charge.
>
> When you come unto one of their Palaces (as indeed some few of the principallest of them live in very magnificent and portly buildings fit for the entertainment of a great Prince) you seem to enter into the Paradise of Venus. For their fairest rooms are most glorious and glittering to behold. As for herself, she comes to thee decked like the Queen and Goddess of Love. Her face is adorned with the quintessence of beauty. The ornaments of her body are so rich, that except thou dost even geld thy affections (a thing hardly to be done) or carry with thee some antidote against those Venerous titillations, she will very near benumb and captivate thy senses. She will endeavour to enchant thee partly with her melodious notes that she warbles out upon her lute, which she fingers with as laudable a stroke as many men that are excellent professors, and partly with that heart-tempting harmony of her voice. Also thou wilt find the Venetian Cortezan (if she be a selected Woman indeed) a good Rhetorician, and a most elegant discourser.
>
> But beware that thou enter not into terms of private conversation with her. For then thou shalt find her the crafty and hot daughter of the sun. Moreover I will tell thee this news which is most true, that if thou shouldst wantonly converse with her, and not give her that *salarium iniquitatis* which thou hast promised her, but perhaps cunningly escape from her company, she will either cause thy throat to be cut by her Ruffiano, if he can after

*ie given the symbolic goats' horns of the traditional cuckold.

Italian courtesans on a balcony. From a painting by Carpaccio, *c* 1500

catch thee in the City, or procure thee to be arrested and clapped up in the prison, where thou shalt remain till thou hast paid her all thou didst promise her.

In 1607 an anonymous English writer explained: 'Your whore is for every rascal, but your courtesan is for your courtier.' A similar distinction was drawn in every European country, and every ruling class maintained its race of courtesans appropriate to the degree of social development their country had attained. In France the glittering new chateaux of Blois and Brissac, Cheverny and Menars—built with no pretence to military necessity, simply for pleasure—were ornamented with ladies like Marion de Lorme, mistress of Cinq-Mars, the Cardinal de Richelieu and other notables, or Ninon de l'Enclos, focal point of a circle of lovers and suitors renowned for their wit and gallantry. Though superficially they resembled the Italian *cortegiane*, these courtesans belong rather in the kept mistress category, passing from one patron to another rather than being generally available; nevertheless they were the pinnacle of their profession to whom every aspiring career-prostitute looked with admiration and envy.

For those who were not members of the ruling class, such ladies symbolised the decadence and luxury of the court. As the merchant and the banker increased in influence, they sought to curb the ways whereby the rulers exploited the rest of the population. Prostitution was clearly a natural target. In 1560 the Parlement of Paris, headed by Michel de l'Hôpital, taking advantage of the fact that King Henri III was only nine—even in France that is on the early side for sexual activity—framed a set of laws which in principle abolished prostitution. At first they were interpreted as meaning that only clandestine brothels and those located outside the traditionally prescribed areas were to go; long-established houses claimed their ancient privileges and expected to stay in business. The courts heard their claims, but allowed no exceptions; no brothel might escape the ban. In principle, that is. In practice it was the usual story. Houses with wealthy owners, or with patrons in influential places, succeeded in making private arrangements, and somehow stayed open. But now it was only on sufferance, not as a matter of right. Thus the system of *maisons de tolérance*—'tolerated houses'—was born; for good or ill, it has ever since characterised prostitution in France.

Across the Channel, things could scarcely have taken a more different course; in Britain the seventeenth century saw the moral pendulum swinging this way and that, reflecting the vicissitudes of official attitudes

Courtesan from sixteenth-century Basel. Holbein

The house of La Schoon Mayken, Brussels. Crispin de la Passe, *c* 1630

and public response to them. Philip of Spain had earlier sent his invincible Armada to bring England back into the papal fold; a happy combination of Drake's fireships and God's scattering wind had thwarted this attempt. The Scarlet Woman of Rome—represented by the daring Guy Fawkes and his backing of sinister Jesuits—had tried for a dramatic come-back and failed. So now the English were all set to conduct their lives very differently from the debaucheries of the Spanish, French and Italian papists; the favourite plays on the London stage portrayed cloaked and daggered Italians indulging in every form of villainy, with incidents of rape and incest shown to be of common occurrence.

The Civil War of the 1640s, culminating in the execution of Charles I, gave doctrinaire religionists the opportunity to impose their moral views on the nation as a whole. For a dozen years or so, theatres were closed—even those which showed papists in so unfavourable a light; prostitution was suppressed and maypoles—the most innocent of phallic symbols—banned. England being England, the puritan repression was never so brutally harsh as, say, in Calvin's Geneva; but in its totally negative approach to natural impulses, its stopping-up of every outlet for recreation, it was a wrong-headed experiment and doomed to failure. The reaction came when Cromwell's Commonwealth collapsed and the monarchy was restored.

It is not easy to take a balanced view of Restoration England. If you are of an abstemious cast of mind and believe that Cromwell's puritans had the right idea and their only mistake was going too far and too fast, then the court of Charles II may seem a cesspool of iniquity. If, on the other hand, you judge Restoration society by the standards of other European nations, what emerges is a permissive class whose easygoing style of living, though admittedly neither praiseworthy nor socially constructive, did little harm to the world.

The beauties of the Restoration court—Nell Gwyn and Catherine Sedley and all those other subjects of Lely's portraits who, whether married or not, bestowed their favours so generously—were career-prostitutes to a greater degree than the French courtesans. Yet they too conducted themselves with wit and elegance, and had regard for social requirements if not for moral dictates. Charles II said of his puritan critics, 'if they don't like the brothels, they needn't go to them'; this laissez-faire attitude was characteristic of the period—as indicated by one of the court's most notable figures, the profligate but talented Lord Rochester:

> I rise at eleven, I dine at two,
> I get drunk before seven, and the next thing I do
> I send for my whore when, for fear of the clap,
> I come in her hand and I spew in her lap.
> Then we quarrel and scold till I fall fast asleep,
> when the bitch growing bold, to my pocket doth creep.
> She slyly then leaves me, and to revenge my affront
> at once she bereaves me of money and cunt.
> I storm and I roar, and I fall in a rage,
> and, missing my whore, I bugger my page.

Although not an attractive picture, it has the rough honesty and humour of a Hogarth painting; these same qualities place the Restoration comedies, for all their questionable ethics, in the top rank of the dramatic repertoire.

For the mid-seventeenth-century man in the street, pleasures were many and various. Pepys' diaries are scattered with references to prostitutes, working either in brothels or as streetwalkers; there were also establishments like Mrs Creswell's, of Lewknor Lane, which would despatch a girl anywhere at short notice. The best place for picking up

Elinor (Nell) Gwyn with her two sons. Henry Gascar, engraved by Stodart prostitutes was the theatre. Dryden, in his prologue to Southerne's play *The Disappointment*, noted:

> The playhouse is their place of traffic, where
> nightly they sit to sell their rotten ware.
> Intrencht in vizor mask they giggling sit
> and throw designing looks about the pit,
> neglecting wholly what the actors say—
> 'tis their least business there to see the play.

Many actresses supplemented their earnings by selling their favours; the career of Nell Gwyn differs from that of many of her fellows only by the degree of her success. At a fairly early age she was probably working for the notorious madam, Mother Ross; and, like many prostitutes, took a job selling oranges in the theatre as a way of gaining admittance to this most rewarding of market places.

While working as an orange-seller she caught the eye of Thomas Lacey, a leading actor of the day; with his help she crossed the footlights on to the stage. Pepys, who saw her act in 1666, assures us that, though less satisfactory in tragedy, she displayed real talent in comic roles. She showed an even greater talent in other spheres, attracting the notice of a succession of aristocratic patrons, culminating in Lord Dorset. Then the Duke of Buckingham—who, for reasons of his own, wished to divert the king's attentions from Barbara, Duchess of Cleveland—decided that Nell might prove an effective distraction. As every schoolboy knows, he was right; Nell Gwyn remained a favourite of Charles until his dying day. Bishop Burnet said of the relationship: 'He never treated her with the decencies of a mistress, but rather with the lewdness of a prostitute.' Nell was not one to complain; she herself—reproaching one of the King's other mistresses, the Duchess of Portsmouth, for her high-and-mighty ways—said, 'As for me, it is my profession, I do not pretend to anything better.'

# 4

# *SALEABLE FOR GOLD*

> Ever the courtesan is the young man's companion,
> common to all as the wayside creeper;
> your body is merchandise saleable for gold.
> (from the Indian of Sudraka, *Mrichchakatika*)

When the first Europeans came to the islands of Oceania in the Pacific they were astonished by the readiness with which the inhabitants permitted their wives, sisters and daughters to have sex with the visitors in return for gifts. Was this simply the local variant of the prostitution the Europeans knew at home? The anthropologist Malinowski, writing at the end of the nineteenth century about the Trobriand Islanders, reported that when a young man received sexual favours from a girl he would then present her with a gift. While a foreigner might interpret this as payment for an act of prostitution, Malinowski saw it as a manifestation of the reciprocal present-giving which was traditional among the Trobrianders.

However, such a tradition was clearly vulnerable to conversion into a more venal arrangement, and this is what happened under the impact of the Europeans' arrival in the Pacific. There must have been tremendous excitement among the natives at the sight of these exotic visitors arriving in their marvellous vessels, with wonderful clothes and astonishing possessions. To offer them food and drink, hospitality and entertainment was a natural thing to do; it was equally natural to offer sex.

The people who enjoyed and suffered the first major impact of Europe on the Pacific were the Tahitians. They were amazed—and amused—when the European sailors insisted on going into the privacy of the woods to make love, for they were perfectly willing to copulate as publicly as they would eat, drink, dance or play games; Captain Cook in his diary

Eighteenth-century English sailors with girls of the Pacific islands. Anonymous French engraving

recorded seeing the natives having sex in the open without any embarrassment. From the age of nine or ten, when they reached puberty, the Tahitian girls would have sex promiscuously, casually and guiltlessly.

When they became pregnant, they usually married. After marriage they were no longer so promiscuous, but sex continued to be taken lightly and a husband would not necessarily be jealous if his wife had sex with another man. So women of whatever marital status gave their favours to the European visitors; sex was also offered at a more official level, as the French navigator Bougainville found in 1768, at a party given by the Tahitian chiefs, where girls were provided along with the food and drink.

The traditional tokens of gratitude would be expected, of course, particularly since their visitors had such wonderful gifts to bestow. Of these the most desirable to the Tahitians were nails, for iron was unknown to them. The sailors soon learned what a nail could purchase; when the ship's carpenter's supply had been exhausted, nails were surreptitiously removed from the vessel itself—even those which held up their hammocks, the men being willing to sleep on the deck. Soon, what had begun as a spontaneous traffic became a regulated one. Captain Samuel Wallis, on his first memorable visit to Tahiti in *Dolphin* in 1767—the first substantial contact between Europeans and the islanders—recorded in his *Journal*:

> Chastity does not seem to be considered as a virtue among them, for they not only readily and openly trafficked with our people for personal favours, but were brought down by their fathers and brothers for that purpose; they were, however, conscious of the value of beauty, and the size of the nail that was demanded for the enjoyment of the lady was always in proportion to her charms. The men who came down to the side of the river, at the same time that they presented the girl, shewed a stick of the size of the nail that was to be her price, and if our people agreed, she was sent over to them, for the men were not permitted to cross the river. This commerce was carried on a considerable time before the officers discovered it, for while some straggled a little way to receive the lady, the others kept a look-out. When I was acquainted with it, I no longer wondered that the ship was in danger of being pulled to pieces for the nails and iron that held her together.

Clearly, by this stage, gift-swapping had turned into prostitution. The native girls, after the first heady delirium, are unlikely to have been so partial to having sex with British sailors that they would do so without hope of reward. So the old tradition was modified. However, what had happened was not, as might superficially appear, the simple corruption of innocent native maidens into guilty harlots by the vicious white man. All that Wallis' men did was introduce an additional dimension of demand into the situation, whereupon the inevitable laws of supply and demand took over.

The price rose as the traffic continued. The demand for girls remained steady, but the demand for nails began to fall. Cook, following in Wallis' wake in 1769, found nails less in demand than clothes; returning from his Antarctic voyage, he noted that now not even clothes were in great demand. The Tahitians were exceedingly struck by some bright red parrot feathers which had been acquired during this last expedition, and these rapidly acquired the status of currency; a chief's wife, with her husband's approval, offered herself to Cook for a single feather. He politely declined.

Cook was a practical man, and ready to look indulgently on a traffic which seemed more beneficial than otherwise in view of his men's need and the natives' readiness to meet it. But in a larger context he saw that evil consequences could follow, and wrote in his journal:

> We debauch their morals, already prone to vice, and we introduce among them wants and perhaps disease which they never before knew, and which serve only to disturb that happy tranquillity they and their forefathers had enjoyed.

Cook's use of the word 'perhaps' in relation to venereal disease reflects a continuing uncertainty about the extent to which the Europeans were responsible for bringing it to the Pacific. Wallis insisted his men were clean; so did Bougainville, and so did Cook. But knowledge of disease was still rudimentary. Sailors habitually frequented prostitutes, and prostitutes were habitually diseased; it is almost inconceivable that none of the sailors from these ships had ever been infected, and, even though they had been inspected before leaving Europe, they could somehow have avoided detection or simply been an undetectable carrier of venereal disease. It seems certain that, along with their nails and their parrot feathers, the Europeans brought disease.

In one respect, however, the effects of European intrusion were beneficial, at any rate to the girls, for previously infanticide of female children had been widespread among the New Zealanders. Now they were spared in order to be hired out as mistresses; European whaling men, for instance, took 'wives' for a season from the native tribes. Similarly, in the Dutch East Indies, sexual facilities were made available, to each according to his need: for the transient sailor, prostitutes in the seaport brothels; for the merchants, planters and administrators, native mistresses, purchased or rented, casually or regularly.

From the accounts of early European visitors to Africa it is clear that prostitution already existed there as an institution, and in forms which—though, as in Europe, they may have had religious origins—had already been modified to meet secular needs. Here is what the Dutch traveller Bosman, in his *Description of the Coast of Guinea* (1705), had to say regarding West Africa in the seventeenth century:

> In these countries are several women who never marry, and who are called whores, being initiated in that trade in the following manner. When the *Manaceroes* [young men of the tribe] find they want a common whore, they petition the *Caboceroes* [elders] that they will please graciously to buy one for the public. The woman so purchased is brought to the market place, accompanied by another already experienced in that trade, in order to instruct her how she should disport herself for the future; which being perfectly accomplished, the Novice is smeared all over with earth, and several offerings offered for her success in her future occupation.
>
> This over, a little boy, yet immature for love affairs, makes a feint or representation of lying with her before all the people; by which 'tis hinted to her that from this time forwards, she is obliged to receive all persons

> indistinguishable who offer themselves to her, not excepting little boys.
>
> Then a little out of the way a small hut is built for her, in which she is obliged to confine herself for eight or ten days, and lie with every man who comes thither; after which, she obtains the honourable name of Abelacre, signifying a common whore; and she has a dwelling-place assigned her near one of her masters, or in a particular place in the town, she being for the remainder of her life obliged to refuse no man the use of her body, though he offer never so small a sum; which seldom amounts to above one penny, and if any body is so well pleased with his entertainment, as to give more, 'tis owing to his civility, for he is not obliged to it.
>
> Each of the above-mentioned towns has two or three of these miserable wretches, according to their largeness. The money that they get they bring to their masters, who return them so much out of it as is necessary to subsist them in clothes and necessaries. As soon as the gain begins to cease, they withdraw their hands, and never so much as take the least care of her; and thus these unhappy creatures come to a miserable end.

Bosman indicates that similar customs prevailed in other West African lands at the time:

> In Whydah, and in all the land of Dahomey, is a very great plenty of these whores, and at a cheaper price than on the Gold Coast. I have seen a vast multitude of huts, not above ten foot long and six broad, placed near the great roads throughout the whole country; in which these women are obliged to ply at their appointed days in the week for the relief of all persons; and these countries being very populous, the slaves vastly numerous, and the married women kept up very strict, these whores on those days must of necessity be very tired: I have been assured that some of them hath lain with thirty men on a day.

Clearly the indigenous African did not need the European to introduce any evil ways; he was perfectly capable of devising and institutionalising prostitution for himself—though it is, of course, dangerous to generalise from such sparse information. If our knowledge of social history in pre-colonial Africa is limited, we are fortunate to have fuller information regarding the great civilisations of Asia.

In the sixth century BC a lady named Ambapali flourished in the Indian city of Vaisali. She was rich, influential, cultivated and famous, so it was only fitting that when Buddha visited that city it should be at her house that he lodged. Yet if Ambapali was celebrated, it was not for her wealth or intellect, but as the paramount courtesan of her day.

In Indian history, in Indian culture, the prostitute has always had a part. Ambapali, who in due course retired from her profession, presented her hard-earned mango groves to Buddha, and attained to *arhat* (a state of holiness), seems at first sight cast in the same mould as the Phrynes and Aspasias of classical Greece. But their cultural environments were essentially different. The Greek attitude to prostitution was a superficial one, viable only because nobody asked too many awkward questions. The Indian attitude was more profound, more philosophically based—yet at the same time more realistic.

The basis of this attitude is to be found in the fatalism which has been a main—perhaps *the* main—ingredient in Indian thought throughout its recorded history. Every Hindu—and this went for the prostitute no less than for anyone else—was considered as having been born into a specific stratum of society, with a role to play in the great scheme of things. *Dharma* (Fate) required some women to be born to be prostitutes, just as others were born to be rajahs' wives or stonebreakers by the wayside. For the women of the three superior castes, prostitution was unthinkable; for those of lower birth, it was acceptable and even, under particular circumstances, a duty.

Just because she had an accepted place in the social structure did not mean the prostitute was not despised. She *was*—but only as refuse-collectors or street-cleaners were despised, on principle, not on moral grounds. A Brahmin—the highest caste of Hindu—would regard the prostitute as unclean, and his priest discouraged him from having anything to do with her; if he did, he was required to ritually cleanse himself afterwards. But this was a spiritual matter and implied no ethical comment; nobody blamed the prostitute for being what she was, nor was she expected to feel any guilt about it.

In India the prostitute had her place in the scheme of things because sex had its place in the scheme of things. Temple sculptures show how sex was integrated into the country's religious life as it has never been in the West: there are no representations of cunnilingus or fellatio at Chartres as there are at Khajuraho or Konarek:

> None of these scenes could have got onto the walls of the Khajuraho temples without universal acceptance of union between the male and the female as the height of spiritual sensitiveness, and of the extension of the pleasure of the body as the vehicle of the soul.
>
> (Mulk Raj Anand, *Kama Kala*, 1958)

As early as 300 BC, a treatise on the art of government—the *Arthasastra* of Kautilya—detailed the duties of the Court Superintendent of Prostitutes. Salaried *ganikas*—the highest grade of courtesan—were part of the establishment, maintained at the ruler's expense and giving him two days' earnings a month in return for his protection. They had their place in the royal household, with statutory rights (such as protection against customers who tried to abuse them) and obligations (they were required to accept all customers, no matter how distasteful). To fit them for their duties, they were instructed in a variety of accomplishments which included a great deal more than the mere giving of sexual pleasure to their companions. In the Sanskrit classic *Dasa Kumara Charita*, the mother of the famous courtesan Kamamanjari gives a description of her daughter's upbringing:

> Since her earliest childhood I have bestowed the greatest care upon her, doing everything in my power to promote her health and beauty. I had her carefully instructed in dancing, acting, playing musical instruments, singing, painting, preparing perfumes and flowers, writing and conversation, and even to some extent in grammar, logic and philosophy.

Formal instruction in sex itself was taken for granted. Indian literature from the earliest times has contained manuals of practical instruction for lovers. The best known is the *Kama Sutra* of Vatsyayana, compiled some time between the first and fourth centuries AD; it embodies material from earlier teachings and was in turn quarried for later manuals, so it should be seen not as a one-off phenomenon but as part of a continuing tradition spanning many centuries. One has only to compare the *Kama Sutra* with the very best of Western writing on the subject—Ovid's *Ars Amoris*, for example—to appreciate the depth and wisdom of the Indian approach. Yet Vatsyayana never forgets that the courtesan is first and last a professional, whose first object is to obtain money from her customer. He devotes an entire chapter to ways of extracting extra money from a lover, such as falsely alleging that her property has been lost, or simulating illness and charging the cost of imaginary treatment—we may assume that the very best of Western writing on the subject—Ovid's *Ars Amoris*, for customers who can be materially useful to the courtesan—officials, ministers of justice, spirit merchants—and those to whom she should resort merely for the sake of love or fame, such as poets, artists and storytellers. Though less likely to offer much by way of monetary reward, they might be better company.

> The duty of a courtesan consists in forming connections with suitable men; attaching the person she has selected to herself; in extracting wealth from her lover; and then, after she has separated him from all his possessions, dismissing him.

This quotation suggests that the *Kama Sutra* preaches the most consummate cynicism; but, in context, this is seen as realism, and such deceits and devious tricks fall into place as the functional guidelines of the courtesans' trade. The real hypocrisy would be to act in any other way.

What Indian prostitution was like in practice, as distinct from what was recommended in the handbooks, is indicated from occasional references. Here is Jakarta's account of a brothel visit during the earliest centuries AD:

> This was the procedure in that brothel; of every thousand pieces of money that were received, five hundred were for the women while the remainder was for the clothes, perfumes and garlands. Customers were supplied with clothes to wear, and stayed all night; next morning they took off the clothes they had been given, put on their own, and went on their way.

From the tenth century AD, India was invaded by the Moslems, whose religious principles, dictated by the Koran, firmly forbade prostitution. But Indian permissiveness was stronger than Moslem piety, and soon the new rulers had acquired their concubines and were playing patron to the dancing girls. As Antony Schorer, of the Dutch East India Company, noted at the beginning of the seventeenth century: 'Moslems buy a female slave for their sons who are grown up but not yet married, to keep them from frequenting prostitutes.' For the general public, prostitution seems to have been organised much as anywhere else. Peter Mundy, an Englishman who visited India around 1630, reported that 'common stewes' were to be found in Agra and other important cities; he saw them as: ' . . . like a faire, where they resort, make their bargains, take and choose the whores sitting and lying on their cots at their balconies and doors'.

Indian prostitution never entirely discarded its religious associations, however; every Hindu community had its temple, and most temples had their *devadasi* (servants of the gods). Tanjore, for example, in the eleventh century possessed 400 of these girls, supported by the temple and supporting it in their turn, each according to her ability. They served in the temple, danced and sang on festive occasions, and prostituted themselves to priests and visitors. In their capacity as entertainers they were

*Devadasi*, Indian temple prostitute. Wall-painting from a cliff temple at Ajunta

often hired out to private individuals, or were employed by the community for special occasions like wedding feasts. Though they did not aspire to the status of the superior grades of courtesan, they took their duties seriously. As late as the 1860s, an English traveller reported that the temple *bayaderes* devoted two hours every day to singing and dancing lessons. Thanks to their professional training, they were frequently the only women of any accomplishment in the neighbourhood.

No less accomplished, in their own way, were the *hinjras*—prostitute-entertainer homosexuals—who specialised in skilful displays of singing and dancing, dressed as women. Generally if not invariably available for prostitution, they were at one time said to artificially enlarge the anus with wooden devices. The *hinjras* are still tolerated, but despised by the rest of society which has traditionally been strongly heterosexual in attitude. The traveller Richard Burton, while serving in India, had the opportunity to observe male prostitution at first hand. In 1845, when Sir Charles Napier had just completed the conquest of Sind and was camped within a mile of Karachi, it was reported to him that in the town were three brothels housing boys and eunuchs, and that the boys cost nearly twice as much as the eunuchs. Burton, disguised as a merchant, was sent to investigate; he confirmed the report, and was able to explain the price differential—boys cost more than eunuchs because 'the scrotum of the unmutilated boy could be used as a kind of bridle for directing the movements of the animal'.

The Chinese, too, approached prostitution in a practical fashion. But, whereas in India prostitution was just one aspect of a positive and all-pervading sexual attitude, thoroughly integrated with other aspects of life, in China it was the mechanical consequence of a totally negative attitude to the female sex. Perhaps nowhere else in the world have women been so inexorably relegated to a secondary social status as in China; confined to the home, required to live in almost complete seclusion, wholly dominated by their menfolk, women of whatever class, whether nominally daughter or wife, widow or spinster, have been little better than slaves.

As is so often the case where such an imbalance exists, the birth of a female child came to be regarded as an affliction. It was accepted that there had to be female children, and nature no doubt knew what she was about in arranging for approximately every second child to be a girl; but every family hoped it would be blessed with sons and that other families would be saddled with the necessary girl children. Female infanticide was prevalent among the poorer classes, and—more constructively—it was often possible to capitalise on misfortune by selling off unwanted daughters as prostitutes; for that, if for nothing else, girl children were well fitted.

This traffic in unwanted girls was the foundation of Chinese prostitution. Itinerant dealers wandered the countryside recruiting girls for the city brothels—a more or less fixed scale related the purchase price to the child's attractiveness. There had been brothels in China from the earliest recorded period; in the seventeenth century BC, Emperor Kwan Chung, of the Chou dynasty, set aside specific areas for prostitution, and these were officially licensed under the T'ang and S'ung dynasties.

The girls, purchased as tiny children, were set to work, when they

Chinese brothel, from an anonymous woodcut

were old enough, as servants of the establishment. In this way they acquired the ancillary skills of a prostitute: how to serve food and drink, how to dress and adorn themselves, how to entertain a visitor. At fourteen they started work properly. If they did their job well, they might succeed in making a reasonable way of life for themselves, perhaps even closing their career by managing a brothel. Although, with exceptional luck, they might thus ensure a comfortable old age, the majority kept at work until too unattractive, and were then relegated to being housekeepers and drudges, or simply thrown out to fend for themselves.

At their best, Chinese prostitutes could be accomplished and attractive courtesans whose company, like that of the *hetairae* of classical Greece, was probably far more entertaining than that of a man's regular wife. Here is Marco Polo, writing of Kin-sai—now Hangchow—in the thirteenth century:

> There are courtesans here in such numbers as I dare not venture to report, and not only near the squares, which is the situation usually appropriated for their residence, but in every part of the city they are to be found, adorned with much finery, highly perfumed, occupying well-furnished houses, and attended by many female domestics. These women are accomplished, and are perfect in the arts of blandishment and dalliance, which they accompany with expressions adapted to every description of person, insomuch that strangers who have once tasted of their charms remain in a state of fascination, and become so fascinated by their meretricious arts that they can never divest themselves of this impression. Thus intoxicated with sensual pleasures, when they return to their homes they report that they have been in Kin-sai, or the celestial city, and pant for the time when they may be enabled to revisit paradise.

While the Chinese could hope to find an earthly paradise, the Moslem had to trust his God's promise that he would enjoy his due share of sexual bliss in the hereafter. Muhammad, in the Koran, is unequivocal on the subject of prostitution: it is quite simply forbidden. He claimed that the Islamic social structure rendered prostitutes unnecessary; there were indeed certain factors operating in Arab society which tended to diminish the need for the professional prostitute. The bedouin—the desert nomads who made up a significant proportion of the Arab world—had a tradition of hospitality which ensured that a visitor was offered a sleeping companion along with other necessities. Furthermore, the prevalence of homosexuality, which met with only the mildest social disapproval, meant that the fiercest desires of the young men could find an alternative outlet.

Nevertheless, prostitution has always been an element in Arab society, whether in the form of brothels, independent prostitutes or entertainers. Even in Mecca, the heart of Islam, prostitutes mingled with the pilgrims and offered their services. Intercourse with a pilgrim was considered by a prostitute to be a pious act. There are accounts of strange practices at the shrine of the Ka'aba itself; women of the Banu Amir tribe, while making the ritual circumambulation of the sacred stone, did so unclothed and chanting obscenely in their own form of devotion. Burckhardt tells of public acts of homosexuality, likewise performed with devotional intent. No doubt such practices were disapproved of by the priesthood and were attributable to only a minute proportion of Moslems. But such instances confirm—as do others reported here from China, from India, from Africa, from the Pacific—that whatever the cultural background, whatever social and religious sanctions are observed, somehow, everywhere, a place is found for the prostitute.

# 5
# SPLENDID MADAMS AND CIVIL NYMPHS

> The splendid Madam at 50 guineas a night, down to the civil nymph with white-thread stockings who tramps along the Strand and will resign her engaging person to your honour for a pint of wine and a shilling . . .
>
> (Boswell's *Journal*, 1763)

Eighteenth-century London was a wide open city, the capital of a nation which was rapidly taking its place as one of the leading world powers. Musicians and painters, writers and dancers thronged to this city where the wealthiest patrons were to be found in conjunction with the greatest social and political stability; and with them came the dancing masters and the singing teachers, the pimps and procurers and prostitutes, and all the parasites of wealth.

When James Boswell, future biographer of Dr Johnson, came from Scotland to London at the age of twenty-two there was no lack of opportunity for business or pleasure. A well-born but none-too-wealthy young man, on his own for the first time, he was dazzled by the prospect of taking his pick of the women of the town—and that there were plenty to choose from is evident from the diaries of d'Archenholz, a German visitor who calculated that there were some 50,000 prostitutes in the city, not including kept mistresses:

> The most wretched of these live with matrons, who lodge, board and clothe them. The dress worn by the very lowest of them is silk, according to the custom which luxury has generally introduced into England. Sometimes they escape from their prisons, with their little wardrobe under their arms, and trade on their own bottoms, when, if they are unfortunate, or happen not to be economical, they are soon dragged to the gaol by their creditors.

Mistress Russell, a noted London courtesan, *c* 1700. M. Laroon, engraved by Lydekker

Boswell's *Journals* give us what is unfortunately so rare—the customer's-eye-view of prostitution.

> 25 March 1763—As I was coming home this night, I felt carnal inclinations raging through my frame. I determined to gratify them. I went to St James Park and picked up a whore. For the first time did I engage in armour* which I found but a dull satisfaction. She who submitted to my lusty embraces was a young Shropshire girl, only 17, very well-looked, her name Elizabeth Parker. Poor being, she has a sad time of it!
>
> 31 March—At night I strolled into the Park and took the first whore I met, whom I without many words copulated with free from danger, being safely sheathed. She was ugly and lean and her breath smelt of spirits. I never asked her name. When it was done, she slunk off. I had a low opinion of this gross practice and resolved to do it no more.
>
> 17 May—Just at the bottom of Downing Street I picked up a fresh agreeable girl called Alice Gibbs. We went down a lane to a snug place, and I took out my armour, but she begged that I might not put it on, as the sport was much pleasanter without it, and as she was quite safe, I was so rash as to trust her, and had a very agreeable congress.
>
> 28 July—As we walked along the Strand tonight, arm in arm, a woman of the town came enticingly near us. 'No,' said Mr Johnson, 'no, my girl, it won't do.' We then talked of the unhappy situation of these wretches, and how much more misery than happiness, upon the whole, is produced by irregular love.

But for those who knew their way around, and whose pockets were better lined than young Boswell's, London had a great deal more to offer than casual streetwalkers. Brothels and night houses, though nominally illegal, abounded. There had, as we have seen, been brothels in London for centuries, but it was only in the eighteenth century that they started to diversify, catering to narrow social groupings and for specialised tastes. Much of the credit should go to Mrs Goadby, whose house in Berwick Street, Soho, opened about 1750, marked the shape of things to come. She had visited the celebrated houses of Justine Paris and Montigny in Paris, and planned her establishment on the same lines; it was business-

*a crude form of condom worn more as a protection against infection than as a contraceptive.

like but also a pleasure to visit in its own right, with hand-picked and elegant girls.

Mrs Goadby's success led to the setting up of well-conducted brothels throughout the West End. King's Place—an inconspicuous turning off Pall Mall, conveniently close to the palaces of Buckingham and St James, the Houses of Parliament and the town houses of the aristocracy—was made up entirely of brothels. It was here that the celebrated Charlotte Hayes maintained her 'Cloister', where the daily business was enlivened by elaborate entertainments. One of these was inspired by the recent voyages of Cook and Wallis in the South Seas; she re-created a 'Feast of Venus' at which, as she chose to interpret the explorers' accounts, young maidens of Otaheite were publicly instructed in the arts of sex. She herself took the role of Queen Oberea, chief instructress; twelve virgins and twelve able youths played the other roles, greatly to the edification of twenty-three high-ranking and high-paying guests, who included five members of Parliament. Some of her audience, unable to contain themselves through the two-hour performance, insisted on taking an active part in the ceremonies.

Many of the fashionable brothels were named in the printed guides available to assist the stranger. We read of Miss Harriott, a Jamaican negress, who had come to England as a slave and opened a house in King's Place when her master died of the smallpox; of Mrs Banks, in Curzon Street, who offered both vigorous men and voluptuous girls to clients of either sex, singly or in pairs; of Mrs Redson, in Bolton Street, whose house of assignation was available for those who preferred to make their own arrangements; of the notorious Moll King, of Covent Garden, whose low establishment was depicted by Hogarth.

In Covent Garden, too, were the bagnios, still playing their ambiguous role; one appreciative customer was the Italian adventurer Casanova, who visited London in 1765:

> I also visited the bagnios, where a rich man can sup, bathe and sleep with a fashionable courtesan, of which species there are many in London. It makes a magnificent debauch and only costs six guineas.

The town's most imaginative brothel was Miss Fawkland's, patronised by such distinguished persons as Lord Bolingbroke and Lord Hamilton, the novelist Smollett and the playwright Sheridan. The establishment comprised three adjacent houses. In the first, the Temple of Aurora, were twelve young girls aged between eleven and sixteen, who for the most

Casanova and friends. From the 1845 edition of his *Memoirs*

part entertained elderly gentlemen; actual sexual intercourse was strictly forbidden. Those who desired more vigorous activity went next door to the Temple of Flora, where were a dozen ladies more mature and more skilled. If your tastes were more specialised, you knocked at the door of the Temple of Mysteries, where any and every whim could be humoured —at a price. The Fawkland girls were well cared for; working conditions were far removed from the rough-and-ready brothels of the past or of less sophisticated neighbourhoods.

Those unable or unwilling to pay Miss Fawkland's or Charlotte Hayes' fancy prices were not, however, reduced to following Boswell into the Park. Almost every pub had its 'tavern players', kept discreetly behind the scenes but available in an upstairs room if called for. The leafy walks of the suburban pleasure gardens—Vauxhall and Ranelagh, Belsize Park and Sadler's Wells—provided a happy hunting ground for the prostitute. And of course the theatres continued to play their traditional role.

Many of the greatest names in the eighteenth-century theatre rose from the ranks of whoredom. There was Anne Bellamy, who declared that she experienced truly satisfactory sexual pleasure only after an evening of intelligent conversation had previously 'freed the soul and transported it to the Elysian Fields'. There was Kitty Fisher, extravagant mistress of the Duke of York, immortalised by a nursery rhyme and by the story of her response when the duke sent her £50 instead of the £100 she expected for a night's pleasure; she sent the banknote to her pastrycook who baked it in a tart which she thereupon ate for breakfast.

Many actresses supplemented their legitimate earnings by prostitution. Nancy Parsons, mistress of the Duke of Grafton, claimed once to have earned, when short of money, 100 guineas in one week—at a guinea a throw. Mrs Williams, of Drury Lane theatre, liked to work in brothels even after she had made a success on the boards. Frances Abington, considered by many the finest actress of her generation, had begun her career as Fanny Barton, working for Charlotte Hayes; no doubt it was there that she acquired her taste for low-cut dresses which caused comment even in those easygoing days—though they didn't prevent her living to be eighty-four.

Homosexuals, too, were catered for; at 'molly houses', like Mother Clap's in unsalubrious Field Lane, clients would gather to choose or be chosen, and retire to a private room to be 'married'. But, even in permissive London, homosexual activity was screened by the severest of taboos; those who catered for 'unnatural lusts', as the contemporary writer Edward Ward characteristically described them, were continually harassed. When Mother Clap's was raided in 1726, the proprietress protested: 'I hope it will be considered that I am a woman, and therefore it cannot be thought that I would ever be concerned in such practices.' But she was convicted of keeping 'a sodomitical house', fined £13 6s $8\frac{3}{4}$d, made to stand in the Smithfield pillory, and imprisoned for two years. In 1726, too, three homosexuals were hanged at Tyburn, and scarcely a year went by without vindictive punishments for this practice being meted out. But persecution could not eradicate the demand—which was sufficiently widespread for Smollett, in his *Roderick Random* of 1748, to make one of his characters suggest that homosexuality, though 'condemned by our laws . . . in all probability will become in a short time a more fashionable vice than simple fornication'—and so the molly houses survived.

While it was the homosexuals who attracted the fiercest criticism, the whole spectrum of London's sex life was an affront to many who were appalled that it was conducted so blatantly and on such a large scale. Solutions were sought—some of them more realistic than others. In 1758 Dr William Dodd, a court chaplain eventually hanged for forgery, founded the Magdalen Hospital near Goodmans Fields, a neighbourhood notorious for its brothels. The inmates were dressed in sober grey uniforms and set to work at sewing; it cannot have offered a

A clergyman accosted by a streetwalker near the Temple, London, 1716. From the *Newgate Calendar*

very attractive alternative to life on the pavement, and perhaps only the least successful whores would have found it a change for the better.

More enlightened was Bernard de Mandeville's brilliantly perceptive *Modest Defence of Publick Stews* of 1724, in which he contended, on purely utilitarian grounds, that a state-approved brothel was the most advantageous solution to the social problem of prostitution:

> Though the Method I intend to propose, of erecting Publick Stews, may seem at first sight somewhat ludicrous, I shall, nevertheless, make it appear the only Means we have now left for redressing this Grievance. Publick Whoring consists in lying with a certain Set of Women, who have shook off all Pretence to Modesty; and for such a sum of Money, more or less profess themselves always in a Readiness to be enjoyed. The Mischief a Man does in this case is entirely to himself, for in respect to the Woman, he does a laudable Action, in furnishing her with the Means of Subsistence. The Damage that he does to himself, is either with regard to his Health, or the Expence of Money, and may be considered under the same view as Drinking, with this considerable advantage, that it restores us to that cool Exercise of our Reason which Drinking tends to deprive us of.

> The Plan I propose is this: Let a hundred or more Houses be provided in some convenient quarter of the City, and proportionably in every Country Town, sufficient to contain Two Thousand Women. Let a hundred Matrons be appointed, one to each House, of Abilities and Experience enough to take upon them the Management of twenty Courtezans each, to see that they keep themselves neat and decent, and entertain Gentlemen after a civil and obliging Manner. There must be a very large house set apart for an Infirmary, and Provision made for two able Physicians, and four Surgeons at least.
>
> For the better Entertainment of all Ranks and Degrees of Gentlemen, we shall divide the twenty Women of each House into four classes, who for their Beauty, or other Qualifications, may justly challenge different Prices.

Though cast in the form of a satire—as was frequently the custom at that time in order to attract readers—it is evident that Mandeville seriously believed that something along his proposed lines was the only viable solution. In an earlier book, *The Fable of the Bees*, he had described with evident approval the attitude of the Dutch authorites:

> Where six or seven thousand sailors arrive at once, as it often happens in Amsterdam, that have seen none but their own sex for many months together, how is it to be supposed that honest women should walk the streets unmolested, if there were no harlots to be had at reasonable prices? For which reason the wise rulers of that well-ordered city always tolerate an uncertain number of houses, in which women are hired as publicly as horses at a livery stable.

Official attitudes varied from one European country to another. In sharp contrast to the enlightened Dutch were the bigoted Austrians. In Vienna, on 24 September 1723, a woman named Anna Maria, aged twenty-eight, was publicly decapitated for prostitution, after previous punishments—two sessions in the pillory, three deportations from the city—had failed to discourage her. Such harshness seems excessive, but it was firmly believed by the Austrian authorities that oppression would ultimately achieve eradication. When prostitutes were caught, their heads were shaved and they were obliged to sweep the streets as a public expression of shame; unfortunately this gave them a perfect opportunity to make further assignations with customers, so instead they were thrown into prison. This, in turn, afforded them an unparalleled chance to enjoy sex with their gaolers and fellow-prisoners, and the resulting pregnancies caused further official embarrassment. They were thereupon set to work in the public laundries; history does not tell us whether this met with any success—but that it failed to wash away sin from the Viennese scene is evident, or there would have been no necessity for Empress Maria Theresa's Chastity Commission of 1751.

It was the Commission's intention to extirpate all forms of sexual irregularity from Viennese life; it began by attacking, logically enough, opportunity and incentive. Short dresses were prohibited; billiard rooms were subject to inspection; waiters were substituted for waitresses in taverns and coffee-houses. It was all rather ridiculous, and the Empress and her commissioners became the laughing-stock for those who dared to laugh. But many of the Commission's actions were anything but amusing. Girls were stopped on the street and questioned, even those who were innocent being locked up until they could prove their blamelessness. Informers and blackmailers flourished; unscrupulous girls made a profitable sideline by acting as *agents provocateurs*, enticing men into the Commission's ambushes.

As for the shrewder professional prostitutes, they simply went underground. The most popular cover was domestic service. The famous painting of *La Belle Chocolatière* by Liotard, in the Dresden Gallery, is not, as it is often said to be, a 'portrait of the Housemaid N.N.' but that of a popular prostitute of the day, named Baldauf, who used this trade as a cloak for her more remunerative occupation. During the same period Goethe's *Werther*—one of the most runaway best-sellers in the history of literature—sold fewer copies in Vienna than a pamphlet by a certain Johann Rautenstrauch simply entitled *Housemaids*.

Official prohibition had been no more successful across the border in Prussia, where in 1690 Friedrich I had shut down the brothels, flogging the girls and sending them packing. In no time they were back, working in taverns and coffee-houses whose names—'Red Pump', 'Little Bride', 'Acute Angle'—were sufficient indications to customers. As time went on, official attitudes relaxed and, in 1765, it was calculated that Berlin alone contained some 1,000 brothels, each employing an average of nine girls. Characteristically, the brothel-keepers subscribed to a Prostitutes' Health Service Fund to cater for the girls' health, an enlightened step born of the period of prohibition when there had been so great an increase in venereal disease that the hospitals had been unable to cope.

In all the major cities of Europe—Berlin, St Petersburg, Moscow, London—there were high-class brothels for the wealthy, which by and large weathered the vagaries of shifting official opinion, and more transient establishments for the lower levels, often masquerading as taverns or hotels. A customer could always get what he wanted, wherever he

Fräulein Baldauf, a noted Viennese courtesan, depicted as *La Belle Chocolatière* by Liotard happened to be; it was only the arrangements that differed. This emerges most clearly when the least regulated country—England—is compared with the most regulated—France. The attitude of the authorities in the two countries could hardly have been in greater contrast; yet in practice a visitor to either London or Paris would find his needs anticipated and catered for in very much the same way. Prostitutes are less liable than politicians to be blown about by winds of change.

The French kings maintained a succession of royal mistresses who, unlike the majority of their English counterparts, have caught the imaginations of writers and readers, playwrights and movie-makers ever since: La Vallière and Maintenon, Pompadour and du Barry, each has become a legend. To classify them as prostitutes is to disregard the structure of court society, where a legitimate queen was a political pawn rather than a selected sexual companion; yet, for all their high rank and influence, that is what these ladies basically were.

One mistress at a time was inadequate to meet the needs of the divinely appointed beings who occupied the French throne, and the provision of additional companions was an important part of the court establishment, often under the supervision of the reigning mistress herself. Thus it was with the *parc aux cerfs*—'deer park' or personal brothel—of Louis XV, surely the most finely feathered sexual nest ever created for the pleasure of one man. Set in the grounds of his palace at Versailles, it was maintained at a cost of £200,000 a year, and its large staff were answerable to Madame du Barry in person. Her recruiting agent, Mère Bompart, the *pourvoyeuse en chef*, saw to it that a continual supply of girls between nine and eighteen was available for the royal pleasure, though it was only during the last three of their years in residence that they were on active service—until then, they were being trained to perform their duties to perfection. After the age of eighteen they were married off or despatched to a convent.

Mere Bompart had no trouble finding recruits. Even comparatively well-born families were not unwilling to give their daughters a start in life which, at the cost of a few years' degradation, could lead to a comfortable marriage or respectable incarceration in a nunnery. So, over a period of thirty-four years, a steady stream of nymphets passed into Louis XV's deer park—a male chauvinist fantasy come true.

The social distress of eighteenth-century France is reflected in the vast numbers of professional prostitutes who catered for the needs of less

Inspecting a virgin. Anonymous French eighteenth-century print

illustrious clients. As always, Paris set the example and the pace for the rest of the country; in the 1760s there were between 20,000 and 30,000 prostitutes in the city, which at the time had a population of around 600,000. In other words, among women of marriageable age, one in eight was a prostitute, whole- or part-time.

In principle, prostitution was illegal in France. The law passed by Charles IX in 1560, when many European nations were giving themselves a superficial clean-up inspired by the Protestant Reformation, had never formally been repealed; on the other hand, neither had it been consistently enforced. Whatever the 1560 law might say, brothels were not simply tolerated by the police but licensed by them, though the licences had no legal force. By and large, the police limited the geographical spread of prostitution by confining brothels and streetwalkers within certain areas. In general, prostitutes were left free to get on with their work, and were bothered by police only when complaints were lodged or conduct became intolerably outrageous. In such cases—because prostitution did not legally exist and there were no statutory penalties—punishment for sexual misdemeanours was left to the discretion of the magistrate; such action was taken under the 1713 Déclaration de Marly whereby a special police corps had been set up with jurisdiction over public morals.

In 1778 further ordinanaces were passed, known by the name of Lenoir, the police magistrate responsible for them; they purported to renew the 1560 act, but did so with a realism typically French. Prostitutes—*femmes de débauche*—were forbidden to exist. If, however, they insisted on existing, they were forbidden to walk in public places or display themselves at windows in such a way as to attract custom; and, if they insisted on doing these forbidden things, they must do them only in certain parts of the city.

Clearly the result—and perhaps the intention—of Lenoir's ordinances was that discretionary powers should be left with the police. For the prostitute and the madam, they confirmed the precariousness of an existence wherein they did not know from one day to the next what might befall them. Periodic round-ups by the police cleared individual houses or complete streets; the victims were frequently sent, like Manon Lescaut in Prévost's novel, to the colonies. But, given the prevailing economic climate of France, there was little danger that such banishment would leave Frenchmen untended. Prostitutes continued to walk the alleys of the forbidden public gardens, to frequent the forbidden pavements, to flaunt themselves naked at windows whispering forbidden invitations to passers-by. The Palais Royal, in the heart of Paris, was the city's most profitable hunting-ground; here the girls lived in tiny rooms on the upper floors of the elegant square, descending to the gardens and arcades to solicit custom and leading their prey upstairs to conclude the bargain. To give themselves a measure of protection, many masqueraded as shopkeepers in the little boutiques of the colonnades; but their clients knew them for what they were, and so did the police.

The police knew all about the brothels, too. They knew of Justine Paris's celebrated establishment in the Faubourg Saint-Honoré, where the services of the chef matched those of the rest of the staff. And they had even better reason to know Madame de Gourdan's house in the traditional prostitutes' district, near the present boulevard Sebastopol. This famous *maison de tolérance* had two entrances; a more-or-less open room in the rue des Deux Portes for those who didn't care if anyone saw them enter or leave, and a clandestine one via an antique shop in the rue Saint Sauveur for those who preferred to be more discreet.

The entertainment provided by Mme de Gourdan aimed to satisfy every taste. One room was kept furnished with common prostitutes, catering at low rates for cheap customers—de Gourdan was no snob. In another,

Manon Lescaut arrested and deported to America. Illustration by Tony Johannot to Prévost's novel girls newly arrived from the country were cleaned up—clients who enjoyed that sort of thing could spy on this interesting process for a certain sum. In the main salons the girls were prepared to slip into all kinds of fancy dress—as fairies, nuns, or in drag—as the client preferred. If he found that his physical faculties were growing sluggish, he might opt for the stimulus of the room known as the Infirmary: scented canes to stir his circulation, Richelieu Pastilles to excite the vital fluids, erotic books and engravings to suggest new approaches to the subject, mirrors ingeniously placed to reflect and multiply. In the Salon de Vulcan was an especially ingenious device—a chair in which the girl was invited to sit, whereupon a set of springs snapped to hold her in place, permitting the client to do whatsoever he chose, though no doubt Madame kept a watchful eye through a spyhole to ensure that things didn't go too far. Finally, there was a room where voyeurs could station themselves and watch and hear all that went on in adjacent rooms; this was of particular interest to the police—a convenient way of building up handy dossiers against potential enemies of the state. This facility, together with the influence wielded by some of her more distinguished clientele, explained why Madame de Gourdan was able for so long to maintain such a lucrative immunity from the penalties prescribed by the laws of France.

In 1789 the old régime collapsed, and with it went, for a while, all legal restraints on such matters as sexual acts between consenting persons. For five years the authorities had too many other things on their minds to bother with anything so trivial as prostitution; besides, what right had the state to interfere in such matters? So licence reigned along with liberty, until matters reached a point where even the most liberated revolutionary began to feel that some measure of control was needed. As so often, official action swung too far in the contrary direction. The brothels were to be shut down completely; the prostitutes were to be forced to abandon their trade. But how could this be reconciled with the aims of the Revolution? Was it liberty, to put brothel-keepers in prison? Was it equality, to harass the prostitute while allowing other people to pursue their professions? Was it fraternity, to close down those splendid social institutions, the brothels?

So the authorities had second thoughts; and, in their own interests, the brothel-keepers and prostitutes took the hint and behaved more discreetly. No formal steps were taken until Napoleon came to power. Even then—for he, too, had many other matters on his mind—his actions, to begin with, consisted chiefly in tidying up the more offensive manifestations of public sex. When he found how much crime was associated

French brothel of 1768. From Restif de la Bretonne's *Nuits de Paris*

with prostitution in the Palais Royal he had its girls banished; and when he found that what habitually held up his carriage at a certain street corner near the Théâtre Français was a popular brothel, he had it closed. In 1811 his Prefect of Police in Paris, Pasquier, got as far as drafting a bill to regulate prostitution, but it was never put into effect. Not until after the monarchy had been restored, and France once again had time to attend to her own affairs, was there any systematic attempt to regulate the position of the prostitute in French society.

# 6
# *SLAVES AND SKITTLES*

In Victorian London a man could find sexual company without the least difficulty. Whatever his tastes, somewhere in the great sprawling city there was someone prepared to minister to them. Visiting royalty or visiting sailors, all found facilities matched to their pockets and predilections—male or female company to be rented by the minute, the hour, the night or the year, in any imaginable shape or size, age or colouring.

The number of prostitutes estimated to be trading in Victorian London varied according to whether those quoting figures wished to play the phenomenon up or down. In 1839 the Commissioner of Police told the Society for the Suppression of Vice how much vice it had to suppress: 7,000 prostitutes, 933 brothels, 848 other disreputable houses; consciously or not, he was clearly trying to give the impression that his men had the situation well in hand. Other estimates, from those more concerned to sound the alarm, ran the number as high as 80,000—at a time when the population was increasing from 2 to 4 million. London's prostitutes were calculated to entertain 2 million clients a week, or twenty-five per girl (if the estimate of 80,000 is accepted), which is clearly far too high an average. Let it simply be acknowledged that Victorian London was swarming with prostitutes eager for trade, and that there were more than enough of them to meet the demand.

It was not a crime to be a prostitute, nor has it ever been in Britain. Keeping a brothel, on the other hand, was illegal, and so was living off a prostitute's earnings—though only for a man; this distinction afforded a convenient loophole for the procuress which, despite much abuse, was for some reason never stopped up. The legal position provided leeway for other forms of exploitation, but it also gave the police room to manoeuvre. As in France, they were able to exercise discretionary powers to keep prostitution under reasonable control, without rigid enforcement of the law which might have had the effect of driving the whole trade underground where the police could not reach it at all. Thus a fairly acceptable equipoise was maintained between letting people do as they liked and at the same time preventing offence being given to the rest of society.

Brothels and houses of accommodation could be closed down or their keepers fined whenever the police found an excuse—and excuses were not hard to find. Public houses, saloons and theatres could lose their licences if they were shown to be 'harbouring' prostitutes and, when the police chose, this could consist simply of selling them a ticket or a drink. So long as a prostitute or madam played along with the system, she could conduct her business with a minimum of interruption; but the moment she started to be awkward, or gave public offence, harassment made her life intolerable. The system placed great responsibility on the police, but despite the complaints of individuals most prostitutes seem to have accepted it as practical and just.

Within the system all kinds of prostitutes were plying their trade. At the top end of the scale was the kept woman who rarely came on to the open market, being passed instead from hand to hand among the wealthy. Below her were infinite degrees of women working—some in brothels and some in the streets, some for pimps and procurers and some for themselves, some for many years and some simply supplementing their earnings during a difficult period, some shrewdly professional and some pathetically amateur. What, if anything, did they all have in common?

In *Darkest England—and the Way Out* (1890), General Booth of the Salvation Army listed the reasons why girls 'fell':

| | |
|---|---|
| Seduction | 33 per cent |
| Bad company | 27 per cent |
| Wilful choice | 24 per cent |
| Drink | 14 per cent |
| Poverty | 2 per cent |

These figures were calculated as a result of information volunteered by girls to the Salvationists and should not be taken as too reliable. That perceptive observer Henry Mayhew—whose *London Labour and the London Poor*, published in the 1860s, quoted prostitutes verbatim—noted:

Prostitutes outside the Victoria Theatre, London. From Mayhew's *London Labour and the London Poor*, *c* 1860

Loose women generally throw a veil over their early life, and you seldom, if ever, meet with a woman who is not either a seduced governess or a clergyman's daughter; not that there is a word of truth in such an allegation —but it is their peculiar whim to say so.

Not only was the conventional account—of the clergyman's daughter seduced by the squire's son, forced to flee her home in shame hugging her swaddled infant as she trudges the snow-covered pavements of the big city, taken in by the kindly lady who turns out to be a scheming procuress and soon traps her into the sinful trade—seen by intelligent observers to be a sentimental fiction; they also recognised that the conventional image of the prostitute was wide of the mark. Dr William Acton, the most acute writer of the period on the subject, claimed that most commonly held beliefs about the prostitute were false. It was not true that 'once a harlot, always a harlot'. It was not true that, once embarked on her career, there was no possible advance for her, either moral or physical. It was not true that her career was short and rapid. In his survey *Prostitution*, of 1869, Acton wrote:

It is a little too absurd to tell us that 'the dirty, intoxicated slattern, in tawdry finery and an inch thick in paint'—long a conventional symbol of prostitution—is a correct figure in the middle of the 19th century. If she is not apocryphal, one must at least go out of the beaten path to find her.

Hundreds of females are at this moment living within a few miles of Charing Cross, in easy if not elegant circumstances, with every regard to outward decorum and good taste, and shocking none of the public who will not attempt unnecessarily close investigation, but for all that 'in a state of prostitution' . . . Prostitution is a transitory state through which an untold number of British women are ever on their passage. By far the larger number of women who have resorted to prostitution for a livelihood, return sooner or later to a more or less regular course of life.

For those who could bring themselves to contemplate the prostitute without prejudice, it was evident that the prime inducement to becoming and remaining a prostitute was the easy money and the good living. James Greenwood, in *The Seven Curses of London* (1869), observed:

Possibly the gay lady may come to the 'bitter end' some day, but at present, except from the moral point of view, she is not an object of commiseration. She has all that she deliberately bargains for—fine clothes, rich food, plenty of money, a carriage to ride in, the slave-like obedience of her 'inferiors'.

'Up in the world—down on her luck'. The vicissitudes of prostitution in Victorian London. From *The Day's Doings*, 1871

*The Times* (1890) concurred:

> The great bulk of London prostitutes are not cowering under gateways, nor preparing to throw themselves from Waterloo Bridge, but are comfortably practising their trade. They have no remorse or misgivings about the nature of their pursuit. On the contrary, they consider their calling an advantageous one, and they look upon their success in it with satisfaction.

For it is important to remember that prostitution is a trade, and a highly competitive one. Some were better at it than others; and those who failed did so for the same reason as dressmakers, actresses or shopkeepers failed—because they lacked the necessary skills or temperament. To feel pity for failure is all very well, but the Actons and Mayhews realised that it was pointless to suppose that every prostitute deserved or even desired pity. The world of Victorian prostitution was in large part seamy and squalid, but it would be a mistake to think that this was the whole picture. A number of those engaged in it clearly had a good deal of fun; and a great many more got on quietly and modestly with a trade which brought them in a useful income and they saw no particular reason to be ashamed of it. Thanks to prostitution, many women were able to live more comfortable and probably happier lives than they would otherwise have done.

The aristocracy of Victorian prostitution comprised the more or less permanent mistresses of peers, businessmen and statesmen. When they changed partners it was often after being recommended by one 'employer' to another, or lured away, more like a cook or a butler. Only when they miscalculated were they reduced to trading in the open market, but most of them would accept a certain amount of casual trade to supplement their regular allowances—as Acton describes:

> On permission to visit her being requested, she would probably take out her pocket book, and, after a careless glance at it, reply that she was full of engagements, but that if the petitioner would call at her house at a given hour that day week, she would, perhaps, spare him some twenty minutes of her society, for which favour she might expect the modest sum of £25.

Though never accepted in the best society, the leading courtesans appeared prominently in public, particularly in the neutral territory of Hyde Park where, popularly known as 'pretty horsebreakers', they would drive or ride in the full knowledge that they were the subject of much

A 'sporting horsebreaker' in London's Rotten Row. From *The Day's Doings*, 1871

comment—approving or reproving, envious or censorious. The journalist Sala chose a tone of gentle cynicism:

> Watch the sylphides as they fly or float past in their ravishing riding-habits and intoxicatingly beautiful hats . . . only these are not all countesses or earls' daughters. She on the bay, yonder, is Lais. Yonder goes Aspasia, with Jack Alcibiades on his black mare Timon; see, they have stopped at the end of the ride to talk to Phryne in her brougham. Some of those dashing delightful creatures have covered themselves with shame, and their mothers with grief, and have brought their fathers' grey hair with sorrow to the grave. All is not gold that glitters.
>
> (*Twice round the London Clock*, 1858)

Sala is being less than sincere. He was man-of-the-world enough to know that his Aspasias and Phrynes probably brought a deal of comfort to their aged parents in the form of a monthly remittance; nor were their own

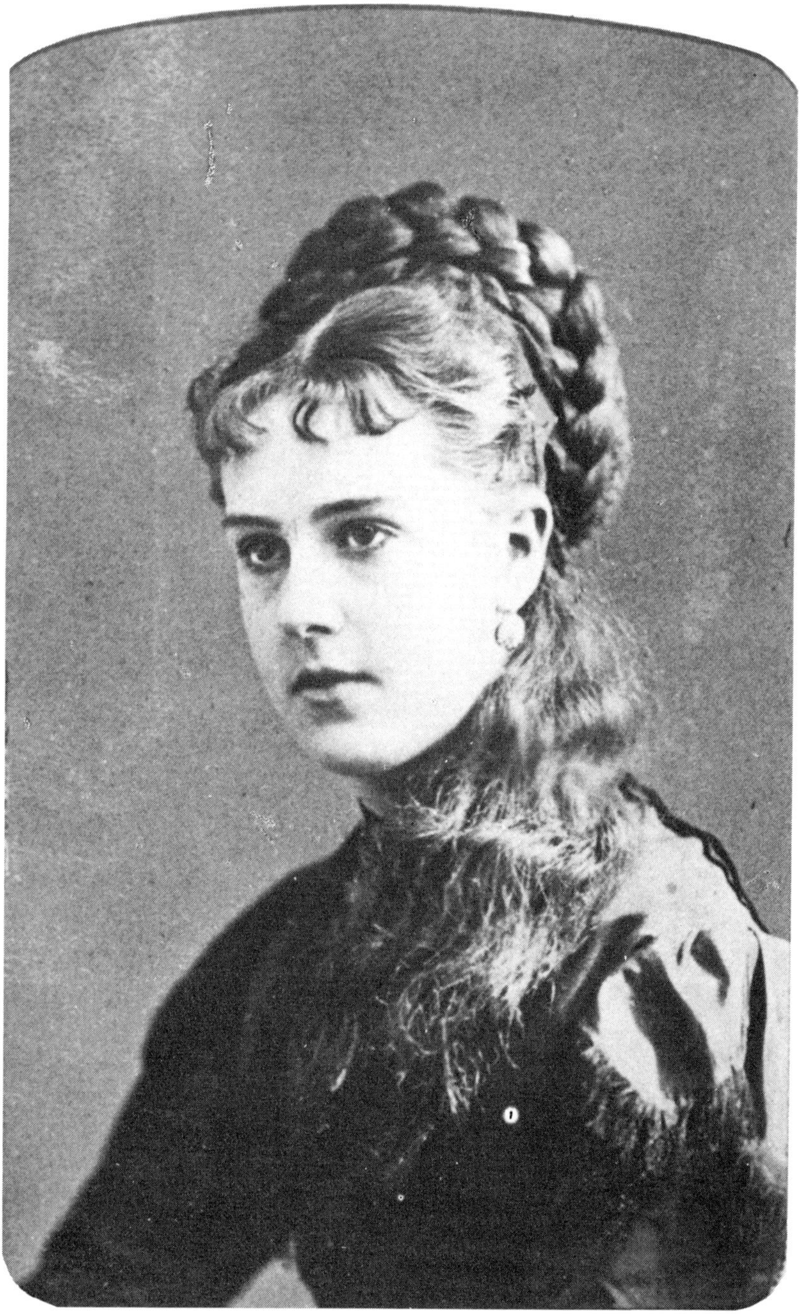

The shopgirl who made it to the top. Mabel Gray once served behind the counter at Jay's mourning establishment in Regent Street, but lived to hear herself praised —she would have taken it for praise—as 'the most notorious, extravagant, vampirish *demi-mondaine* of her day'

fates necessarily tragic. A few careers ended in catastrophe, but the majority of these courtesans managed to provide for their sunset years with commendable shrewdness. Those, like Cora Pearl and the legendary 'Skittles', who were in this category were patronised by the wealthy few. Most men seeking relief from the claustrophobic atmosphere of Victorian domestic life turned to the streetwalker and the brothel girl. On this less exalted plain, too, there were gradations to suit every taste and purse:

> In the fashionable brothels the younger women are carefully secluded: when they walk out they are accompanied: they do not solicit, they merely show themselves. The men who frequent such houses are rich. Brothels of this high class avoid publicity, and by discretion seek to escape prosecution. There are not many of them, and they are located where they are least likely to be noticed as a nuisance. Their clientele is private and personal; those who seek them know where to find them.
>
> Below these are a large number of less fashionable but still mostly West End houses, well known to the police, those who keep them being frequently prosecuted and the brothel closed. This does not seriously affect them. The house is closed, the fines paid, and a fresh start promptly made somewhere near. In some cases the same proprietors keep more than one house, and can transfer the inmates; in others a friendly understanding between two proprietors serves the same end.
>
> The girls from these houses walk the streets or frequent public places. Activity is maintained by the frequenting of public places in the evening and until late at night, but each house has also its regular connection, and while some of the inmates are out, others stay at home to receive their visitors. The girls themselves keep their fees, and from night to night or week to week meet very varying fortune. Some can and do save, but as a rule whatever they have after paying for their board is spent on dress.
>
> (Charles Booth, *Life and Labour of the People of London*, 1890s)

While in some brothels the girls lived in, at others they came in for the working day, hiring dresses finer than they could themselves afford. When these 'dress lodgers' went out on to the streets they were accompanied by a 'watcher'—generally a retired prostitute—to see they didn't make off with the dress. Mayhew spoke to a watcher working in the Strand:

> We, that is, Lizzie and me, the girl I'm watching, came out tonight at nine. It's twelve now, ain't it? Well, what do ye think we've done? We have taken three men home, and Lizzie, who is a clever little devil, got two pound five out of them for herself, which ain't bad at all. I shall get something when

Street girls in the Haymarket, London. From Mayhew's *London Labour*

we get back. We ain't always so lucky. Some nights we go about and don't hook a soul. Lizzie paints a bit too much for decent young fellows who've got lots of money. They aren't our little game. We go in more for tradesmen, shopboys, commercial travellers and that sort.

Few London brothels made any pretence of luxury; there were none to continue the great eighteenth-century tradition or to rival those of Paris where, because such houses were more or less officially tolerated, fine furnishings and elaborate equipment were a worth-while investment. In London the price of survival was continual discretion—except in the East End, in districts so rough that the police seldom put in an appearance let alone sought to impose more than the loosest of control. Here, round the docks, open and brazen, were hundreds of brothels of indescribable squalor catering chiefly for seamen. This was the district where Jack the Ripper did his ripping, gutting a succession of prostitutes with surgical precision and always escaping detection.

Even in the West End, the lightest purses were catered for, though the customer needed a strong stomach if he chose to frequent the street and park women, whose place of business was any conveniently ill-lit alley wall or tree trunk or, for the horizontally inclined, the bushes of Hyde Park. As Mayhew noted, such obscure places favoured the ugly and the elderly:

They will consent to any species of humiliation for the sake of acquiring a few shillings. They are old, unsound, and by their appearance utterly incapacitated from practising their profession where the gas lamps would expose the defects in their personal appearance and the shabbiness of their ancient and dilapidated attire.

Such derelicts had also to face the competition of the amateurs—shopgirls and housewives supplementing their meagre earnings by moonlighting. In the 1880s Havelock Ellis spoke to a thirty-two-year-old widow with two children to feed:

She was earning 18 shillings a week in an umbrella factory in the East End: she occasionally took to the street near one of the big railway stations. A comfortable and matronly person, who looked quite ordinary except that her skirts were shorter than normally worn. If spoken to she would remark that she was 'waiting for a lady friend', talk in an affected way about the weather, and parenthetically introduce her offer. She will either lead a man into one of the silent neighbouring lanes filled with warehouses, or will take

> him home with her. She will take what she can get—sometimes £1, more often only 6d; on an average she earns a few shillings an evening. Though not speaking well of the police, says they don't interfere as much as with the regulars; never gave them money, but sometimes gratified their desires to keep on good terms.

The dollymops, as amateurs were often called, were likely to be nurse-maids and servant girls after a bit of fun as well as extra money; they were particularly popular with soldiers, who could not afford to go with regular prostitutes. The professionals resented the additional competition—as if there wasn't enough already!—and accused the amateurs of being more likely to be diseased, which was probably true.

The Haymarket and its surrounding streets, lined with theatres and cafés, were thronged with prostitutes. After leaving the theatre, men would go on to some such place as the Argyll Rooms in Great Windmill Street, Soho, which were licensed for music and dancing and nominally supervised by the police. Although notorious as places for meeting prostitutes, they maintained high standards of behaviour so as not to jeopardise their licences. These licensed premises were required by law to close at midnight, and it was then that the cigar divans and the night houses took over. Since, nominally, they offered no alcoholic drink, music or dancing, these places did not have to be licensed; in practice, drinks were not only available but obligatory, at exorbitant prices, being swiftly concealed when the look-out warned of approaching police—who, having been suitably squared by the proprietor, took care to give ample advance warning of their arrival. There was no entertainment; the sole attraction was the girls, who would keep a customer company for as long as he continued to fork out for drinks, then take him home to their lodgings or to one of the many convenient accommodation houses in the neighbourhood.

Of all London's night houses, none was better known than Kate Hamilton's, in Prince's Street off Leicester Square. When her portrait was lithographed for the racy *Nicholson's Noctes* in 1842 Kate was already of ample proportions; a quarter of a century later, when Mayhew included a view of her establishment in his great survey, she was frankly very fat indeed. She was also very prosperous. Her house was open from midnight till dawn; she presided over the company from a rostrum where she sat enthroned, sipping champagne hour by hour. Supper was cold beef, and a bottle of Moselle, for which Kate had paid a few pence, cost her customers twelve shillings; but they didn't care, for Kate's house had class and the

Kate Hamilton. Lithograph by W. Clark in *Nicholson's Noctes*, 1842

Kate Hamilton's night house. From Mayhew's *London Labour*

others hadn't. Even the prostitutes were conscious of the distinction, and a girl who wouldn't deign to be seen anywhere else would permit herself to visit Kate's.

Another area where prostitutes could be found at appropriate hours was Marylebone—not so pricey as Mayfair nor so rough as dockland; in 1858 the rector of Marylebone's Trinity Church stated that four out of five houses in nearby Norton Street were brothels, and described how naked girls would flaunt themselves at the windows while others rushed half-dressed into the streets to drag in passers-by by brute force. In outlying suburbs the pleasure gardens—Cremorne, Highbury Barn, Rosherville—were popular hunting grounds for professional and amateur alike.

In short, London provided every kind of prostitution for every kind of customer, and for the girl it offered the possibility of fame and fortune no less than the prospect of misery and squalor:

> And what will be the future of this girl?
> She may be married—one is—to an earl.
> She may her earnings squander, and come down
> among the lowest women of the town.
> She may be careful, on her means retire
> and from her carriage preach about hell fire.*
> She may in time—it is not great the fall—
> keep on her own account a house of call.
> She may, stung by remorse which never dies,
> leap into Lethe from the Bridge of Sighs.
>
> (Anon, *The Siliad*, 1875)

Most that is written about prostitution comes from historians and sociologists; while the first-hand accounts gathered by Mayhew have a more immediate impact, it is rare to hear from the other party to the bargain—that shadowy anonymous figure, the client. *My Secret Life*, published privately in the 1880s by a man-about-town calling himself 'Walter', is thus one of the most important documents in the story of prostitution. It is virtually the diary of a man who seems to have had no interest in anything whatsoever except sex; its 2,000 or more pages are devoted single-mindedly to accounts of sexual encounters. What makes such a mass of monothematic material palatable is the fact that Walter writes with an astonishing honesty and detachment:

*the reference is to Laura Bell, a courtesan who ended a successful career as a reformer seeking to save her former fellow workers.

> At London I at first took fancy again for women in the suburbs, punks who would let me have them for half a crown, and several jolly fucks I had. Then suddenly I took to those clad in silks and satins, and wondered at my recent low tastes. My intercourse with these poor women gave me a curious insight into life, and makes me think what a godsend having a cunt is to many women, who would starve without it. And what a comfort that is to men who cannot marry, and who if they couldn't get a cheap fuck, must either frig themselves, or bugger each other, both of which habits are most objectionable, and to be avoided if possible. But surely the seed in a man's testicles will and must come out by some process, natural or unnatural.

High philosophy it is not, but what a wholesome corrective to the bulk of Victorian literature—to the novels of Dickens, for example: for all their greatness and vision they manage discreetly to skirt a phenomenon which, as he well knew, was only too prominent a feature of the Victorian scene.

A great many of Walter's encounters were with what he calls 'the fair mercenary ones':

> To their class I owe a debt of gratitude: they have been my refuge in sorrow, an unfailing relief in all my miseries, have saved me from drinking, gambling, and perhaps worse. I shall never throw stones at them, nor speak harshly to them, nor of them. They are what society has made them, and society uses them, enjoys them, even loves them; yet denies them, spurns them, damns, and crushes them even whilst frequenting and enjoying them. In short, it shamefully ill-treats them in most Christian countries, and more so in protestant England than in any others that I know.

His conscience rarely troubled him; but his cynicism is of its time, and there is no reason to doubt his sincerity when he writes:

> Some say that harlots are sick of their business, and hate the erotic whims and fancies to which they minister. Such is not my experience. I believe that most of them like bawdy tricks, and that directly their lust is aroused, they rejoice in them. Nature is the same in them as in other women who want fucking daily.

Walter rarely flew higher than the £1 to £2 girls, but there were exceptions:

> Having had my game with the cheap women, I went to the opposite extreme and had the dearest; those who said 'I never take less than a fiver' and were

> not satisfied with that. I had half a dozen well-known courtesans. Baby Johnson was one: Skittles took a fancy to me, but her foul tongue shocked me. I had a thin and lovely lady with exquisite eyes, since married to one of the rich ones of the land (and still alive and living in a square, and who shall therefore be nameless).

The compliant landlady of an accommodation house permitted Walter, for a consideration, to watch her guests through a secret spyhole. The couples paid 3s 6d to 5s for a half-hour occupancy of the room; one night, Walter reported, it was used by seven couples between 8pm and midnight, giving the landlady an income of £10 a week per room One girl took 5s from her first customer and £2 from another, for the same services and length of stay; except for those who were very tough or confident, most girls would settle for what their clients offered.

A typical middle-range street girl could expect to earn between £20 and £30 a week, or £1,000-£1,500 a year. By the standards of the day, that was a very good sum, even when allowing for the outlay on clothes, lodgings, protection money and so on. Salvationist General Booth had reluctantly to admit:

> Terrible as the fact is, there is no doubt that there is no industrial career in which for a short time a beautiful girl can make so much money with so little trouble as the profession of a courtesan . . . The profession of a prostitute is the only career in which the maximum income is paid to the newest apprentice. Giddy girls are told that if they will but 'do as others do' they will make more in a night, if they are lucky, than they can make in a week at their sewing; and who can wonder that in many cases the irrevocable step is taken?

Is it true that Cora Pearl was paid £200 a night; that Lord Clebden paid out £1,000 for a single night with Bessy Howard, later the mistress of Napoleon III; that Lord Hertford gave £40,000 to the Countess Castiglione for one session—from which she had to spend three days in bed recovering! These were the legends which circulated in the fashionable clubs. But theirs was a very different world from that of the desperate creatures Mayhew found around the slums of Drury Lane: 'their countenances were stolid, and their skin hostile to the application of soap and water. They would go home with a man for a shilling, and think themselves well paid, while sixpence was rather an exorbitant amount for the temporary accommodation their vagrant amour would require'. As twenty-seven-year-old Swindlin' Sal said to him:

Cora Pearl. Anonymous photograph

> Well, I'll tell yer, one week with another I makes nearer on four pounds nor three—sometimes five, I 'ave done eight and ten. Sometimes I get three shillings, half-a-crown—five shillings, or ten occasionally, accordin' to the sort of man.

One of the prostitute's basic functions is to cater for customers whose unusual sexual impulses their regular companions are perhaps unable or unwilling to gratify. The most common of these is flagellation, which not only has the physiological effect of arousing sexual urges but also has strong psychological undercurrents. In England it is traditionally linked with the educational system. In Shadwell's eighteenth-century comedy *The Virtuoso*, the old roué Snarl is asked by a brothel girl why he chooses this form of sexual gratification: 'I wonder that a thing which I like so little should give you so much pleasure.' Snarl replies: 'I got so used to it at Westminster School that I have not been able to do without it since.' However, *le vice anglais*, as it is known, is by no means exclusive to England, as we know from the Paris of Proust's Baron Charlus and the Berlin of Isherwood's Mr Norris.

Brothels specialising in flagellation existed at least as early as the Regency period. When George IV, as Prince of Wales, visited Mrs Collet's in Covent Garden it is not known whether the royal wrist wielded the whips or the royal buttocks submitted to them. Perhaps it was due to his patronage that Mrs Collet was able to move house from shady Covent Garden to classier Bloomsbury. But it was her rival, Mrs Theresa Berkley, who won the greater notoriety for the care she lavished on equipping her premises at 28 Charlotte Street, Soho. An astonishing arsenal of implements was available; besides the simple canes, stored in water to keep them green and supple, the anonymous author of *Venus Schoolmistress*, published in 1830, tells us that she could offer:

> . . . a dozen tapering whip thongs, a dozen cat o' nine tails studded with needle points, various kinds of thin supple switches, leather straps as thick as traces, curry combs and ox-hide straps studded with nails, which had become tough and hard from constant use, also holly and gorse and a prickly evergreen called 'butcher's bush'. During the summer, glass and Chinese vases were kept filled with green nettles with which the 'dead were often brought to life again'.

Her greatest invention, the 'Berkley Horse', was first demonstrated in 1828; this was an adjustable frame on to which the customer was strapped —there were openings for his head and genitals. While he was being

Flagellation. Aubrey Beardsley, frontispiece to John Davidson's *The Wonderful Mission of Earl Lavender*, 1895

operated on with whatever instrument he had selected from Mrs Berkley's catalogue, a girl could sit beneath him and 'manualise his embolon', as the author delicately puts it. The fame of this device brought Mrs Berkley clients from far and wide, and when she died in 1836 she was said to have left a fortune of £10,000.

In an exposé published in 1813, *The Phoenix of Sodom*, an account was given of a homosexual brothel maintained at the Swan Inn in Vere Street, Clare Market:

> One of the rooms was equipped with four beds, another was furnished in the style of a lady's boudoir with dressing table and all conveniences, paint, powder, etc. A third room was called the 'Chapel', where marriages were celebrated, sometimes between a 'feminine' grenadier, six foot tall, and a 'petite maître' who was half the height of his 'beloved wife'! These weddings were celebrated in proper style with bridesmaids, best man, etc., and the nuptial night was often spent in the same room with two or three other couples . . . Prominent men of honourable professions could be seen with lads of the lowest type 'in' or 'supra lectum'. A gentleman from a respectable house in the City often visited one of these inn-brothels, staying there for several days and nights, during which time he usually enjoyed himself with eight, ten or even a dozen different men and boys. Sunday was the usual great day for appointments, to which some came from a long distance, sometimes thirty miles from London, in order to take part in festivities and elegant amusements with grenadiers, servants, waiters, drummers, and the whole band of catamites in human form, from the sweepings of Sodom to the refuse of Gomorrah.

A noted brothel-owner of the day, Mary Wilson, whose establishments offered flagellation as well as 'straight' prostitution, in 1824 outlined her plans for an 'Eleusinian Institute':

> Any lady of rank and means may subscribe to this Institute, to which she shall always have the entry incognito; the married to commit what the world calls adultery, the unmarried to obey the commands of all-powerful nature. I have bought a very convenient piece of land, lying between two main streets, from both of which it can be reached through shops in which only women's goods are sold. In this space, between two rows of houses, I have erected a very elegant temple, in the centre of which are large salons surrounded by charming and comfortable boudoirs. In these salons, arranged according to their class, can be seen the most attractive men of all types that I may obtain, expert in all forms of pleasure to suit all tastes, and all in a state of great exaltation produced by good living and inertia.
>
> The ladies never enter the salons, but are shown the occupants through

'Before the flagellation'. Florian in *Le Courrier Français*, 1888

darkened windows in the boudoirs. In one room can be seen beautiful, elegantly dressed young men, playing cards or music, in others, athletically built males, completely naked, wrestling or bathing. In short, there are so many kinds of these animals for them to look at, that they cannot tell which to choose. As soon as their minds are made up, they ring for the chambermaid, call her to the window and show her the object of their desire, and he is forthwith brought to the boudoir.

Mary Wilson speaks of her establishment as though it were already in existence, but no other reference to it has ever been found. Did it exist only in her imagination or did her customers, in their own best interests, manage to conceal it behind a mantle of discretion?

Of all the specialised services provided by London's brothels, the most lucrative was catering for those whose passion was the defloration of virgins. Back in 1760, the author—again, anonymous—of *The Battles of Venus* had written:

> I hold truly that the enjoyment of a virgin, from the point of view of the physical as well as the psychic experience of the seducer, is the highest peak of sensual pleasure . . . A man's fancy will be inflamed by the prospect of the enjoyment of a woman who has never before been in bed with a man, in whose arms no man has yet lain, and whose virgin charms he will be the first to see and triumphantly enjoy. This exquisite work of the fancy prepares the body in the highest degree for sensual pleasures.

Virgins were at a premium throughout the period; brothels housing children aged fourteen or less were a standard feature of the London underworld. Located for the most part in the squalid area of London's dockland, houses like Maxwell's in Betty Street and Catherine Keeley's in Dock Street were shady establishments, despised by the more respectable and shunned by all who did not share this particular penchant. Some, like William Sheen's, provided young boys as well as girls, in any combination the client might fancy.

The 'straight' end of the prostitution trade condemned these dubious establishments on practical as well as on moral grounds. For it was not the everyday traffic but its extreme manifestations which were to stir the Victorian conscience, and led to the 'social problem' being discussed by respectable people and in the columns of respectable journals.

In his ballad, 'Two Women', George Sims reflects the dual attitude of society:

> Tonight is a midnight meeting, and in from the filthy street
> they are bringing the wretched wantons who sin for a crust to eat;
> there's cake to be had, and coffee, as well as the brimstone tracts
> that paint in such flaming colours the end of their evil acts.
>
> Tonight is a midnight meeting, and out of the rain and dirt
> there creeps in a sinful woman; drenched is her draggled skirt,
> drenched are the gaudy feathers that droop in her shapeless hat,
> and her hair hangs over her shoulders in a wet, untidy mat.

She hears of the fiery furnace that waits for the wicked dead,
of the torture in store for the outcast who sins for her daily bread;
she hears that a God of mercy had built, on a sunlit shore,
a haven of rest eternal for those who shall sin no more.

Anon by the silent waters she kneels with her eyes upcast,
and whispers her Heavenly Father, 'O God, I have sinned my last.
Here, in this cruel city, to live I must sin the sin;
save me from that, O Father!—pity and take me in!'

A plunge in the muddy river, a cry on the chill night air,
and the waters upon their bosom a pilgrim sister bear;
she has laved the stain of the city from her soul in the river slime,
she has sought for the promised haven through the door of deadly crime.

Tonight is a midnight meeting—a hall in a Western square—
and rank and fashion and beauty and a Prince of the Blood are there.
In the light of a thousand tapers the jeweled bosoms gleam,
and the cheeks of the men are flushing, and the eyes of the women beam.

But fair above all the women is the beautiful Countess May,
and wealthy and great and titled yield to her queenly sway.
Her they delight to honour, her they are proud to know,
for wherever the Countess visits, a Prince of the Blood will go.

The story is common gossip; there isn't a noble dame
that bows to the reigning beauty, but knows of her evil fame.
She is married, had sons and daughters when she honoured a Prince's whim;
but her husband is proud of her conquest—the Prince is a friend to *him*.

The bishop who christens her babies, the coachman who drives her pair,
the maid who carries her letters, the footman behind her chair,
the Marquis, her white-haired father, her brothers, the gossips say,
all know of the guilty passion of the Prince and the Countess May.

She is crowned with the world's fresh roses; no tongue has a word of blame;
but the woman who falls from hunger is a thing too foul to name.
She is blessed who barters her honour just for a Prince's smile;
the vice of the Court is *charming*, and the vice of the alley *vile*.

So, world, shall it be for ever—this hunting the street girl down,
while you honour the titled Phryne, and hold her in high renown.
But when, at the great uprising, they meet for the Judgment Day,
I'd rather be that drowned harlot than the beautiful Countess May.

A midnight meeting for fallen women. From Mayhew's *London Labour*

The 'Countess' may simply be an archetype, but it is more likely that the author had in mind Daisy, Countess of Warwick, one of the more notable mistresses of the Prince of Wales. The moral of these verses found an echo in the minds of a growing number of Victorians; cynicism and hypocrisy were equally unacceptable and they therefore had no option but to confront the problem of prostitution despite the traditional taboos surrounding the subject. Good intentions, however, were clouded by ignorance and prejudice. To give one example: in 1854 George Henry Lewes, biographer of Goethe, applauded the Lord Chamberlain for refusing to license Dumas's *La Dame aux Camélias* (on which Verdi's *La Traviata* was based) for the English stage, describing it as 'an unhealthy idealisation of one of the worst evils of our social life' and adding 'Whatever might be suitable for Paris, London, thank God, has still enough instinctive repulsion against pruriency not to tolerate them.' Yet Lewes himself felt no 'instinctive repulsion' against living with the novelist George Eliot even though she was not his wife.

The arguments and the figures provided by such men as Acton, Greenwood and Mayhew would have enabled anyone to take up the fight who had the will for it; but the reforming zeal was not yet there in sufficient strength, as was proved by the scandalous Jeffries case. Mrs Jeffries was the best-known and wealthiest brothel-owner of the day. She had four houses in Church Street, Chelsea; at Rose Cottage, Hampstead, she ran a flagellation establishment said to have been patronised by the poet Swinburne; in her Grays Inn Road house under-age girls could be sodomised by those who enjoyed that sort of thing; at Kew she had a country house where virgins were stored before being shipped off to the Continental market. To protect herself she paid £550 a year into police funds; her main insurance was the influence of her high-ranking customers.

In 1885 a letter addressed to her was accidentally delivered to a Miss Mary Jeffries, who read with astonishment a request in Italian for a lively girl of sixteen years with a nice complexion and a pretty bosom to live with the writer as his mistress; by way of reference, he gave the name of King Leopold of the Belgians. When Mary Jeffries took the letter to the police, it fortunately came into the hands of officers who were not concerned to protect the brothel-owner. Word reached a group of reformers, including the dauntless campaigner Josephine Butler, who took out a writ against Mrs Jeffries for keeping a disorderly house.

Mrs Jeffries called upon her friends, and was not disappointed. She drove to the trial in a carriage lent her by a member of the House of

Procuress with child prostitute. Félicien Rops

Lords and escorted by officers of the Guards. In court she was loudly cheered and the judge made no attempt to suppress demonstrations in her favour. Wisely, she pleaded guilty, and was fined a derisory £200, which was immediately paid by her wealthy clients. Afterwards her carriage was drawn through the streets by her faithful guardsmen.

The Jeffries case, technically a victory for the reformers, had advanced their cause not a step. Paradoxically, they were soon to win a more decisive victory by what was technically a defeat—the Stead case. William Thomas Stead, thirty-six-year-old editor of the *Pall Mall Gazette*, was a somewhat confused journalist of mystical tendencies; whatever his psychological motivations, however, his zeal for reform was unquestionably sincere. The Jeffries fiasco inspired him to look more closely at the way prostitution was managed in London and, with the help of the National Society for the Prevention of Cruelty to Children, he saw a girl of seven who had been abducted and raped in a fashionable brothel, and was told the case could not be taken to court because she was too young to give evidence on oath. He was also shown a girl aged four and a half who had been lured into a brothel and raped twelve times; on this occasion those responsible had been arraigned, but the case had collapsed for lack of legal evidence.

Stead discovered a lot about Victorian prostitution. He learned that in a fashionable house little of the profit came from straight adult prostitution; the real money was in virgins, true or fake, selling at £25 a throw, or the rape of very young children which could bring in as much as £100. He learned that there were brothels, like the notorious house in Half Moon Street, off Piccadilly, which had soundproof rooms for the flagellation and rape—normal or sodomite—of under-age victims. He learned that the victims were gagged, drugged, strapped down, even chloroformed, and that death was not infrequent. He learned that every fashionable brothel maintained a doctor to repair damage and to restore lost virginities. And he learned that the brothel owners had friends everywhere—in the police, in government departments, in parliament. When one of Stead's investigators approached the Archbishop of Canterbury's establishment at Lambeth Palace, the official misunderstood his request and supposed that the man was anxious to dispose of an unwanted mistress; he offered to have her abducted and transported to a Belgian brothel for £10, and no questions asked.

Stead resolved to act, and to use his editorial position to publicise his action. He saw that the vital requirement was for evidence that would stand up in court, and he planned to provide this by demonstrating the process whereby innocent girls were recruited into prostitution. In the summer of 1885 a series entitled *The Maiden Tribute of Modern Babylon* appeared in his paper; in the first of four articles, headed 'A Girl of 13 bought for £5', his readers were told:

> It occurred to these persons to demonstrate that such a traffic was being carried on; that it was possible to get hold of a child of tender years, to get her examined by a midwife, to introduce her to a brothel, to administer chloroform so that a vile purpose could be accomplished, and finally to deport the child from this country without leaving a trace.

With the co-operation of the Salvation Army, Stead found a procuress who helped him purchase a girl named Eliza Armstrong for £5. A midwife guaranteed her virginity; Eliza was taken to a brothel, where it was

Street girls bribing the beadle to let them walk in the Burlington Arcade, Piccadilly, London. From *The Day's Doings*, 1871

established that drugging and violation could have been effected, and thence she was smuggled to France. Stead thought he had taken every precaution to demonstrate the purity of his intentions, but one technicality had been overlooked: the fact that Eliza's mother had accepted the money was not legally sufficient. Though the father was no longer living with his wife and daughter, his permission should have been obtained; this was the loophole needed by those who resented Stead's interference. He was prosecuted for the very offence he was seeking to oppose, and sentenced to three months in Holloway prison.

From the publicity point of view, nothing could have served his cause better. His articles had roused public opinion and the feeling of outrage was reinforced by the fact that he had been imprisoned for revealing the truth. The Criminal Law Amendment Act of 1885 was directly influenced by the Eliza Armstrong case. Stead had shown that, even in the face of determined opposition, an equally determined pressure group could achieve results.

But the reformers were also divided on a fundamental question. All agreed that prostitution, as it existed in Victorian England, was open to abuse and exploitation which should be remedied—but was the solution to accept the fact of prostitution and subject it to official regulation, or to reject the fact and seek to abolish it altogether? As Harriet Martineau, one of the English reformers, wrote in a letter to the *Daily News* in 1870:

> This admission of the necessity of vice is the point on which the whole argument turns, and on which irretrievable consequences depend. Once admitted, the necessity of a long series of fearful evils follows of course. There can be no resistance to seduction, procuration, disease, regulation, when once the original necessity is granted.

She and her colleagues advocating total abolition were opposed by men like William Acton who argued that prostitution would exist whatever governments decided, and so it was better that it should operate openly and legally, and be subject to regulation and control which would prevent abuse and exploitation, than that it should operate illegally and clandestinely, where the authorities could not prevent abuse. It is an argument which permeates public attitudes towards prostitution throughout the rest of history, and has still to be resolved. In Victorian England the two points of view divided the reformers and hampered their efforts; today we can see the begged questions and false premises underlying such views as Harriet Martineau's, but at the time they convinced the authorities who, unlike the French, refused to approve the recognition and regulation of prostitution.

The leading reformer in England was the redoubtable Josephine Butler; she toured the country indefatigably, speaking at public meetings against regulation despite newspaper criticism of her as 'an indecent maenad, a shrieking sister, frenzied, unsexed, and utterly without shame . . . worse than a prostitute'. She was one of the heroines of the women's movement, patently sincere if not always practical; consider, for instance, this exchange when she was being examined by a sympathetic member of the Royal Commission of Inquiry into the Contagious Diseases Acts:

| | |
|---|---|
| Massey | Efforts made by private persons like yourself are very inadequate to meet the evil. |
| JB | If there were a sufficient number of private persons to act as I do, you would require no government machinery. |
| Massey | How would you induce so many to be as devoted as yourself in the matter? |
| JB | By showing them the example of Christ. |

Yet, when attacking specific abuses, Josephine Butler achieved excellent results. Her efforts to halt the export of ignorant girls to brothels in Belgium show her at her best, fighting officialdom with relentless determination and ultimately curtailing this degrading traffic. An English girl named Adeline Tanner had been abducted and taken to a Belgian brothel, where it was found that she was built too small for normal sex. For a while she was compelled to perform other types of sexual act; then it was decided to try surgery at a Belgian government hospital. She told Josephine Butler:

> They did not even give me chloroform, but the students held my hands and feet, whilst the operator seemed to cut and tear away my living flesh. This was repeated at intervals about seven times, and during the operations my screams and appeals to my tormentors for mercy were heard, as the other patients told me, over the whole building, and the other girls who were there used to cry at the sight of my sufferings.

By fortunate chance, an English investigator visited the hospital at the same time on another matter; the authorities panicked and shipped

The Promenade of the Empire Theatre, Leicester Square, London. From *Living London*, 1900

Adeline back to England. Josephine Butler passed her story on to the Home Office, who hesitated—but some allies of the reformers saw to it that the allegations were printed in a Belgian newspaper. In Belgium the police chief implicated in the affair sued the paper for libel, and this brought the whole case into the open. As a result, thirty-four English girls were released in Brussels alone and the traffic in prostitutes was halted. One small pocket of sexual exploitation had been cleaned out.

If Josephine Butler and her colleagues had confined their efforts to the remedying of such abuses, they would have won whole-hearted public sympathy for their cause. Unfortunately their ranks included many who believed that prostitution should be attacked on all occasions and in all its aspects; sometimes this led not to reform but to ridicule.

The Promenade of the Empire Theatre, Leicester Square, was one of the best-known haunts of high-class prostitutes in London—a shop window where they could display themselves to best advantage. Surely prostitution was less offensive here, where any misconduct would be dealt with by the theatre management, than on the open pavement? But in 1894 the reformers launched a campaign to force the London County Council to refuse the theatre's licence unless the Promenade was closed. This was done, to the accompaniment of derisive satire; but it was not long before the barriers were removed and the girls were back. When the reformers launched a second attack, the city fathers, fearing further ridicule, refused to back them. It was not until World War I, when the question of Moral Danger to Our Soldier Boys gave reformers a convenient new weapon, that the Empire Promenade was finally closed.

Victorian prostitution needed reforming and, if some of the reformers were muddle-headed, others were successful in removing the worst aspects of the trade. On the fundamental issues—was prostitution to be officially recognised or not? and, if recognised, was it to be officially regulated or not?—opinion remained divided.

# 7
# *SPLENDOURS AND MISERIES*

The best-known brothel in literature is La Maison Tellier, the provincial French establishment whose Madame takes her staff into the country to celebrate her niece's first communion. Though Maupassant's account is of a fictional house, he gives us a unique glimpse of 'everyday' brothel life in nineteenth-century France:

> One went there every evening about eleven, just as one might go to the café. Six or eight of them, always the same, used to gather there; no debauchees, but respectable men—tradesmen, young fellows of the town. One sipped one's chartreuse while teasing the girls a little, or else one chatted seriously with Madame, a lady whom everyone treated with respect. And then, before midnight, one went home; sometimes the younger fellows stayed on.
>
> Madame, born of a good peasant family, had accepted this profession just as she might have gone into millinery or lingerie. The shame attached to prostitution, so violent and outspoken in the towns, simply doesn't exist in the Normandy countryside. 'It's a good profession,' the peasant will say, and send his child to manage a harem of girls as though he were sending her to run a school for young ladies.
>
> The house had come by inheritance from an old uncle. Monsieur and Madame had been innkeepers near Yvetot, but closed down the inn at once, reckoning the business at Fécamp a better proposition. They were good people who soon won the approval both of their staff and of their neighbours. Monsieur died of a stroke after two years. Since her widowhood, Madame had been courted in vain by every one of her clients, but her conduct was said to be absolutely irreproachable, not even her girls had managed to discover the slightest blemish on her reputation.
>
> The house had two entrances. At the corner, a sort of low café opened in the evening for common folk and sailors. Two of those who performed the

La Maison Tellier. Illustration by René Lelong to the 1903 edition of Maupassant's story

> duties of the house were assigned to the needs of this section of the clientele. The three others (for there were only five of them altogether) formed a sort of aristocracy, and were reserved for the upstairs company, unless they were needed downstairs and there were no visitors above.
>
> The Jupiter Room, where the bourgeois of the neighbourhood gathered, was papered in blue and decorated with a large picture depicting Leda stretched out beneath a swan. To reach this room, one came by a spiral staircase, leading from a narrow door, modest in appearance, giving on to the street, and over which there shone, all night long, behind a griddle, a little lamp like those that in some towns are lit at the feet of madonnas.

The brothel of Fécamp represents the permissive approach at its most human; by means of this club-like institution, a social need was met in a way which gave little or no offence to the community. Such houses as Maupassant describes were to be found in every French town, performing their social function for the most part without scandal or abuse.

The picture was not always so rosy. In contrast with Britain, where prostitution was legal but the police had such wide discretionary powers that they could in practice prevent any girl from plying her trade, in France prostitution was technically illegal, but it was left to the police whether or not they invoked the law. While the French policy had certain pragmatic advantages, it also offered infinite opportunities for graft, blackmail and other abuses. A series of attempts to impose control over prostitution culminated in 1843 with the inauguration of the Service des Moeurs—'moral service'—which persisted with minor changes until after World War II. The basic principle was that prostitution would be tolerated—hence brothels became known as *maisons de tolérance*—but within carefully defined limits. Brothels, being more easily supervised, were preferred to other forms, but not to the extent of persecuting the streetwalker so long as she behaved herself. There were still anomalies and room for abuse, but the system worked well on the whole. Dr William Acton, comparing the two capitals in the 1860s, said: 'In London a man has prostitution thrust upon him; in Paris he has to go out of his way to look for it'—a tribute to the success of the system adopted in France.

A common prostitute was known as a *fille soumise* because she had submitted to the regulations, a *fille inscrite* or *enregistrée* because her name was inscribed on the official register of the Bureau des Moeurs, or a *fille en carte* because she carried a card identifying her profession. These were some of the regulations she was obliged to follow:

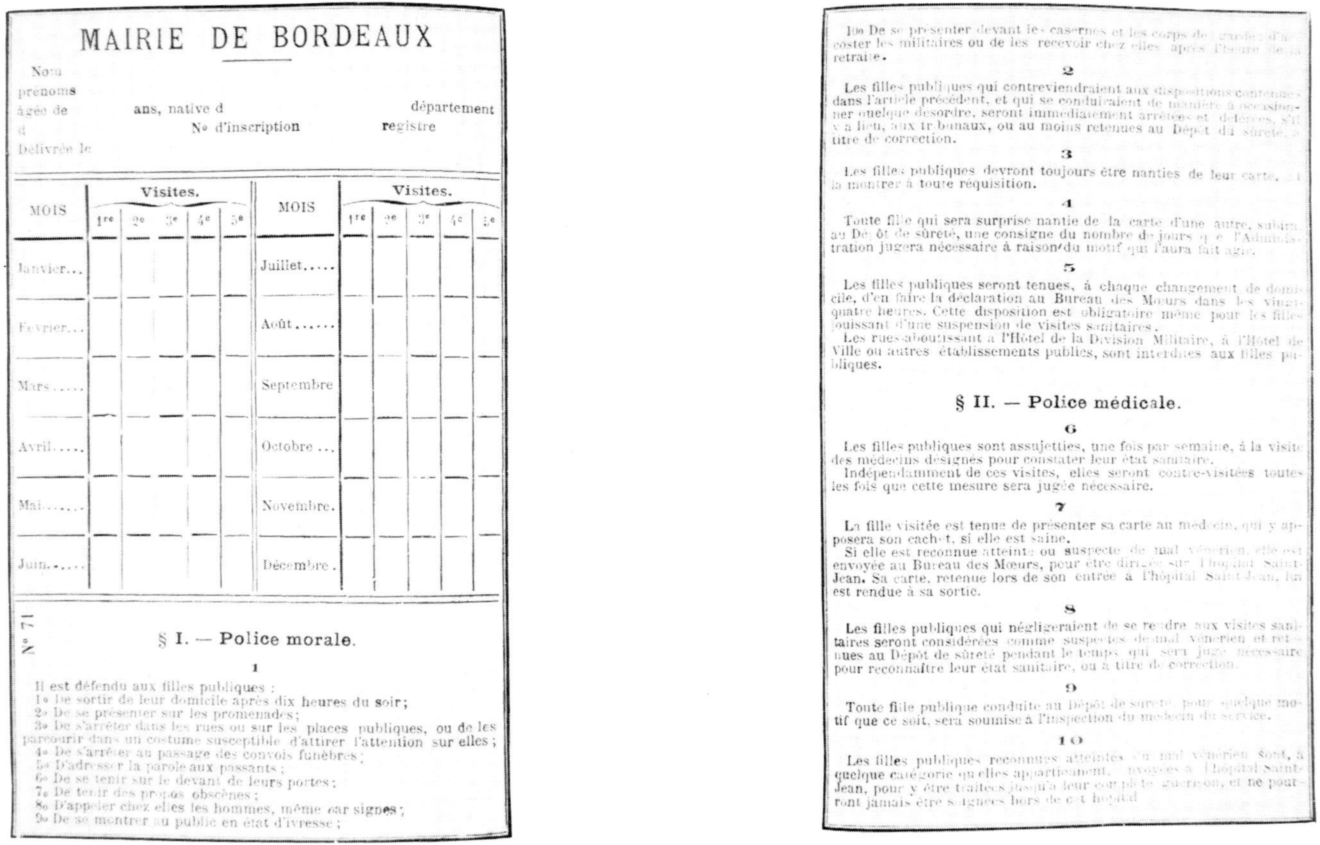

# MAIRIE DE BORDEAUX

Nom
prénoms
âgée de ans, native d département
d N° d'inscription registre
Délivrée le

| MOIS | Visites. 1re | 2e | 3e | 4e | 5e | MOIS | Visites. 1re | 2e | 3e | 4e | 5e |
|---|---|---|---|---|---|---|---|---|---|---|---|
| Janvier... | | | | | | Juillet..... | | | | | |
| Février... | | | | | | Août...... | | | | | |
| Mars..... | | | | | | Septembre | | | | | |
| Avril.... | | | | | | Octobre ... | | | | | |
| Mai...... | | | | | | Novembre. | | | | | |
| Juin..... | | | | | | Décembre. | | | | | |

N° 71

## § I. — Police morale.

**1**

Il est défendu aux filles publiques :
1° De sortir de leur domicile après dix heures du soir;
2° De se présenter sur les promenades;
3° De s'arrêter dans les rues ou sur les places publiques, ou de les parcourir dans un costume susceptible d'attirer l'attention sur elles;
4° De s'arrêter au passage des convois funèbres;
5° D'adresser la parole aux passants;
6° De se tenir sur le devant de leurs portes;
7° De tenir des propos obscènes;
8° D'appeler chez elles les hommes, même par signes;
9° De se montrer au public en état d'ivresse;
10° De se présenter devant les casernes et les corps de garde, d'accoster les militaires ou de les recevoir chez elles après l'heure de la retraite.

**2**

Les filles publiques qui contreviendraient aux dispositions contenues dans l'article précédent, et qui se conduiraient de manière à occasionner quelque désordre, seront immédiatement arrêtées et déférées, s'il y a lieu, aux tribunaux, ou au moins retenues au Dépôt de sûreté, à titre de correction.

**3**

Les filles publiques devront toujours être nanties de leur carte, et la montrer à toute réquisition.

**4**

Toute fille qui sera surprise nantie de la carte d'une autre, subira au Dépôt de sûreté, une consigne du nombre de jours que l'Administration jugera nécessaire à raison du motif qui l'aura fait agir.

**5**

Les filles publiques seront tenues, à chaque changement de domicile, d'en faire la déclaration au Bureau des Mœurs dans les vingt-quatre heures. Cette disposition est obligatoire même pour les filles jouissant d'une suspension de visites sanitaires.

Les rues aboutissant à l'Hôtel de la Division Militaire, à l'Hôtel de Ville ou autres établissements publics, sont interdites aux filles publiques.

## § II. — Police médicale.

**6**

Les filles publiques sont assujetties, une fois par semaine, à la visite des médecins désignés pour constater leur état sanitaire.

Indépendamment de ces visites, elles seront contre-visitées toutes les fois que cette mesure sera jugée nécessaire.

**7**

La fille visitée est tenue de présenter sa carte au médecin, qui y apposera son cachet, si elle est saine.

Si elle est reconnue atteinte ou suspecte de mal vénérien, elle est envoyée au Bureau des Mœurs, pour être dirigée sur l'hôpital Saint-Jean. Sa carte, retenue lors de son entrée à l'hôpital Saint-Jean, lui est rendue à sa sortie.

**8**

Les filles publiques qui négligeraient de se rendre aux visites sanitaires seront considérées comme suspectes de mal vénérien et retenues au Dépôt de sûreté pendant le temps qui sera jugé nécessaire pour reconnaître leur état sanitaire, ou à titre de correction.

**9**

Toute fille publique conduite au Dépôt de sûreté, pour quelque motif que ce soit, sera soumise à l'inspection du médecin du service.

**10**

Les filles publiques reconnues atteintes de mal vénérien sont, à quelque catégorie qu'elles appartiennent, envoyées à l'hôpital Saint-Jean, pour y être traitées jusqu'à leur complète guérison, et ne pourront jamais être soignées hors de cet hôpital.

*Carte* of a registered French prostitute. Bordeaux, *c* 1890

> Public women must present themselves at the dispensary for examination at least once every 15 days . . . They are forbidden to practise their calling during daylight, or walk in the streets until at least half an hour after the public lamps are lit, or at any season of the year before 7pm or after 11pm . . . They must be simply and decently dressed so as not to attract attention by the richness, striking colours or extravagance of their dress. They must wear some sort of cap or bonnet, and not be seen bareheaded . . . They are strictly forbidden to address men accompanied by females or children . . . They may not exhibit themselves at windows . . . They must not station themselves on the sidewalk, form or walk in groups, or walk to and fro in a narrow space . . .

In practice, so long as a girl conducted herself with reasonable discretion, she was likely to avoid police harassment. Most independent prostitutes would have a ponce; among Paris girls the preference was often less for a tough from the criminal class than for a student or budding artist of the bohemian world—such a companion, known as a *paillasson*, would be fed and kept by his girl but would escape the execration heaped, in France as elsewhere, on the professional pimp.

A street girl would get 5 francs a trick if she was lucky—say, £2.50 today—but would often have to settle for less. Not surprisingly there was considerable inducement for a girl to work in a brothel where, though expenses were greater, she would receive 5 to 20 francs from each customer as well as a tip of 'glove money' from a satisfied client.

The registered brothels of Paris—there were 2,000 or more in the 1850s—were equally subject to official control. There were strict limits as to the area where a brothel might be located. Two such houses were not permitted side by side. Each girl must have a room of her own with her own washing facilities. Windows had to have curtains or shutters and must not be fully opened. All girls had to be medically inspected once a week. But again, so long as the proprietor conducted himself well, he could trade in relative peace. Acton, who was in favour of similar regulation in England, described a Paris brothel of the 1860s in terms which suggest that his professional objectivity was tinged with admiration:

> The visitor discovers, on entering, scenes of sensual extravagance to which his eyes are unaccustomed in England. Here vice finds a retreat of voluptuous splendour, to which in soberer climes she is a stranger. The visitor is received by the mistress of the house, and ushered into a sumptuous ante-room: on a curtain being drawn aside, a door is revealed to him, containing a circular piece of glass about the size of a crown piece, through which he

Raid on a brothel. From *Le Petit Journal*, 1895

can reconnoitre at his ease a small, but well-lighted and elegantly furnished drawing-room, occupied by the women of the establishment.

They are usually to be seen seated on sofa chairs, elegantly attired in different-coloured silks, with low bodices and having their hair dressed in the extreme of fashion; the whole group being arranged artistically, as in a tableau vivant, and the individuals who comprise it representing the poses of different celebrated statues, selected apparently with the object of showing off to the best advantage the peculiar attractions of the different women.

From the room of observation the visitor can, if he pleases, select his victim, in the same way as the traveller in Galway, on his arrival at a certain hotel, can choose from a number of fish swimming about in the tank the particular salmon on which he would prefer to dine. If this somewhat cold-blooded process of selection is distasteful to him, and he desires to become acquainted with the women in a less summary manner—or if the object of his visit is merely amusement, or the satisfaction of curiosity without any ulterior aim—he can enter the room, and enjoy the society of its occupants, and will find that the terms of the invitation addressed by the old women at the street-door to passers-by are strictly carried out—'Si vous montez voir les jolies filles, cela vous n'engage à rien!' ('Come up and see the lovely girls—no obligation to purchase!')—all that is expected from him being to stand a reasonable amount of champagne, or other refreshment, and make himself generally agreeable.

The life of these women must be monotonous enough. They rise about ten, breakfast at eleven, dine at half-past five, and sup about two: they seldom go out walking, and when they do it is in the company of the mistress or sub-mistress.

Acton was a doctor, and it was on medical grounds that he championed the introduction of regulation in England. He pointed out that, while in the British Army one man in three suffered from venereal disease, in France not only were the girls inspected at least once a fortnight but the men were examined before and after going on leave, with the result that only one man in ten was infected. No such figures are available for civilian customers; but whereas one in four of the girls in London were found to be infected, any French girl whose weekly inspection revealed symptoms was forbidden to trade until she had been cured, on pain of losing her licence. Even allowing that a girl could be infected between one inspection and the next, and that some would trick the inspector or go undetected, it is evident that the customer was much safer in Paris than in London.

No wonder, therefore, that the French police were so active in their harassment of the *clandé*—the casual or clandestine girl—who did not

Customer inspecting brothel girls. Anonymous French print, *c* 1890

want to register as a professional, perhaps because she was an amateur moonlighting from another job or because she didn't want her activities known by her family, friends or neighbours. A special force of agents, known as *mouchards*, were employed to track down these freelance prostitutes; the system was open to abuse, but there was sound medical justification for hounding the casual girl who was far more likely than the professional to pass on infection. None the less, amateurs continued to flourish, and the shopgirls of Paris—particularly the *midinettes* from the milliners' workrooms—acquired a worldwide reputation for their amiable dispositions.

But there was another class of prostitute whose names would not appear in the registers of the Service des Moeurs. Ranking higher than the inmates of even the most luxurious and expensive brothels were the aristocrats of harlotry who never peddled their flesh on the open market and so never came within the jurisdiction of the police. These were the legendary women for whom the French, with their gift for elegant directness, found the *mot juste: les grandes horizontales*. There were other names for them; unkind observers might speak of them as *les degrafinées*—the unbuttoned ones—or as members of *la haute bicherie*. Behind such derogatory phrases was concealed a certain admiration, for these girls had made it to the top in a tough and highly competitive profession.

Among the courtesans of Paris, as among the horsebreakers of London, the prostitute with charisma could rise to extraordinary heights; but because there was less hypocrisy in France, and perhaps because French society, being largely post-Revolutionary in origin, was less liable to put on airs, the courtesan was more generally accepted in society. A further contributory factor was the greater formality of the marriage relationship in France, where the arranged marriage continued to be prevalent throughout the nineteenth century; its socio-economic basis relieved the married partner from the sense of obligation normally felt in Britain or America, making infidelity comparatively venial. The mistress was a more or less openly condoned element in a French gentleman's life in a way her English counterpart had never been, even in the permissive eighteenth century. Similarly, for a Frenchwoman to take a lover was, even in the highest society, by no means unacceptable so long as certain conventions were not flouted.

The *grandes cocottes* made no attempt to gatecrash polite society's innermost sanctums, but at the Opéra, driving in the Bois, racing at Longchamps or dining at Maxim's they were the focal point of attention; their activities were daily reported in the frothier press as though they had a real standing in society. They had friends among the influential, but it was upon the rich that they ultimately depended—the South American millionaire, the German banker, the Russian prince or the English peer. For the most sought-after courtesan—'not by the hour but by the quarter-hour'—such a man would casually part with twenty-five gold

Marguerite Bellanger

louis (about £500 today). Not many girls earned that kind of money; these high-flying birds of paradise were few in number compared with the thousands of *filles soumises* walking the streets or the *filles de maison* awaiting their evening visitors—but they were what every *fille publique* aspired to be, if only in her dreams. For, just as every one of Napoleon's soldiers carried a marshal's baton in his pack, so every sidewalk tart pictured herself as the celebrated Liane de Pougy—'notre courtisane nationale'.

Born Anne de Chassaigne, the daughter of a soldier and a bourgeois mother, Liane married a naval officer—who fired two shots into her thigh for reasons that can only be guessed; later in her career she would tell her more privileged admirers: 'If you doubt my words, you can feel the bullets!' She started as a piano teacher, then gave lessons in English, but it was at the Folies Bergère—where she was seen by the Prince of Wales—that she found her true vocation. As a Folies girl she had little difficulty in securing a wealthy patron, and soon Liane was rising rapidly in the ranks of high-class whoredom. So many remarkable tales were told of her that it is impossible to disentangle truth from legend: did Henri Meilhac, Offenbach's librettist, offer her 80,000 francs simply to see her naked? And did she take her jeweller with her when she visited Russia so that he would be on hand whenever an admirer wished to purchase a little memento for her? She was said to have become a postulant nun in her thirties under the name of Soeur Madeleine de la Pénitence; then, having second thoughts, she resumed her decolleté gown and pearls, only to take up her vows again after she was seventy.

Another whose story stretches the imagination was Marguerite Bellanger. A simple streetwalker, catering for the needs of junior military officers, she chanced, when caught in the rain in the Bois de Boulogne, to attract the attention of the Emperor Napoleon III driving past in his carriage. He threw his cape out of the window for her to protect herself against the elements; after spending the night wrapped in it, she presented herself at the palace and insisted on returning it to its owner in person. The consequence was that for two years she was the emperor's official mistress; shrewdly she made a graceful retirement and lived her later years quietly in the château he gave her, becoming known for her good works.

Léonide Leblanc, the mistress of the Prince d'Orléans, son of King Louis Philippe, would take favoured customers—for, like many courtesans, she did a little trading on the side—to peep through a crack and see, from behind, the prince at work in his study. The subsequent proceedings—not to mention Léonide's fee—were considerably enhanced by the client's knowledge that he was deceiving a prince of the blood who, moreover, was actually on the premises! None suspected that the wily Léonide was in fact deceiving the deceiver—what her customers saw was only a wax figure of her patron.

The courtesan's attitude towards money was often an ambivalent one—

Léonide Leblanc

her acquisitiveness being offset by extravagance. It was as if she owed it to herself to demand the highest fee for her favours and then despised what she had earned once it was in her possession. None displayed this duality more than Cora Pearl; born Emma Elizabeth Crouch in 1842, she was one of the few English girls to successfully challenge the French courtesans on their own territory. Seduced at fourteen, she rose vulgarly and

La Belle Otéro. Drawing by Paul Rieth in *Jugend*, 1900

vivaciously via—in her own phrase—'a golden chain of lovers' until she reached the bed of Prince Jerome Bonaparte, cousin of the emperor. He installed her in a mansion costing the equivalent of today's £400,000—or so she claimed; the 12,000 francs—say, £6,000 today—she is said to have charged for a night in her company may also be an exaggeration. There is, however, no doubt that money came Cora's way in prodigious quantities and that it slipped through her fingers at an equally prodigious rate. The story was told of how a group of students clubbed together, each putting in a louis to make up her fee, then drawing lots to find which of them would enjoy the experience of a night with her. Afterwards, Cora gave the winner back his louis, telling him that he had pleased her and she wished to give herself to him for nothing. (But she kept all the rest!)

Fantasy reached perhaps its greatest heights with La Belle Otéro, a Spanish gipsy dancer whose career, like Cora's, began at the age of fourteen. She was kidnapped by a perceptive chief of police; after being rescued she made her way to Monte Carlo, where she had a lucky win on the tables that enabled her to migrate to Paris. Like many others of her profession, she appeared at the Folies Bergère. It was perhaps her friendship with the young Colette which inspired her to write her autobiography—a highly coloured tale scattered with men who are supposed to have shot themselves on her account. In at least two cases this seems to have been true: the Comte Chevdole of the Jockey Club discovered that life wasn't worth living after he had squandered a fortune on her, and an unnamed explorer felt the same way after she had declined his offer of 10,000 francs. According to her memoirs, Vanderbilt offered her a yacht and Dion an automobile; d'Annunzio wrote a poem about her and Renoir painted her portrait; German barons competed for her with offers of bigger and better schlosses and the Kaiser commissioned a pantomime for her; the Grand Duke Nicolai abducted her and Prince Peter of Russia cried 'Ninouchka, ruin me but never leave me!' In 1948 she was living in Nice; but she had lost her fortune where she had first found it—on the gaming tables.

The *grandes horizontales* of France were unique, as perhaps were those friendly neighbourhood brothels described by Maupassant. There was, of course, a less attractive face of prostitution and, when it came to the seamier side of the trade, there was little to choose between France or any other country in Europe—Russia for instance. In *Resurrection*, Tolstoy sets the scene most vividly:

After many fruitless attempts to find a situation, Katusha returned to the registry office; here she met a woman with bracelets on her bare, plump arms and rings on most of her fingers. Hearing that Katusha badly needed a place, the woman gave her address and invited her to come to her house. The woman received her very kindly, and set cake and sweet wine before her. In the evening a tall man, with long grey hair and white beard, entered the room, and sat down at once near Katusha, smiling and gazing at her with shining eyes, and began joking with her. The hostess called him into the next room, and Katusha heard her say 'A fresh one from the country'. Then the hostess called Katusha and told her he was an author with a great deal of money, and that if he liked her he would grudge her nothing. A few days later the author sent for her . . .

Next door lived a jolly young shopman, with whom Katusha soon fell in love. She told the author, and moved to a little lodging of her own. The shopman, who promised to marry her, went to Nijni on business without mentioning it to her, having evidently thrown her up, and Katusha remained alone. She meant to continue living by herself, but the police told her she would have to get a prostitute's card, and submit to medical examinations. She returned to her aunt but, seeing her fine dress, her hat and mantle, her aunt no longer offered her laundry work: as she saw it, her niece had risen above that sort of thing. Katusha looked pityingly at the hard-worked laundresses, some already ill with consumption, and thought with horror that she might have shared their fate.

It was just at this time that a procuress found her. She produced all sorts of dainties, and while Katusha drank, she offered to place her in one of the largest establishments in the city, explaining all the advantages. Katusha could choose between going into service, to be humiliated and probably annoyed by the attentions of the men and occasional clandestine sex, or an easy secure position, sanctioned by the law, and open, well-paid, regular sex—and it was the second way she chose. In this way, it seemed to her, she could revenge herself on her seducer, on the shopman, and on all who had injured her. She was tempted, too, and finally persuaded by the procuress telling her she might order her own dresses—velvet, silk, satin, low-necked ball dresses, whatever she fancied.

From that day a life of chronic sin against human and divine laws commenced for Katusha Maslova—a life which is led by hundreds of thousands of women, and which is not merely tolerated but sanctioned by the Government, anxious for the welfare of its subjects; a life which for nine women out of ten ends in painful disease, premature decrepitude, and death. Heavy sleep till late afternoon followed each night's orgies. Between 3 and 4 o'clock came the weary getting up from a dirty bed, soda water, coffee, listless pacing up and down the room in bedgowns and dressing jackets, lazy gazing out of the windows from behind the drawn curtains, indolent disputes with one another—then washing, perfuming and anointing of the body and hair, trying on of dresses, disputes about them with the mistress of the house, surveying of oneself in the mirror, painting the face, the eyebrows; fat, sweet food; then dressing in gaudy silks, exposing much of the body, and coming down into the ornamented and brightly lit drawing-room—then the arrival of visitors, music, dancing, sex with old and young and middle-aged, with half children and decrepit old men, bachelors, married men, merchants, clerks, Armenians, Jews, Tartars, rich and poor, sick and healthy, tipsy and sober, rough and tender, military men and civilians, students and mere schoolboys, of all classes, ages and characters. And shouts and jokes, and brawls and music, and tobacco and wine, and wine and tobacco, from evening till daylight; no relief till morning, and then heavy sleep; the same every day and all the week.

Then at the end of the week came the visit to the police station, as instituted by the government, where doctors, sometimes seriously and strictly, sometimes with playful levity, examined these women, and gave them written permission to continue in the sins they had been committing all the week. Then followed another week of the same kind, always the same, every night, summer and winter, working days and holidays . . .

# 8

# *BASIN STREET BLUES*

'They have harlots and honest women: the harlots never marry, or else are widows' This tantalising reference to the Indians of Virginia and New England by Captain John Smith—he who was so romantically rescued by Pocahontas in 1607—is the solitary indication that any form of prostitution existed on the North American continent before the arrival of the Europeans.

The new inhabitants did not have to wait long for the prostitute's services to be established. Boston was well supplied by the 1670s, while Philadelphia's riverside haunts catered to some of the most eminent men of the day—Benjamin Franklin being a regular customer. By the middle of the eighteenth century, it was reckoned that one in thirty of New York's female population earned her living from prostitution. New Orleans, with its French connections, catered for its sailors and slavers with a panache lacking in the northern communities. The inalienable right to the pursuit of happiness claimed by the Founding Fathers of the new federation in 1776 led, among other effects good or bad, to a flourishing trade being conducted almost unhindered in every sizeable community—sometimes sober, occasionally elegant, but for the most part matching in squalor and indignity the worst examples of vice traffic to be found anywhere in the world.

In the 1830s an English visitor to New York reported: 'There is not a dance hall, a free-and-easy, a concert saloon or a vile drinking-place that presents such a view of the depravity and degradation of New York as the gallery of a Bowery theatre.' As in any big city, the theatre was a natural rendezvous for the prostitute and her client; the difference was that in New York the girls did not require the customer to move on somewhere else but performed their function on the spot, thus enabling the customer to see the rest of the show without wasting his ticket.

Bordello on Almond Street, St Louis. Anonymous print of 1878

The beer gardens were no less obliging, providing back rooms where the waitresses could entertain clients; they were thus competing with the brothels and street girls who were themselves in fierce competition one with another. The diversity and ubiquity of New York prostitution were as remarkable as its sheer quantity. By 1872 there were some 600 brothels in the city, backed by around 5,000 streetwalkers and an untold number of part-timers.

The New York brothels ranged from the elegant parlor house to the squalid dives of the Five Points district. William Sanger, in his *History of Prostitution*, gave this vivid account of a fashionable New York parlor house in the 1850s:

The houses are furnished with a lavish display of luxury, scarcely in accordance with the dictates of good taste, however, and mostly exhibiting a quantity of magnificent furniture crowded together without taste or judgment for the sake of ostentation. Large mirrors adorn the walls, paintings and engravings in rich frames, vases and statuettes add their charms. Carpets of luxurious softness cover the floors, while sofas, ottomans, and easy chairs abound. Music has its representative in a beautiful pianoforte, upon which some professed player is paid a liberal salary to perform. In such an abode probably dwell from three to ten prostitutes, each paying weekly for her board from 10 to 16 dollars. Their active life comprises about twelve or fourteen hours daily, ranging from noon to midnight or early morning. Their visitors are mostly of what may be called the aristocratic class; young, middle-aged and even old men of property, of all callings and professions; anyone who can command a liberal supply of money is welcome, but without this indispensable requisite his company is not sought or appreciated.

None of the disgusting practices common in houses of a lower grade are met with here. There is no palpable obscenity, and but little that can outrage propriety. Of course there is a perfect freedom of manner between prostitutes and visitors, but so far as the public eye can penetrate, the requirements of common decency are not openly violated. There is no bar room or public drinking place in the house, but it is a general custom for

At this dive in Spring Street, New York, children of fourteen or less solicited custom—until raided by the police. From the *National Police Gazette*, 1886

each visitor to invite his *pro tempore inamorata* and her companions to take champagne with him, which is supplied by the keeper of the place at three dollars a bottle. Excessive drunkenness is rare, both prostitutes and keepers trying to suppress it, because an intoxicated man would be likely to give them trouble, damage their furniture, and injure the reputation of the house.

Chicago streetwalkers disguised as shoppers. From *National Police Gazette*, 1886

'Tempting to ruin! How Gotham's Palaces of Sin are garrisoned out of the hovels —the gaudy spider spreading her webs for the flies who make her loathsome trade profitable.' From the *National Police Gazette*, 1882

But such brothels were, as everywhere, the exception; James McCabe, in his 1872 exposé *Lights and Shadows of New York Life*, reckoned there were only fifty or so in the highest category. Girls stayed in these select houses for a year or two; then, unless they had managed to break out via a fortunate marriage or gone into business for themselves, they started to descend the ladder to establishments where youth and beauty were not so all-important. Working conditions in the middle range of houses were largely dictated by their ethnic character; a German brothel in New York was described by Sanger:

> There is a public bar-room opening directly from the street, where can be obtained lager beer and German wines. This is the reception room of the establishment, and a stranger who might walk in to get a glass of beer without knowing the character of the place, or being aware of the significance of the crimson and white curtains festooned over the windows, would find himself followed to the bar by some German girl, who would ask him in broken English if he would 'treat her'. If he feels inclined to gaze around and study human nature in this place, he sees that the room is very clean: a common sofa, one or two settees, and a number of chairs are ranged round the walls, there is a small table with some German newspapers upon it; a piano, upon which the proprietor or his barkeeper at intervals performs a national melody; and a few prints or engravings complete its furniture. Two or three girls are in different parts of the room engaged in knitting or sewing; for German girls, whether virtuous or prostitute, seem to have a horror of idleness, and even in such a place as this are seldom seen without their work.
>
> The visitor is surprised at the entire absence of all those noisy elements generally considered indispensable from a low-class house of prostitution. He can sit there and smoke his cigar in as much peace as at any hotel in the city, and if he once tells a woman he does not wish to have any connection with her, he will scarcely be annoyed again. If he thinks proper to enter into conversation with the proprietor, he will be certain of a courteous reply, and will frequently find him an intelligent and communicative man. Finally, concluding to resist the temptations around him, he leaves the place in the most perfect security, and without the least fear of being insulted.

It was quite otherwise in the Irish houses, according to McCabe:

> The girls are, without exception, the nastiest, most besotted drabs that ever walked the streets. In the company there is a large preponderance of the cub of seventeen or eighteen. Some of these boys are the sons of merchants and lawyers, and are 'seeing life'. If they were told to go into their kitchens at

'Pure American girl abducted with unspeakable intent'. From *The Day's Doings*, 1871

> home and talk with the cook and the chambermaid, they would consider themselves insulted. Yet they come here and talk with other Irish girls every whit as ignorant and unattractive as the servants at home—only the latter are virtuous and these are infamous.

But whatever the conditions of work, the incentive to become a prostitute was not easy to resist. Sanger estimated her average weekly earnings are not lower than $10 (roughly equivalent to $100 today), a figure which takes in the lowest grades of prostitute, trading in cents rather than dollars, as well as the higher ranks. It doesn't sound like wealth until the amount is placed alongside another of his statistics—in the 1850s one quarter of the women in respectable occupations were earning one dollar a week or less. As Sanger comments: 'No economist, however closely he may calculate, will pretend that fourteen cents a day will supply any woman with lodging, food and clothes.' While in Victorian England it was largely economic advantage which drew girls into prostitution, in New York it was sheer necessity.

> The miners came in forty-nine,
> The whores in fifty-one,
> and when they got together,
> they produced the native son.
> (Anon)

When the Gold Rush of 1849 began to draw men to California from all over the world, prostitutes were inevitably among those who flocked to prey on the prospectors. It was a seller's market: in San Francisco the pioneers made their fortunes: one capable French girl is said to have banked a clear profit of $50,000 in her first year. The town expanded rapidly if inelegantly, and its red-light district grew to match. Almost every dance hall or saloon designed for entertaining sailors, prospectors and all the others attracted by the promise of the get-rich-quick boom catered also for their sexual needs. Upstairs or downstairs a large room would be partitioned into cubicles just large enough to hold a rudimentary bed or, in the sleaziest joints, a pallet on the floor; sometimes there were not even curtains or partitions to separate one couple from the next.

Crime flourished. If a man had any money on him, the girl or her associates would get hold of it by fair means or foul, stopping at nothing—drugging, slugging or mugging. One notorious pair of Mexican girls

'The result of following a streetwalker'—the customer blackmailed. From McCabe, *Lights and Shadows of New York Life*, 1872

habitually worked together; when they reached the cubicle, the customer was asked to choose between them and, while he went to work on his preference, her partner belted him from behind. It was their proud boast that none of their customers had ever achieved the sexual satisfaction he paid for.

Not all the girls were so prudent, and often they were themselves the victims:

> If one of 'Bull Run' Allen's pretty waiter girls or performers became unconscious from liquor, as frequently happened, she was carried upstairs and laid on a bed, and sexual privileges were sold to all comers while she lay helpless in a drunken stupor. The price ranged from 25c to $1, depending upon the age and beauty of the girl. For an additional quarter a man might

watch his predecessor, an extraordinary procedure which was supposed to give an additional fillip to the senses. It was not unusual for a girl to be abused by as many as thirty or forty men in the course of a single night.

(Herbert Asbury, *The Barbary Coast*, 1933)

Prostitution also flourished in San Francisco's Chinatown. Girls were purchased or kidnapped in China by agents of the Californian brothels; in the 1870s a pretty Chinese girl could be purchased for a few hundred dollars. Once bought, she was virtually a prisoner for life. She was confined to the house at all times, except for occasional excursions under strict guard; she received not a cent of the proceeds of her work, was

Episcopal minister lured to sin. From the *National Police Gazette*, 1886

never rewarded in any way and was punished for the slightest offence. Branding, whipping and other forms of torture were reported. It is no surprise to learn that the average life expectancy of a Chinese brothel girl in San Francisco was only six years. From the customer's point of view, a few of the better Chinese brothels were as well-appointed as the parlor houses, but the majority were as squalid as any along the Barbary Coast.

While most American clients appeared to prefer their sex straight and simple, a few had elaborate tastes which were catered for by the more exclusive houses. Madame Gabrielle's 'Lively Flea' boasted a Virgin's Room cunningly lined with mirrors and peepholes. Here a gullible client, who paid handsomely enough for the privilege, would encounter che 'house virgin'—a girl still young enough to look the part yet suffipiently knowledgeable to act like a terrified novice. Besides the strange tleasure experienced by the client, he provided vicarious joy to delighted voyeurs who watched his performance through peepholes on payment of \$5-\$10. At the same house a girl did an interesting double-act with a Shetland pony. In another of Madame Gabrielle's houses spectators could watch white women performing with black men—arousing heaven knows what complexity of conflicting emotions! Fetishists were catered for at Madame Marcelle's 'Parisian Mansion'. During the 1890s, a respectable middle-aged man arrived there each morning, changed into a housemaid's uniform, and swept and dusted the house from top to bottom; he paid a dollar a day for the privilege. His identity was known only to Madame Marcelle, who never betrayed his confidence.

At the other extreme, in the low cribs, the client was not expected to remove any of his clothing except his hat, the aim being to get him out of the place, his orgasm achieved and his money taken, in the shortest possible time. So he stood in line, his hat in one hand and his money in the other, awaiting his brief encounter with a girl who might receive a hundred different men on a busy Saturday night.

San Francisco's Barbary Coast displayed prostitution at its lowest, girls and customers alike at their most degraded; its closing down at the onset of World War I was a matter of little regret except to those who had made a fat living from the lusts and miseries of others.

In most of America's towns prostitution was a scaled-down version of the New York experience; but in New Orleans—as perhaps nowhere else on the North American continent—the trade acquired some of the finesse which was taken more or less for granted in Europe. While the city's

France's loss, America's gain: French prostitutes forcibly despatched to New Orleans. *La Triste Embarquement des Filles de Joie*, anonymous print of 1684

prostitution was a native product derived as much from the slave trade and its geographical location, it owed its distinctive quality to its French origins. The women taken in police raids in France and shipped across the Atlantic to populate the new colonies continued to practise the profession they knew best, so that New Orleans was from the start furnished with more experienced whores than any other city in the New World. Not everyone was delighted; but when, about 1715, the church suggested that the moral tone of France's colonies would be improved if the immoral women were expelled, Governor Lamothe Cadillac of Louisiana replied:

> If I expel all the immoral females, there will be no women left here at all: this would suit neither the wishes of the King nor the inclinations of the people.

Not all the French girls who came to America were prostitutes; some were from respectable families, sent over as part of colonial policy and each presented with a chest containing clothing and other necessities to serve as a dowry when she arrived. These 'casket girls' were, one may reasonably suppose, somewhat plainer in appearance than their sailing companions; they were making the voyage because they reckoned on a better chance of marriage in a land where women were fewer. Herbert Asbury, who chronicled the New Orleans underworld with the same dedication he brought to the Barbary Coast of San Francisco, noted with some irony how these 'founding mothers' came to be regarded by their descendants:

> By some queer physiological mischance none of the correction girls, apparently, ever bore a child. On the other hand, the casket girls would seem to have been extraordinarily fertile, each becoming the mother of at least a hundred children. Proof of these biological miracles is furnished by the fact that practically every native family of Louisiana is able to trace its descent in an unbroken line from one of the *filles à la cassette*.

During succeeding decades, New Orleans shifted from French to Spanish hands then back to French again, but continued to merit its reputation of easygoing morality; and when, in 1803, Louisiana came into United States' possession, the American people acquired a legacy they have never altogether been able to absorb. Throughout the nineteenth century New Orleans, an expanding seaport and terminal for the

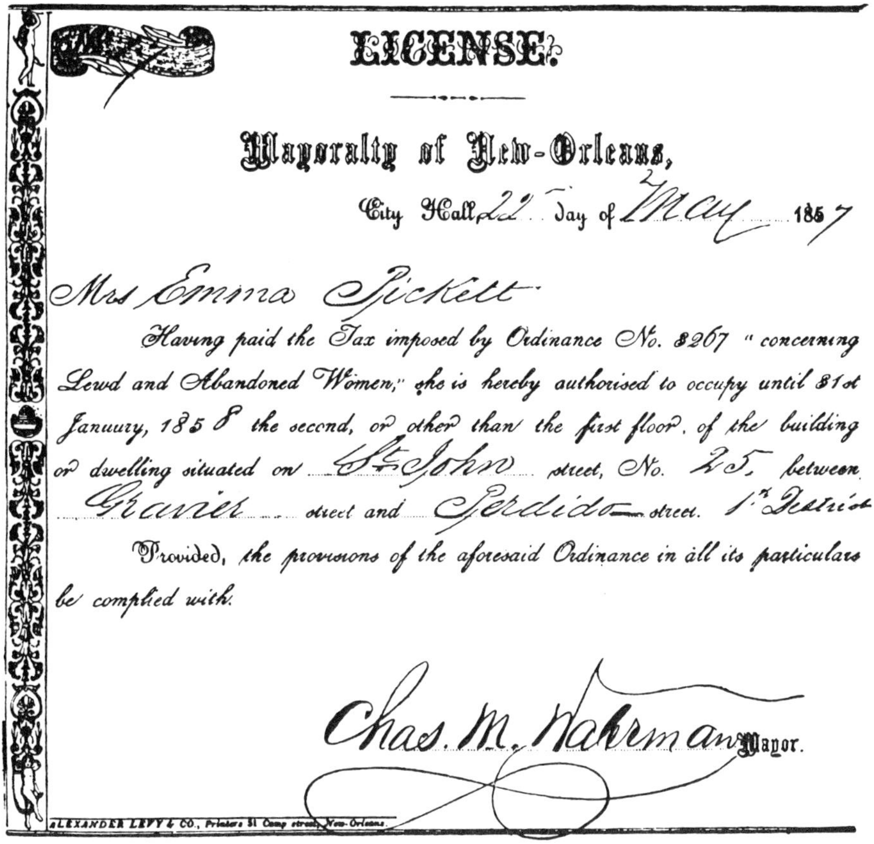

LICENSE.

Mayoralty of New-Orleans,

City Hall, 22 Day of May 1857

Mrs Emma Pickett

Having paid the Tax imposed by Ordinance No. 8267 "concerning Lewd and Abandoned Women," she is hereby authorised to occupy until 31st January, 1858 the second, or other than the first floor, of the building or dwelling situated on St John street, No. 25, between Gravier street and Perdido street. 1st District

Provided, the provisions of the aforesaid Ordinance in all its particulars be complied with.

Chas. M. Waterman Mayor.

ALEXANDER LEVY & CO., Printers 31 Camp street, New-Orleans.

Licence for a New Orleans brothel, 1857

Mississippi river traffic, catered for vast numbers of sailors and merchants, travellers and immigrants of all nationalities, as well as its own rapidly growing population. As the city sprawled, control of prostitution was becoming an urgent necessity.

In 1857 the city fathers decided that the French system of licensed prostitution was the most efficacious; apart from enabling some degree of supervision, it would bring in around $100,000 per annum to the city coffers, for each girl was to pay $100 for her licence, each brothel $250. But New Orleans was now an American, not a French, city. Barely had the authorities started to put their scheme into operation than lawyers hired by the underworld called the legality of the scheme into question. The enterprise was abandoned without a conclusive legal decision, prematurely closing what might have been an edifying experiment in social control.

For the next four decades, the red-light districts of New Orleans flourished without hindrance. Basin Street—immortalised in one of the

# Miss Josie Arlington

THE ARLINGTON

NOWHERE IN this country will you find a more complete and thorough sporting house than the Arlington.

Absolutely and unquestionably the most decorative and costly fitted-out sporting palace ever placed before the American public.

The wonderful originality of everything that goes to fit out a mansion makes it the most attractive ever seen in this or the old country.

Nothing daunted, Miss Arlington, after suffering a loss of many thousand dollars through a fire, has refurnished and remodeled the entire place at an enormous expense, and the mansion is now the most gorgeous in the Southwest.

Within the great walls of this mansion will be found the work of great artists from Europe and America. Many articles from the Louisiana Purchase Exposition will also be seen.

PHONE MAIN 1888

# 225 N. Basin

Advertisement for Josie Arlington's house in Basin Street, New Orleans. From the New Orleans *Blue Book*—a guide to the brothel quarter

greatest of jazz blues—has vanished from the map, half of it buried beneath a railway station; but in its heyday almost every building was a house, not a home. The first big brothel in Basin Street was Kate Townsend's at No 40, opened in 1866, a year after the South's defeat in the Civil War. Kate's success was imitated by others, and soon New Orleans could boast a number of high-class houses where only wine and champagne were drunk, where the girls wore evening gowns and could be seen by appointment only, and where 'refined and artistic entertainments' were featured on the evening programme. Asbury has described a visit to Kate's:

> When a gentleman arrived he was met at the door by a uniformed negro maid. If he was one of the steady clients, many of whom had charge accounts,

he was ushered ceremoniously into the drawing room, where he was expected to buy wine—at from $10 to $15 a bottle—for the assembled company. If a stranger, he was shown into an ante-room and questioned by Kate, who also drank a glass with him—at $2 a glass. If his credentials were in order, he was escorted into the drawing-room and formally presented to the ladies. If one of the girls struck his fancy, he communicated his desires to the Madame, who conferred with the lucky strumpet. If the latter was willing—and there is no record that one of them was ever otherwise—she discreetly retired to her boudoir. Thither, after a seemly interval, the gentleman was conducted. The tariff for such an adventure was $15: Kate herself was occasionally available for the entertainment of a particularly distinguished client, at a price which is said to have been $50 an hour.

There were many houses at the other end of the scale of sophistication; Josephine Killeen's, at no 45 Basin Street, for instance, where in 1870 clients could rent not only Molly Williams but also her ten-year-old daughter at an all-in price of $50 a night—until even the easygoing New Orleans police decided this was going too far, and took the child away from her. They stepped in too when Kate Smith advertised that none of

The parlour of Josie Arlington's house

Police raid Madam Willett's 'Crinoline Factory' at 21 Bleecker Street, New York, and rescue girls aged between twelve and fifteen. From the *National Police Gazette*, 1886

the girls working for her was more than seventeen years of age; among those 'rescued' was a sixteen-year-old who declared she had been a prostitute for four years. Things were worse still in the Canal Street district, where the price of copulation was 20 cents; yet even this was not the lowest, for there were streetwalkers whose working premises were a bit of worn carpet, which—for 10 cents a throw—they would stretch on the ground in full public view, while the neighbours shouted advice and encouragement.

By the 1890s, New Orleans was in danger of becoming one vast brothel. But at the same time, the reform movement was growing in strength to such a degree that the city authorities had to choose which they were going to fight, the brothel-owners or the reformers. They chose to contain and control prostitution—an action that was to create an American legend. Alderman Sidney Story made a study of methods employed in Europe and in 1897 put up a proposal that prostitution in New Orleans should be confined within a specific area, and that within that area it should be tolerated though not actually legalised.

Inevitably such proposals were bitterly opposed: there was moral opposition from those who insisted that legislation implied approval and that such a scheme would be giving vice the green light as well as the red; while more material opposition came from those reluctant to see a large section of a great city turned over to prostitution and all that went with it. But the merits of the scheme outweighed such objections, and the new district—baptised 'Storyville'—became the largest and most colourful of its kind.

The anxieties of those concerned with property values were fully justified; rents doubled in the selected area, while elsewhere houses were left untenanted. Eventually thirty-eight blocks were allocated as brothels, assignation houses, saloons and cabarets. Jazz pianist Jelly Roll Morton described the scene:

> This tenderloin district was like something nobody has ever seen before or since. Hundreds of men were passing through the streets day and night. The chippies in their little-girl dresses were standing in the crib doors singing the blues. Some were real ladies in spite of their downfall, and some were habitual drunkards, and some were dope fiends . . . They had everything in The District, from the highest class to the lowest. Creep joints where they'd put the feelers on a guy's clothes, cribs that rented for about $5 a day and had just about room enough for a bed, small-time houses where the price was from 50c to $1, and they put on naked dances, circuses and jive. Then, of course, we had the mansions where everything was of the highest class. These houses were filled up with the most expensive furniture and paintings. It was in these mansions that the best of the piano players worked.
>
> (Shapiro and Hentoff, *Hear Me Talkin to Ya*, 1955)

The 'sporting houses' were gaudy, lavish establishments emulating the French style. This publicity hand-out conjured up a fantasy vision:

> The New Mahogany Hall was erected specially for Miss Lulu White at a cost of $40,000. The house is built of marble and is four storey: containing five parlors, all handsomely furnished, and fifteen bedrooms. Each bedroom has a bath with hot and cold water and extension closets. The elevator, which is built for two, is of the latest style.
>
> In describing Miss Lulu, as she is most familiarly called, it would not be

amiss to say that besides possessing an elegant form she has beautiful black hair and blue eyes, which have justly gained for her the title of the 'Queen of the Demi-Monde'. Her establishment is unquestionably the most elaborately furnished house in the city of New Orleans. She has made a feature of boarding none but the fairest of girls—those gifted with nature's best charms, and would, under no circumstances, have any but that class in her house.

As an entertainer Miss Lulu stands foremost, having made a life-long study of music and literature. She is well read and one that can interest anybody and make a visit to her place a continued round of pleasure.

Many features of Storyville—not only its elegant heights but also its squalid depths—are reflected in the titles of jazz classics. 'Barrel House Boogie' and 'Gut Bucket Blues' recall the primitive barrel houses where for a nickel customers filled their glasses from a cask and the spigot dripped whisky into a gut bucket on the floor—and where the girls were hardly more costly than the drink. Other titles recall individuals—like Mamie of 'Mamie's Blues'—and countless sweet poppas who end up by taking the 2.19 train and leave their women to sing the blues. No other red-light district was ever so immortalised.

But Storyville itself proved not to be immortal. Corruption continued but within controllable limits; so far as the city authorities were concerned, Alderman Story's solution worked, and statistics confirm their judgement. Though the population of New Orleans increased by 50,000 during the first two decades of the twentieth century, the number of brothels declined from 260 to about 100, and the 2,000 known prostitutes to 450, half of them part-time; these figures support Asbury's verdict: 'The operation of the New Orleans experiment over a period of twenty years proved that segregation with strict police supervision was unquestionably the best method ever devised for the control of vice.'

Unfortunately there were others who thought otherwise. New Orleans was a naval base and, when America entered the war in 1917, the authorities decided that Storyville was a menace to the morale of servicemen and ordered it to be closed. On 2 October the mayor, Martin Behrman, declared:

Our city government has believed that the situation could be administered more easily and more satisfactorily by confining prostitution within a prescribed area. Our experience has taught us that the reasons for this are unanswerable, but the Navy Department of the Federal Government has decided otherwise.

So the great mansions, lavish as Habsburg palaces, were closed down and their sumptuous furnishings auctioned off. The girls were rounded up for inspection; the jazz players took the train to Chicago. From then on prostitution in New Orleans, as elsewhere in the United States, was to be wide open to every form of racketeering, exploitation, abuse and corruption.

# 9
# *FLOWER BOATS AND CHERRY BLOSSOM*

When enjoying a virgin of thirteen, the Chinese called it 'trying the flower'; if she was fourteen—'cultivating the flower'; if she was fifteen—'gathering the flower'. No doubt the girls had other terms for it; but, as the whole weight of Chinese tradition was in favour of absolute feminine submission, they may have accepted their degrading lot without realising that any alternative was possible. A life of prostitution was at least a life, whereas before the nineteenth century one Chinese girl-child in three was killed off as a 'useless mouth' that would contribute less to the family earnings than it would consume. Then, as contact with the rest of the world encouraged an export trade in young girls, their market value was recognised and children who would formerly have been quietly murdered were ceremonially apprenticed to the brothels. A European traveller noted: 'The little victims are seen constantly passing on their way to the habitations of their purchasers, gaily dressed out as though for some great ceremony or happy festival.'

In the brothels of Shanghai and Canton the children would be trained in etiquette and the necessary arts, but their passivity was not always to the liking of Western visitors, one of whom, Jacobus, found the fare lacking in spice:

> Unfortunately, for those who like voluptuous pleasures, the Chinese prostitute has one immense fault—her frigidity. Copulation with her is accomplished mechanically: it is a commercial transaction which brings her in a piaster, and that is all. Never expect from a Chinese girl any refinement of voluptuousness—she is incapable of it.
>
> (*Untrodden Fields of Archaeology*, 1898)

It is possible, as the anthropologist Henriques suggests, that this reluctance to display enthusiasm was due less to inherent frigidity than to concern about disarranging an elaborate hair-style on which the girl may have lavished hours of work—appearance being all-important in the Chinese tradition of social conduct.

Though no doubt the majority of the 3,650 brothels which catered for sailors in Amoy were as primitive and brutal as those in seaports the world over, there were also more refined establishments. The better class of *tsing-loo* or 'blue houses'—so named from the traditional colour of their window-blinds—were purpose-built and sumptuously furnished. At dusk the blinds would be raised, lamps would be lit, music would play; such brothels were favourite places for merchants to congregate, and the talk would be as much about commerce or politics as about sexual matters.

A picturesque variant was the flower boat, partly café and partly brothel; there were fleets of them in the Pearl River at Canton. A party of men could hire one for the evening, paying £30 (at today's prices) for supper, music, and a girl apiece. After the meal, there would be games and music for a while, then couples would discreetly adjourn to one of the smaller boats moored alongside. It all sounds charming and, if the girls compared their lot with what it might have been in some other line of business, perhaps they counted themselves well enough off; they were, however, little better than slaves, utterly at the disposal of their owners.

Male prostitution in China is a subject on which virtually no information is available from native sources and only scanty testimony from occasional European travellers who were willing to defy the taboos of both Eastern and Western cultures. Although evidence exists for a class of male prostitutes who formed their own guild and were officially recognised, no details have been published; Schlegel, writing of Canton in 1880, makes the remarkable assertion that the homosexual brothels came near to outnumbering the heterosexual houses. Whatever the facts of the matter, the silence surrounding the reporting of homosexual behaviour was at least as prevalent in China as in Europe.

———◆———

When Captain John Saris was sent out to Japan in 1613 by the East India Company, he was diverted by the discovery that prostitutes were an essential item in the evening entertainment which, then as now, cemented business transactions. He noted a few facts about their working conditions:

> These women are as the slaves of one man, who putteth a price which every man shall pay that hath to do with any of them; more than which he is not to take upon pain of death, in case the party injured shall complain. It is left to his own discretion to price her at the first, but rise he cannot afterwards, fall he may. Neither doth the party bargain with the wench, but with her master, whose command she is to obey. The greatest of their nobility travelling hold it no disgrace to send for these panders to their inn, and do compound with them for the wenches.

Saris, like all European travellers in the Far East, had to come to terms with attitudes towards women and sex very different from those of the West. In Japan, a man would be no more ashamed of going to a brothel

European sailor with Japanese prostitute. Anonymous Japanese woodcut, mid-nineteenth century

than to a tavern; and a prostitute might feel more shame at being a girl than she did for practising her profession. Except among the lower classes, prostitution was treated more ceremoniously. The ultimate aim might be the same, but the preliminaries were very different; the ritual as performed in Tokyo made even the most sophisticated mating dances of Paris look crude and boorish.

In Japan a prostitute would have been apprenticed to the trade by her own family, in her teens or even earlier; thus she had enjoyed no other prospect and her only options were whether to seek to do well or to get by as effortlessly as might be. A high-class house in Tokyo or Nagasaki would contain between seven and thirty such girls, who would all have gone through years of elaborate training before being permitted to practise the trade. Sometimes a girl would be apprenticed for a certain period in order to earn a dowry, after which she would return to a respectable life, well-endowed financially and culturally. At its worst, the Japanese system was no better than the sex slavery of China; but at least a certain respect was shown in Japan for the girl as a human being.

The celebrated Yoshiwara in Tokyo, an 18-acre site which had, with government approval, been dedicated to prostitution in 1626, was described by visitors as the most beautiful brothel quarter in the world. Its entrance gateway bore this inscription:

> A DREAM OF SPRINGTIDE WHEN THE STREETS ARE FULL OF CHERRY BLOSSOMS : TIDINGS OF THE AUTUMN WHEN THE STREETS ARE LINED ON EITHER SIDE WITH LANTERNS.

To a surprising extent, the Yoshiwara lived up to this flamboyant introduction. Though doubtless corruption and exploitation thrived there, the façade at any rate was decoratively maintained, and even the lowest grade house could be described in purple prose:

> In the dusk of the evening, when all is chilly and lonesome, the deep-toned curfew bell fills the heart with a vague sense of gloomy sadness. Just when the temple bell is reverberating over hill and dale, the women of the Yoshiwara file into their cages. Decked in all the splendour of coral and tortoise-shell, they sit for hours exposed to the gaze of the passer-by. The *o shaku kabu*, leading beauty of the house, sits lazily smoking her long red bamboo pipe, pretending not to see the crowds swarming in front of the cage, feigning to be absorbed in the perusal of an epistle supposed to have been received from one of her numerous admirers.
>
> (Anon, *The Nightless City*, 1900)

A brothel in the Yoshiwara, Tokyo. From *The Nightless City*, 1900

The process of getting together with a top-class girl was far more complicated than choosing a bird from the cage; it was a process as meticulously hallowed by tradition as the tea ceremony. As a first step the customer went to a tea-house of the class known as 'leading-by-the-hand houses', just outside the main gate of the Yoshiwara. Conducted indoors, he would be asked which brothel he wished to patronise and whether there was any particular girl he was anxious to meet. If this was a *shokwai* (first meeting) the proprietress would suggest a candidate from her *shashin-mitate-cho* (photographic album for facilitation of selection of lady), enlarging on the girl's particular charms and talents and indicating her fee. He would also specify what ancillary delights he wanted. If he was doing the thing in style, he would request a *geisha*—an entertainer, not a professional prostitute, though some certainly did a little of the other on the side.

Servants were sent to warn the courtesan and the geisha of the client's imminent arrival. He would then be led to the brothel, together with the geisha and a servant bearing her instrument, his own night apparel and a bottle of *sake*. At the brothel the servant would act as go-between with the *obasan* (Auntie) in all the necessary preliminaries, such as entering the transaction in the police register; this document enabled the authorities to check on every visitor and, justly distrusting names and address which can be faked, required details of the client's nose, ears and mouth.

In a top-grade house there were separate rooms for each stage of the subsequent proceedings. The customer met the lady of his choice in the 'introduction apartment'. Formal bows, a certain reserve, were in order at this stage; *sake* was produced, cups exchanged; the girl uttered the conventional phrases of the nuptial ceremony and for the next few hours they were man and wife.

Next came 'honourable change of garments'. The girl left the room. More *sake*. The geisha tuned her *samisen*. The girl returned for the formal meal—usually only a token affair, with microscopic helpings, though some houses were celebrated for their food and a full banquet might be ordered by a client who liked to gratify as many senses as possible. Meanwhile the geisha began her performance, accompanying the eating and drinking. She might be praised for her skill, but so also must the courtesan, for every girl would have some personal accomplishment—flower arrangement, the art of burning incense, the tea ceremony—which was her own speciality.

Finally, having drunk sufficient *sake* and enjoyed enough of the geisha's performance, the client would signify his readiness for the 'honourable retirement'. Another change of clothes while he was conducted to the sleeping apartment. Here it was etiquette to simulate sleep, from which the girl would pretend to awaken him; as for the rest—well, she had been trained from childhood to ensure his pleasure and satisfaction.

Perhaps it was all a bit of a sham, but the world of prostitution is one of illusion in any case—a substitute for a more ideal relationship. From the elaborate fancy dress of the fetish specialist to the phony grunting of the streetwalker, when paid enough to throw in a fake orgasm as an additional fillip to the proceedings, pretence is an integral part of the job. What, then, could be more appropriate than the way the prostitute was integrated into Japanese social life by way of ceremonial? At intervals throughout the year, the Yoshiwara would be enlivened by festivals and processions; some, like the formal greeting of the cherry blossom in spring, were shared with the rest of the community, while others were unique to the prostitute's profession. The *Tayu-no-michiyuki* festival was an annual procession where the girls would parade in their finest clothes; another speciality was the *hachi-mon-ji-ni-anka*, or 'figure-of-eight walking', in which an elaborately costumed courtesan performed a highly sophisticated walk, repeatedly imprinting in the dust with her clogs the figure '8'. In Japan this is, it seems, a phallic symbol; no doubt the man in the street got the message.

# 10
# *FACING UP TO THE MASTER PROBLEM*

Social evil, master problem—call it what you will, by 1900 the time was past when the question of prostitution could be swept under the mat. In every civilised community in the world it stood high on the list of things that somebody should do something about. But what should be done, and who should do it?

Broadly speaking, there were three alternative policies that were both practicable—that is, enforceable—and morally acceptable to at any rate the more enlightened sections of society:

1 To make brothels illegal and prostitution a criminal offence as in the United States.

2 To make brothels illegal but to allow prostitution within defined limits, as in Britain.

3 To allow both prostitution and brothels, within defined limits usually involving compulsory registration, as in France and Germany.

In making their choice between these options, governments were swayed less and less by moral and religious doctrine, more and more by social and sanitary arguments. But everywhere the reformers were hampered by moral pressure groups; some believed, for instance, that the syphilis virus was one of 'God's little allies' sent as a deterrent to indiscriminate and unsanctified sexual congress. A substantial proportion of people held that prostitution was an unmitigated evil and that any attempt to regulate it implied recognition and therefore some measure of acceptance. For those who took this view, the only policy they could countenance was one of total suppression.

Nowhere was this no-compromise school of thought more effective than in the United States, where vice had flourished virtually uncontrolled in every city, with the consequence that by the turn of the century influential people in most communities were ready to concede that some form of regulation was necessary. In 1900 the 'Committee of Fifteen' was appointed to investigate prostitution in New York and make recommendations as to how it should be regulated. Two years later its findings were published in *The Social Evil*, which remains one of the most enlightened documents ever issued on the subject. Despite attempts by police and other interested parties to hamper the efforts of the investigators, they had no difficulty in establishing the nature and extent of the problem and indicating the anti-social consequences, ranging from the corruption of young children to that of the highest-ranking police officers.

The committee concluded that the system of toleration and regulation, as practised in France, would not be appropriate for New York, but it did put forward a number of sound proposals, such as the setting up of a 'morals police' and free treatment of venereal disease. These would have been helpful first steps towards an effective programme, but public acceptance of even such mild recommendations was not forthcoming. Only the committee's negative proposals were implemented, thus opening the way to more sophisticated forms of corruption.

The effect of the new provisions was to be seen at its worst in the infamous night courts, where prostitutes were charged as a result of the investigations of the vice squads—the one provision of the committee's recommendations which had been enthusiastically welcomed by the police. Policemen, posing as customers, trapped prostitutes into open solicitation and accompanied them to their apartments or rented rooms. Once an offer was formally made, and the couple had undressed, an offence had been legally committed; the member of the vice squad thereupon revealed his identity and charged the girl. She might protest if she chose, but it was improbable that the magistrate would accept her word rather than that of the police. These night courts became a regular public spectacle, respectable husbands taking their wives to see how the other half conducted itself. A few people protested against a system which required policemen to act as *agents provocateurs*; it was suggested that no decent man would take on such a task or that, if he did, he would not remain decent for long if he spent his working hours taking off his trousers in prostitutes' bedrooms. But despite these objections—and the recurrence of cases where informers threatened blackmail or extorted protection money—the degrading practice continued.

And so, throughout the United States, did prostitution, in all its forms.

There were brothels for every American, of whatever race, colour or creed: negro brothels for negroes and negro brothels for whites; white brothels for whites and white brothels for negroes; Japanese brothels for whites, white brothels for Chinese—in short, whatever was wanted, at an average fee of one dollar for each loveless orgasm.

Those who could afford it, might patronise the Everleigh Club on South Dearborn Street, Chicago, which had some claim to be ranked first among the great cat-houses of America; there was an art gallery, a library, a Turkish Ballroom with a real fountain, and a Gold Room with cuspidors of real gold. Fresh roses exuded their perfume in the Rose Parlor; on gala nights butterflies were released in the salons. Actors like John Barrymore, sporting heroes like Jim Corbett, visiting celebrities like Prince Heinrich of Prussia, all contributed to the considerable fortunes made by the Everleigh sisters.

For one-fiftieth of what he paid at the Everleigh Club, a client could visit a 'dollar house', where business was so brisk that every girl had a card which was punched by the management each time she entertained a customer, the totals being totted up at the end of the day. This is the record of four days in one such house in Chicago:

| | Sunday | Monday | Tuesday | Wednesday |
|---|---|---|---|---|
| Alice | 20 | 16 | 11 | 15 |
| Vere | 16 | 17 | 14 | 16 |
| Kitty | 24 | 14 | 12 | 9 |
| Mina | 36 | 22 | 12 | 10 |
| Edith | 11 | 15 | 15 | 4 |
| Florince (sic) | 20 | 23 | 21 | 21 |

If a dollar was more than a man could afford, he could, if he had the stomach for it, find relief for half that sum:

> The rooms are dirty, the creaking floor is covered with matting which harbours filth and vermin . . . the atmosphere is laden with vile odours, the small windows are seldom open . . . the small bedrooms are damp and unventilated and reek of stale tobacco, medicated drugs, and inferior disinfectants. Into such places common men crowd. The wooden bench ranged against the wall of the receiving room was full of customers, while others stood about the room, all being unashamed and unabashed. At the foot of the stairs which led to the bedrooms above, a man was stationed. Every time a visitor came groping his way down the stairs, the businesslike and aggressive announcer would cry out, 'Next!' At the word the man on

the bench whose turn it was, rose and passed up, and so the endless Saturday night sacrifice of honour and virtue went on.

(James Marchant, *The Master Problem*, 1917)

According to Marchant there were in Manhattan twenty houses charging 50c a trick; eighty charging $1; forty charging $5 or $10; and a handful where the rate might be as high as $100. Every one of them was illegal; every one of them was known to—and paying money to—corrupt police, corrupt health officials, corrupt politicians; and every one of them was frequented by men of this class or that, this income bracket or that, who were democratically responsible for the laws which forbade the brothels to exist.

Few in Europe favoured the American approach. To stigmatise the prostitute as a criminal seemed both unjust and inhuman, and the right of a woman to prostitute herself was generally, albeit regretfully, conceded. It was another matter when it came to ponces, pimps and procurers. Most European legal systems had sanctions against those who exploited the prostitute or lived parasitically off her earnings, even though she submitted voluntarily to such an arrangement.

This led to a dilemma when it came to deciding whether to legalise a brothel which provided a living for both prostitute and procurer. Was it any worse to be the madam of a brothel than the landlady of a hotel where prostitutes lived? The advantages of the brothel, from officialdom's point of view, were evident. It was easily supervised and could be inspected, taxed, closed down at will; it was possible to ensure that those employed there enjoyed reasonable working conditions and were not operating under compulsion or fear, and also that health safeguards were observed. At the same time, the brothel system was open to abuse, especially if the police were corrupt. In many countries, legislation did not seem to work; Norway suppressed brothels in 1890; Denmark in 1901; Finland in 1907; Spain in 1910; Bulgaria and Holland in 1911—and so on, until on the eve of World War I only one European country in three tolerated the brothel.

In Britain, where brothels had been officially illegal since the sixteenth century, the prohibition was never strictly enforced but was used by the police as a means of controlling vice. Following the scandals of the Victorian age and with the reform movement gradually gaining strength, brothels had to maintain a low profile; those houses that continued to

Prostitute and potential customer. Phil May, 1891

do business needed an ever larger return on their investment. More and more they tended to be specialist establishments for homosexuals, flagellants and so forth; the straight heterosexual brothel was becoming a rarity, except in the form of an apartment leased by a handful of girls working discreetly and avoiding publicity.

At the same time, prostitutes working outside brothels found that if they conducted themselves unobtrusively they could work with a minimum of harassment; this again led them to avoid the brothels unless the rewards were exceptionally high. So street prostitution flourished, though so discreetly that a spokesman for the National Vigilance Association was able to say in 1917: 'Today London is an open-air cathedral compared with what it was forty years ago.' Anomalous and imperfect as it was, Britain's solution came close to balancing control with justice and humanity; and other countries were moving in the same direction.

Brothels were tolerated in Russia and in several parts of Germany—where a system of local option prevailed—but it was chiefly to France that the rest of the world looked to discover whether the policy of legalising brothels constituted an effective solution. The answer was unequivocal: whatever might be the advantages in principle, as practised in France it led to appalling abuse, exploitation and injustice. The Police des Moeurs were thoroughly corrupt and totally unsympathetic to the spirit of the law. The system afforded them infinite opportunities for blackmail and bribery, as well as individual indulgence in cruelty, extortion and inhumanity of the most sadistic nature. Women who were patently virtuous were forced to submit to a humiliating medical examination—a nauseating procedure which those in the know were, by means of a timely bribe, able to avoid.

A mounting series of scandals led to the setting up of a Commission du Régime des Moeurs in 1903. Vast numbers of witnesses, from both Paris and the provinces, testified to the way the system was being abused. So devastating were the revelations that the prefect of police had no choice but to plead guilty on behalf of his force. The next step was to draw up proposals to prevent the recurrence of such abuses, but no appreciable progress had been made by the outbreak of World War I.

In the meantime, at the upper end of the social ladder, life continued in much the same spirit as during *la belle époque*. The pavements of the rue St Denis were thronged with the same kind of merchandise that had been offered there in the Middle Ages, while more expensive versions of

French streetwalker in the rue Asselin, early twentieth century. Photo Atget

the product could be found in the neighbourhood of the Champs Elysées or the Bois de Boulogne. At the House of All Nations in the rue de Chabanais, Mademoiselle Kelly performed interesting aquatic feats in a bathtub of gleaming copper for the edification of members of the Jockey Club gathered around. Amélie Hélie, whose flamboyant hair earned her the sobriquet of 'Casque d'Or', became a legend to match her most eminent predecessors. The girls of the rue d'Amboise, of No 6 rue des Moulins, and of the Perroquet at 2 rue Steinkerque were being recorded for posterity by the hand of Toulouse-Lautrec. Paris was still a long, long way from being an 'open-air cathedral' when her men went off to war.

> The army brothel was round the corner in the main street of Béthune. I had seen a queue of a hundred and fifty men waiting outside the door, each to have his short turn with one or other of the three women in the house. My servant, who had been in the queue, told me that the charge was ten francs a man—about eight shillings at that time. Each woman served nearly a battalion of men every week for as long as she lasted. The assistant provost-marshal had told me that three weeks was the usual limit, 'after which the woman retires on her earnings, pale but proud'.
>
> (Robert Graves, *Goodbye to All That*, 1929)

It was the same in Rouen, in Calais, in every French town behind the lines to which the troops withdrew for a brief respite. A blue lamp showed officers where to go, while their inferiors followed the red; sometimes the NCOs enjoyed slightly less squalid facilities than the other ranks. Few mothers, wives or sisters back at home ever realised that provision had been made for their fighting men to assuage their sexual lusts with the assistance of some officially licensed mademoiselle from Armentières. Indeed there were many who believed that war would drive from men's minds all considerations of anything so trivial as sex.

Hirschfeld's classic *Sexual History of the World War* cites two German professors, Kuhn and Möller, who declared that the Fatherland had a right to expect sexual continence from its fighting men. A writer named Müller described the feelings of a young Austrian soldier on the Eastern Front, face to face with the Russians:

> If Liane were now to bend over me, Liane the beautiful, for whom I once yearned with all the fibres of my being—if she were now to let her golden hair fall over me, I would brush it from my eyes in order not to miss the first light of dawn which will be the signal for our drive on Ostrowa Palcze.

The reality was epitomised by Ernst Jirgal:

> Only the brutish side of love, no, less than that remained. The female merely acted as a fast and automatic deflector of lust.

Whatever dreams the man in the trenches might cherish, the authorities —even in England, which Hirschfeld aptly terms 'the classical land of sexual hypocrisy'—were more realistic. Facilities for sex had to be organised; if a brothel survived the shelling, it was inspected and authorised for military use; if the populace fled before the enemy advance, then girls must be recruited and premises improvised. One way or

Entente cordiale at Paris during World War I. From Hirschfeld, *Sexual History of the World War*, c 1930

another, the army must be given access to women just as it must be supplied with food and drink. Behind every battle-front, in every town to which the men retired for recuperation, it was somebody's job to ensure that women were available for them.

But those queues of trench-weary soldiers, representing sex in its most vivid wartime setting, must nevertheless be seen in a wider context. Hirschfeld's underlying thesis, with which few psychologists or sociologists are likely to disagree, is that war is itself erotic. The perennial attraction of a uniform, even a khaki one, and the unequivocal phallic symbolism of the gun, are the surface expression of a complex interplay between sex and death which is as deeply rooted in the subconscious as any other of our motivating impulses. The warrior half in love with death, the woman in love with the warrior because he is in love with death, contributed to what Hirschfeld calls 'a sort of war nymphomania' which sanctioned a release from the rules of peacetime life. A man could legitimately dream of an infinite number of sexual partners, picture himself marching through a world in which conquered womenfolk would yield submissively to his victorious virility, where liberated women would

## PREIS-VERZEICHNIS.

**A. Getränke:**

| | | |
|---|---|---|
| Sekt Henkell Trocken . . . à Flasche | 18,— | Mark |
| Bordeaux Château Lafitte . „ „ | 6,— | „ |
| Ungarwein . . . . . . . . . „ „ | 8,— | „ |
| Bier, eine große Flasche . . . . . . . . | 1,50 | „ |
| Kaffee, Tasse . . . . . . . . . . . . . . . . | 1,— | „ |
| „ ein kleiner Krug, 6 Tassen . . | 6,— | „ |
| „ ein großer Krug, 12 Tassen . | 12,— | „ |
| Tee, ein Glas . . . . . . . . . . . . . . . . | 0,60 | „ |
| Selter, kleine Flasche . . . . . . . . . . | 0,30 | „ |

**B. Beischlaf:**

| | | |
|---|---|---|
| für die ganze Nacht . . . . . . . . . . | 30,— | Mark |
| für 2 bis 3 Std. zur Abend- u. Nachtzeit | 20,— | „ |
| für 1 Stunde . . . . . . . . . . . . . . | 10,— | „ |
| für jede beliebige Zeit von 9 Uhr vorm. bis 6 Uhr nachm. . . . . . . . . . | 10,— | „ |

Lodz, im März 1917.

**Die Sittenpolizei.**

Tariff in a German military brothel, Lodz, 1917

embrace him in gratitude, where his own womenfolk would welcome him home with unstinting admiration. A woman created a fantasy-world in which clerks and factory workers were transformed into uniformed heroes who, because by tomorrow they might have given their life's blood for her protection, deserved today all the encouragement and solace it was in her power to give.

The immediate result was, primarily, a vast increase in non-commercial sex; the abrupt rise in the number of marriages represents only the respectable peak of increased sexual activity. But, because not every man had access to a willing partner, the secondary outcome was a corresponding increase in commercial sex. In Paris the number of arrests for clandestine prostitution rose by some 40 per cent; but, allowing for greater leniency on the part of the authorities, the actual increase may have been very much higher.

Soldiers on leave in Paris make friends, *c* 1916. From Hirschfeld, *Sexual History of the World War*

In enemy-occupied countries, the additional factors of poverty and starvation drove women to join the ranks of prostitution. In the streets of Ghent and Brussels, girls dressed in rags, aged only twelve but heavily made-up to add a few years to their appearance, accosted German soldiers with the plea 'Monsieur, pour un livre de pain!' ('for a loaf of bread'), while mothers hired out their daughters for half a kilo of sugar.

One inevitable consequence of so much sexual activity was that a high proportion of those on whom the nurses lavished their ministrations were in hospital for ailments contracted not in the trenches but in bed. Venereal disease had always been one of the most redoubtable foes the generals had to face. Before 1914, the armies in Europe were nearly all infected to some degree; Blaschko gives these figures:

| | per cent |
|---|---|
| Germany | 2.5 |
| France | 4.2 |
| Austria | 6 |
| Italy | 8.5 |
| England | 17 |

The remarkable discrepancy between England and the others is simply explained: in the British Army the men received no instruction whatever in the avoidance or treatment of venereal disease.

A survey taken of British soldiers on leave in Paris showed that in 1916 nearly 30 per cent were infected; put another way, in those familiar photographs of World War I soldiers, at least one in four of those smiling for the camera is infected with VD. At a time when every available man was needed at the front, the military authorities decided to ignore public opinion at home—where VD was still widely considered to be 'God's own deterrent'. Prophylactics in the form of calomel tubes were issued to men going on leave during the winter of 1917, and the infection rate dropped to 3 per cent.

It was further revealed that, of that 3 per cent, at least one man in three wished positively to contract VD in order to be invalided out of the combat. This unsavoury aspect of the business was also to be found back in England, where infected girls would charge soldiers a higher rate because of the chances of their catching the disease and thus avoiding front-line service; American doughboys in transit were accused of this squalid transaction. English tommies were caught selling venereal discharge in order to pass on the disease, while others deliberately infected their own eyes, not realising that this was likely to lead to blindness. These unpalatable facts, which were to be well attested—notably by Dr Ettie A. Rout in the *British Medical Journal* (November 1922)—would have been very hard for the people at home to stomach.

It might have seemed, however, from the dramatic drop in the incidence of venereal disease among the men on leave in Paris, that an unanswerable argument had been made in favour of similar prophylactic measures being officially encouraged in Britain. Despite government appeals from Canada, Australia and New Zealand, whose troops in England were being infected in considerable numbers, diseased women were not isolated or controlled in any way. The moralists, disregarding what had been achieved by preventive action on the part of the military authorities, were determined that, whatever might be enforced behind the battle lines, nothing of the sort should be put into effect back in Britain.

# 11
# GOOD TIMES AND BAD

Morally, intellectually, politically, culturally, people's attitudes were changed by World War I. In facing moral issues, postwar society became at the same time more permissive and more serious. The characteristic image of the period—the beaded flapper dancing the Charleston on a piano-top—was the measure of prevailing trends; such behaviour would not have raised any eyebrows in Cora Pearl's Paris or Kate Townsend's New Orleans. But though society might have less regard for the moral conventions of an earlier generation, it was also less casual about its own mores and less hypocritical about what it expected of others. If there was more sexual activity of a kind which would formerly have been termed immoral, it was on a higher interpersonal level and involved more mutual respect.

Indirectly such attitudes affected prostitution by altering the make-up of the clientele. Men who would once have resorted to prostitutes, because they made sex available when others did not, now found it easier to get it elsewhere. A greater proportion of clients now were likely to be those with psychological or emotional hang-ups; or with special requirements which could not readily be satisfied in 'normal' life; or with so little time available that they could not afford to invest it in the courtship of a non-professional who might or might not be willing to provide what they were looking for.

In most countries prostitutes were now more discreet and better behaved. Tougher control had made them more professional. They had a longer working life, were less liable to end up drunk or diseased; and their attitude towards their work was more perceptive. In a survey conducted in London in 1921 a number of prostitutes were asked why they had taken up the trade:

| | per cent |
|---|---|
| economic reasons | 26 |
| because it 'suited them' | 25 |
| seduced and abandoned | 13 |
| drink | 9 |
| husbands made them | 8 |
| they liked the 'easy life' | 6 |
| they had been raped | 1.5 |

Today these superficial statements would be looked at more closely: were those who opted for the 'easy life' so very different from the ones who found that the life 'suited them'? And those who cited 'economic reasons' might well have been driven as much by necessity as by a desire for a larger share of the good things of life.

A close examination would also be made of the report on 'rescue work' issued in 1919 by the Committee for Social Investigation and Reform, which investigated prostitute activity around Piccadilly in London:

> Almost without exception they are able and willing to give a man a 'good time' and to say that they are happy and feel gay. But it is not generally recognised that all this is a necessary part of saleswomanship in this market,

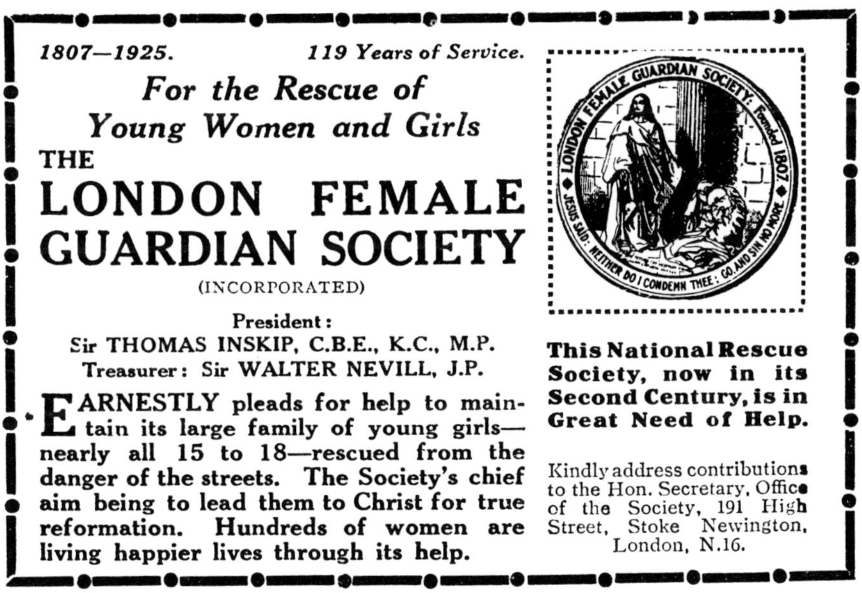


'Rescue work': advertisement for the London Female Guardian Society

*At Sunset*. George Grosz, 1922

> and that not far below the surface is to be found in these girls a very different feeling . . . These girls never lose some consciousness of the fact that they are social outcasts and failures, nor do they lose memories of better days, of higher aspirations.

Did such regrets exist only in the minds of those who compiled the report or, if genuinely voiced, were the girls simply saying what they knew the investigators wanted to hear?

The earnings of a London prostitute in the early 1920s could well be £15-£20 a week, at a time when £2-£3 was the wage for 'honest' work. Certainly little sense of failure comes through from one of the first convincing autobiographies by a prostitute—Sheila Cousins' *To Beg I am Ashamed* (1953)—which indicates a very realistic approach:

> I am not begging for sympathy. I chose with my eyes open to do what I am doing today. And I know that I have never enjoyed such self-respect as I do now. I have escaped from emotional sponging. I cannot be put upon. If you want my body, you must pay for it. However odd the adjective may sound, there is, to me, something clean about that. What I am doing is a job like any other, a way of keeping alive.
>
> I regret that I came on the streets in the age when I did. Thirty years ago, the streetwalker's client was the normal man who had yet to persuade his friend's sister that his intentions were honourable. Today, with honourable intentions at a discount everywhere, my pick-ups are the rejects, the neurotics, the cast-outs who, for all the general promiscuity, have been unable to find a real woman for themselves. There are times when I feel that the prostitute today needs to be half a psycho-analyst.

Her attitude to her work was thoroughly professional:

> Within a week it was as if I had never been doing anything else but prostitution. I would go down to Piccadilly at 8 in the evening, as I had gone down to the office at 9 in the morning. Except when I stayed with a man for the night, I never returned home after 12. I rarely had to walk more than 10 minutes before making a pick-up, and then I didn't always accept the first-comer. I was attractive enough to be able to choose my own man. My earnings averaged from £20 to £30 a week without my having to make the least effort, for it was only occasionally that I would go out twice in a night.
>
> The men I dropped within a few days into accepting and enduring almost unconsciously. The flashed-on smile brought one to a halt: half your attention was fixed on his face while the other half roamed over his dress for evidence of his likely wealth. A worn raincoat and a stammering approach

> might mean that he was not worth your while to go with, but they might also mean that he spent all his money on Saturday night hunts for street women. With half your ear you listened to the familiar phrases: 'You're awfully young to be doing this.' All the while at the back of your head your real thoughts flashed by, 'Clicked pretty quickly tonight. Might have been a good deal worse . . .'
>
> I wasn't a good prostitute. I hadn't sufficient detachment from what I was doing to be able to pretend feeling for my clients. Never have I been so hard and bitter, never have I hated men so much as in those first few weeks on the streets. I gave what I was paid for—but I shrank back in loathing from giving a thing more. I evaded the hurried fumblings in the dark cab: I had flaming quarrels with men who, not content with possessing me, wanted to make love to me as if I were a mistress and not a tart.

Her realistic approach to her work was shared, she found, by her companions, though they might not share her objectivity:

> For most of them their profession had been a rise in the world. If they had gone straight they must have contented themselves with a 70-shillings-a-week husband and a semi-detached house in the suburbs. They would have had to pinch for their cheap finery, and within a few years a brood of squalling children would have surrounded them. On the streets they make five times what a husband would have brought them.

For those who were able to organise their lives efficiently, prostitution was still a lucrative trade. A Scotland Yard officer wrote in 1931:

> On the evening of 24th November last, I passed a house in Maida Vale which I suspected of being a high-class brothel. I went in to make inquiries, and was received by Madam, a handsome woman of 55 or thereabouts, wearing a diamond ring worth at least £300. 'You cannot touch me,' she smiled. 'I have four houses of this kind and I never use any one for more than four consecutive nights.' The law says that before a brothel can be raided it must be kept under observation for six nights, so she had cleverly put herself beyond the reach of Scotland Yard.
>
> This woman will send a girl at 10 minutes notice to a flat in the West End of London, or to any outlying suburb. She knew I was harmless and rather enjoyed my questioning. 'Business is increasing every month. I believe I have 60 girls on my books, but my secretary attends to all those details. I take a 20% commission on all business I find for my girls, and when a client leaves five £10 notes, as one did yesterday, I do not do badly. My average profits never fall below £30 a week: indeed, at specially favourable times I have made as much as £200 to £300.'
>
> (Cecil Bishop, *Women and Crime*)

Across the Channel, where brothels were legalised, prostitution was still operating in the time-honoured way. From all over the world customers came to Paris to visit houses like 'The Sphinx', built in 1930 near the Gare Montparnasse, where the business of sex was conducted in a manner so different from the working world of Sheila Cousins that the two seem to be participating in an altogether separate trade. Yet here, too, a new self-assurance was to be found among the girls; the under-manageress of The Sphinx, interviewed in 1939, declared:

> I have never felt that our girls are ashamed of a profession they have freely chosen. Quite the contrary: they have nothing but scorn for women who work yet earn only a tenth of what they do. Girls cloistered against their will? Kept by force by the brothel keepers? Don't make me laugh! We get

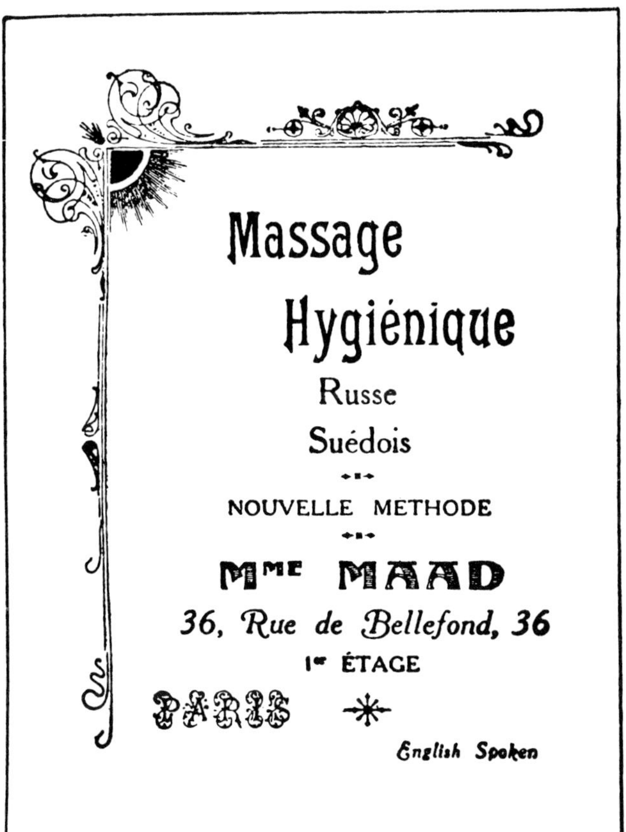


Trade card of a French brothel

at least ten letters a week from prospective candidates begging us to admit them.

The Sphinx employed some sixty girls, who between them catered for around 500 clients a day—about nine per girl, which Sheila Cousins and her colleagues would consider heavy going. During the Paris Motor Show—there is something about motor cars which inspires men to prove their virility—The Sphinx had to cater for ten times its usual number, and recruited additional staff.

The Sphinx was a straight business venture, run on strictly commercial lines; wealthy men invested money in it and drew their dividends in the usual way. Bizarre and kinky tastes were not catered for. Minors were not employed, though this is not to say that clients were never led to believe otherwise. Girls were expected to conduct themselves as befitted a high-class establishment; if they misbehaved they were sent to another house under the same management in a working-class district. 'The black sheep are sent there for a week, and after her three-hundredth go I can assure you that the girl is tamed'—the words of the under-manageress hardly consistent with her earlier comments about the 'freely chosen' trade. But, for girls who behaved, conditions were good. There were two official medical inspections a week, and a resident specialist to deal with such emergencies as clients who died on the job. After five or ten years, if a girl was *sérieux*, she could have saved enough to purchase a bar or a shop, or even go into business herself as a madame.

The Sphinx was something of a rarity even in France, herself the odd-girl-out among European countries in the 1930s. In 1929 the League of Nations had condemned those which still officially tolerated brothels; they had been closed down in Vienna in 1921, in Berlin and Budapest in 1927. Much interest was being directed towards Russia: did the Bolsheviks possess the magic formula that would solve every social problem, prostitution included? At first it seemed as though they might.

In 1919 a Committee for the Suppression of Prostitution was inaugurated at the Public Health Office in Moscow. Its operations were conducted not against the girls—seen as unwilling victims of the czarist regime—but against the capitalist-created institution itself; since the causes could be diagnosed as purely economic, the remedy lay in economic solutions. So the girls were sent away to labour colonies to be trained as nurses or re-educated in other trades—and that should have been the

Street girl and customer in Berlin. Anonymous photo, 1922

end of prostitution in Russia. But by 1922 it had begun to re-emerge, as was admitted by the official newspaper *Izvestiya*. Blame was attributed to those of the former upper and middle classes—perhaps correctly, for, deprived of their sources of income, they must have been hard put to it to find any means of surviving. Those who were caught were sent to official 'prophylactoria' where they were re-trained for better things. Workrooms were attached to hospitals where infected girls were treated; they were rehabilitated 'in a proletarian spirit' and sent to work in state factories.

Nor was there any place for the prostitute in the ideological world being created by the National Socialists in Germany. She was a threat to the purity of the family, she distracted men from more important tasks, and she distorted the ideal of patriotic motherhood. She must go.

But, as does tend to happen, one such principle came into conflict with another. The Nazi leaders were also convinced that homosexuality was a threat to the nation. The day after prostitution was banned, on 22 February 1933, homosexual bars were closed—the first step in a campaign against homosexuals which culminated in enforced sterilisation. Before that, however, efforts were made to re-educate the homosexual in the hope that he could be made useful to the fatherland; a dedicated prison commandant would seek to 'cure' his homosexual prisoners by using aversion therapy, after which prostitutes were employed to arouse the subject to a healthier frame of mind.

When war came, sexual exploitation by the Nazis was seen at its worst in the uses made of the brothels—and of the women of occupied Europe who were forced into prostitution. Rictor Norton writes:

> In decrees issued on 9 September 1939, and on 16 March 1940, medically-supervised brothels were officially set up on the front for the use of Himmler's unmarried SS men. In 1943, 600 women from Paris, Poland, Bohemia and Moravia were recruited to supply 60 brothels, each of which served 50 clients a day. Some were used for biological experimentation: in the Klosterstrasse brothel in Stuttgart, for example, the women wore special sheaths to collect the semen, which was then gathered for tests to devise a plasma substitute. The brothels were supplemented by the Nazi stud-farms, called 'Founts of Life', huge child-producing factories for the élite, of which there were 13 in 1944.

More dedicated to liberty than any other nation on earth, the Americans have shown themselves capable of greater demonstrations of self-imposed restrictions than any other people. If the Jazz Age hit the United States more violently than most other countries, it was largely because they chose this moment to perform an experiment in social self-discipline which even Communists or Nazis might hesitate to initiate—the nationwide prohibition of alcoholic beverages.

In principle there need be no link between drink and prostitution; in practice they are intimately associated. Men in the mood for drinking are likely to be in the mood for other forms of indulgence; if they are not, then drinking may well make them so. Taverns and bars have been the prostitute's most rewarding hunting ground throughout history, and in brothels in all cultures it is customary for the customer to order drinks for the girls.

America's National Prohibition Act, forbidding the sale of beverages containing more than 1 per cent alcohol, was passed over President Wilson's veto on 28 October 1919. Clandestine drinking establishments quickly became part of the American scene; with alcohol as well as prostitution forbidden by law, these places—even when not actually doubling as brothels—became the natural habitat of the prostitute. In 1926 the night clubs and speakeasies of New York City were investigated by the Committee of Fourteen who found that 132 out of 157 establishments had connections with prostitution. Sometimes the girls were on the bar's payroll, employed nominally as hostesses; others were freelancing for what they could get, encouraged by the management both as an attraction to entice drinkers into the place and as aids to increased consumption of bootleg liquor.

Inevitably, organised crime, which had a virtual monopoly of the illegal drinks business, found itself involved in prostitution also. If a speakeasy paid a gang protection money, that protection covered its prostitutes along with the rest of the merchandise. By the mid-1920s prostitution in most large American cities was controlled by organised crime, which supplied the brothels with girls and arranged for them to be shifted from one house to another, particularly over state lines, just as it organised the shipment of alcohol. The biggest syndicate of brothels in the United States was operated by a Chicago gang reputedly headed by Al Capone. A chain of houses, purporting to be hotels, stretched from Chicago westwards to Seattle; girls were passed along from house to house, spending two weeks or so in each. The continually changing faces not only made for safety but stimulated trade. The girls turned over a proportion of their earnings to the syndicate; any who refused were punished just as were refractory bar-owners.

Capone's name was specifically linked with the Speedway Inn in Burnham, a suburb of Chicago; until its closure in 1934, it must have qualified as about the most businesslike—and least appealing—brothel ever devised. After passing a bar and a cigar franchise, the customer came to a turnstile where, having paid from $2 to $5, he was handed a towel and soap. Upstairs, he was assigned to one of the fifty prostitutes who each had a small room. Having had his pleasure, he left by a second staircase so as not to hold up the traffic. Each girl's output was periodically evaluated, and those who didn't achieve a satisfactory turnover were replaced. It was, perhaps, an inevitable development in the nation which invented the assembly line.

Some idea of how prostitution outside the larger cities was conducted can be gleaned from *Middletown*, a classic study of a 'fictitious' medium-sized American town which was subjected to a comprehensive analysis by the Lynds' team of sociologists. They found that 'Middletown' had a flourishing red-light district which, taking relative size into account, was comparable to that of New York. Before 1915 there had been twenty-five brothels with between four and eight girls in each. Although, following wartime reform, they had all supposedly disappeared, in fact there was still a well-defined district—with brothels containing as many as fifty girls—known to the majority of citizens and tolerated more or less openly by the police and councillors; just before election time, however, there was apt to be a vote-catching clean-up.

It was much the same picture across the States, though with some regional variations. In the South, negroes had their own brothels, and there were houses with negro girls catering for white customers; but only north of the Mason-Dixon Line were white girls provided for black clients. In Natchez it was illegal for white prostitutes to accept negro customers, notwithstanding the fact that by law there were not supposed to be any prostitutes anyway! Special circumstances called for special solutions; in Butte, Montana, a police officer admitted:

> We have to tolerate a red light district here, otherwise we should never be able to prevent assaults on women and children. Butte is full to overflowing of vigorous young miners, who are unmarried and can't do without females. Quite recently certain religious bodies persuaded us to close the district. But it didn't work. Too many offences against morality occurred, and we had too few police to deal with them all. So we were obliged to ignore the prohibition and re-open the area. But juveniles are not allowed to enter it, no alcohol is sold there and the girls undergo regular medical examination. These conditions have proved satisfactory.

In most American communities brothels operated with the knowledge and connivance of the police. Polly Adler, most celebrated of all New York madams, declared: 'My apartment became a hangout for the police themselves. On many an evening I should have had a green light out in front as well as the red one which tradition says should be there.' She quoted figures given her by Madam Rose, owner of a small local brothel, who paid one-third of her earnings in protection to the police, plus an average of $1,000 a month in bails and fines. Even setting aside the moral issues involved, these figures represent a bitter indictment of the folly of making prostitution a criminal offence. For who was making most out of what Madam Rose's girls earned? Not the girls themselves; not the madam; but the police who had been entrusted by the community with the prevention of the activity in the first place.

In the 1930s, in belated response to such blatant abuse of the law, the New York authorities investigated the links between vice and organised crime in the city, and exposed a system of corruption which ramified through every branch of the administrative and legal system. Bribery, fixing, protection rackets, extortion, framing of the innocent, *agents provocateurs*, police on the take, lawyers on the take, judges on the take, health officials on the take—you name it, somebody was doing it. Sometimes the methods were extraordinarily crude. One of the methods uncovered by Roosevelt's commissioners was the 'Doctor Racket', whereby a stool-pigeon employed by the police waits till he sees a doctor leaving his surgery; then, posing as a patient, he enters and asks for treatment. He is shown into the doctor's office and asked to wait. As soon as the nurse is out of the room, he places a sum of money in a conspicuous spot and starts to undress; he then calls for the nurse. A moment later the waiting police officers burst in and arrest her on a prostitution charge.

That so crude a trap would be taken seriously by the courts seems unbelievable, yet this and others equally clumsy were employed—sometimes for simple blackmail, sometimes to make up a satisfactory quota of arrests for moral offences so that the public could see how zealously their paid representatives were upholding the law. Such are the consequences when a community insists on making illegal an activity which it is powerless to eradicate.

The situation in the southern half of the American continent could hardly have been in greater contrast. For it was Latin America, more than any other part of the world, which became the focus of the most sensational bogey in the story of prostitution—the White Slave Trade.

From the earliest times, one of the richest sources of prostitutes had been slavery—a spin-off from wars of conquest when women were taken into captivity by their victors. When a girl was already a slave it was not difficult to persuade her to prostitute herself in return for better living conditions. As wars of conquest gradually died out, slave trading continued as a commercial venture. It was all but eradicated in the course of the nineteenth century; but another trade, which had hitherto been only a tiny trickle, gradually grew to be a business enterprise in its own right—the international traffic in prostitutes.

Its basis was quite simple: to get hold of a girl by fair means or foul, and

Cover of *Horrors of the White Slave Trade*, c 1912

persuade or coerce her into a situation where her only choice was between prostitution and death. It was, in effect, compulsory prostitution; the girl did not prostitute herself, she was prostituted—in any meaningful sense of the word, she was a slave. During the nineteenth century, this trade flourished in Europe, notably between England and Belgium, France and Italy, although girls were being shipped to and fro in all directions, particularly from countries where conditions were wretched, such as Russia, or where the girls were considered particularly attractive, such as England.

By the close of the nineteenth century, traders were starting to look farther afield; this was in part the natural expansion to be expected in any commercial enterprise, in part the consequence of tightening legal controls within Europe. Reformers like Josephine Butler had compelled the authorities to take action and, however half-heartedly the new procedures were implemented, the sex traffickers were finding the European market too restrictive.

By contrast, the overseas trade in girls proved to be one of the most remunerative criminal enterprises of the twentieth century. In the Far East, in Latin America, in North Africa, the demand for European girls was insatiable. But the conducting of such an international operation called for substantial investment in a network of agents and a complex structure of recruiters, couriers, transit houses and sales staff, so that the girls could be passed from hand to trusted hand without arousing the suspicion of any authorities whose co-operation had not been purchased in advance. In 1902 an organisation, endearingly named Association Amicale des Patrons et Patronnes des Maisons Sociales but more generally known as *la Grande Force*, was formed to protect the interests of the traffickers—the first of many syndicates to move into the field. Some idea of the scale of their operations can be gained from the fact that Simon Rubinstein, who at one time supervised the Argentine end of *la Grande Force*, had an army of 700 agents to help him run what was just one terminal of an international spider's web along whose threads 'parcels'—as the girls were referred to—were despatched with all the efficiency of a well-run export business. At one point the police of Buenos Aires had 1,414 prostitutes listed on their files, of which only 272 were natives of the Argentine; the rest were mostly Europeans who had *la Grande Force* to thank for launching them on their careers.

There were many roads to Buenos Aires, but typically it went like this: a girl in London, perhaps working on the insecure fringes of show business, learns of a job as a dancer, with good money and prospects; she applies and is accepted, being told that first she must go to Paris for training. It seems a fine opportunity, so off she goes, quite voluntarily—and the organisation has achieved the first major step of getting her out of her own country, willingly and without fuss. After training in Paris—still as a dancer, all above board—she is offered a well-paid job in Marseilles, which she naturally accepts. Here, without her knowledge, she is 'viewed' by a Latin-American agent—perhaps through a hole in the bathroom wall in her hotel. He makes his offer: in the 1920s, a 'fresh' English girl would fetch between £1,000 and £2,000. She is then told that the dance troupe has been booked for a tour in the Argentine—all expenses paid, a good salary. The chance of earning so much, and seeing an exotic part of the world into the bargain, is irresistible; off she goes, though seldom on a British ship whose officers might ask inconvenient questions. Then, on arrival, oh dear, there's been some mistake, the club where they were to perform has closed, the manager has vanished, there is no money . . . They owe for lodgings, for food . . . At this point the courier in charge of the troupe tells the girl that a rich land-owner is interested in her; a meeting is arranged; she is invited on a visit to his country estate; the courier discreetly vanishes and the girl is left stranded in a strange house in a strange country. For a while she will be the Argentinian's mistress; then, when he is tired of her, she will be sold to a brothel in Buenos Aires. A less fortunate girl, confronted by the courier with a choice between prostitution and starvation, with a threat of prison for the money she owes for food and lodging, will reach the brothel by a more direct route. If she has her wits about her, she will go to the British consul—but of course the slavers will be on the watch to prevent this if possible.

Cecil Bishop, a Scotland Yard detective, described how he had been detailed to recover a young English girl who had been taken abroad by an Italian to be sold to the highest bidder—not that she knew that; she thought he was genuinely attached to her:

> When I picked up the trail I followed it to Calais, from Calais to Boulogne and from Boulogne to Paris, Marseille, Cherbourg, Le Havre, back to Paris, Brussels, Ostend, Antwerp, Paris, Berlin, Vienna, Budapest, and finally recovered the girl in Paris. On several occasions Florence had been sold temporarily to raise money to pay hotel expenses. But, finding that ducking from place to place did not throw me off his trail, the Slaver bolted in panic just before completing a remunerative sale with a South American agent.
>
> (*Women and Crime*)

Bishop made it clear that what had all the makings of sensational fantasy was a very down-to-earth reality:

> To the average person the White Slave Traffic is as unreal as was the Bogeyman of childhood. It is supposed that the influence of public opinion, combined with the efforts of the police, has destroyed the traffic in women so far as Great Britain is concerned. This is not the case. Improvements in the passport regulations have made the abduction of women more difficult, that is all. But the demand for girls increases steadily, and whereas before the war little effort was needed to procure scores of good-looking girls, today great pains and much money are used to procure twice the number.

Strictly speaking, a prostitute is a woman who voluntarily and knowingly sells herself, however much she would prefer not to. Sex slavery, white or black, is different; more often than not, the girl is coerced into prostitution, often by direct physical means. The sex slave trade represents the most extreme form of exploitation of women by their fellow creatures of both sexes.

# 12
# *BRAVE NEW WORLD*

At 10pm on Tuesday 4 August 1942, forty-eight agents of the Wisconsin State Beverage Tax Division, together with state health officials and United States federal agents, abandoned the pretence that they were a bowling group from out of town and moved in on Silver Street, Hurley, Wisconsin. In a matter of minutes they had arrested fifty-one men and women either for being or for harbouring prostitutes. A local newspaper, the *Capital Times* of Madison, reported:

> If a Hollywood movie director were to make a picture combining all the features of a Klondike boom town, the Barbary Coast of California's gold rush days, and the Hell's Kitchen of old New York, he would have something very closely resembling the mess which investigators found when they started here last Thursday night. Unless you have seen Hurley, it might be difficult to believe that such a place could exist in the 20th century, in 1942, in the state of Wisconsin—or in the United States.
>
> Houses of prostitution operated as openly as grocery stores along both sides of two blocks of the city's 'main drag'. In one of these blocks, on one side of the street, every door was a tavern and nearly every tavern had prostitutes soliciting business.

John W. Roach, chief of the state's Beverage Tax Division and mastermind of the operation, insisted that it was not part of 'a moral crusade' but was conducted solely in the interests of the war effort:

> Our sole interest is to wipe out prostitution, which spreads venereal disease among our war industry workers, slows production, takes men out of production work, and thereby hinders the war effort. In addition there is a great danger that such a place may be the seat of much fifth column activities. The dives in Hurley would provide an excellent place for espionage agents and other subversive elements to hide out, and to obtain information from war workers, soldiers, and others who may come to these places.

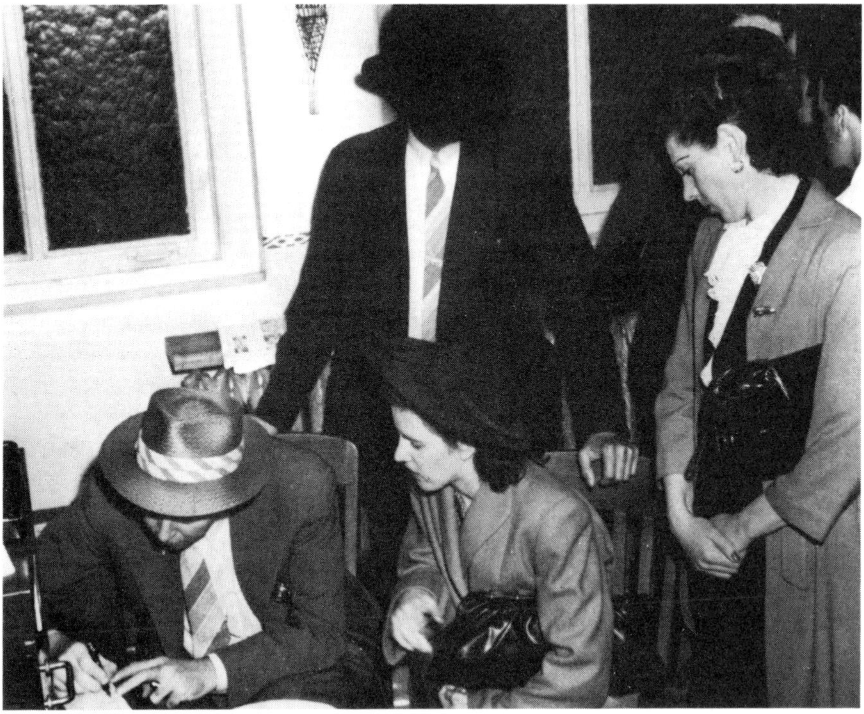

Prostitutes booked after raid at Hurley, Wisconsin, August 1942

It is true that Hurley was conveniently located to serve defence workers and others whose work was important to America's war effort. But how serious a menace were the activities of those fifty prostitutes to the productivity of the 10,000 miners and factory workers of the district?

In time of war, nations as well as individuals are apt to revert to archaic patterns of behaviour. A notable example is the way warring states seek to 'purify' themselves, after the manner of ancient warriors ritually preparing for battle. The rationale—insofar as reason is involved—is that God will grant us victory only if we deserve it: accordingly we must show ourselves worthy. The consequence is that a highly advanced society, which has armed itself with the full panoply of sophisticated hardware designed to kill the greatest number of human beings in the shortest possible time, throngs the churches, renews its allegiance to traditional symbols such as flags and kings and national anthems, and performs, as a bribe to the God of Battles, such moral ablutions as were carried out in Hurley that night in 1942.

France, in 1946, went through a different emotional process, but the mechanism was similar and the end result the same. The traumatic defeat of 1940, the shame of Vichy, the failure of the old régime, inspired a severance from the past. The true causes of the French débâcle were complex and deeply embedded in the social structure; but in these acts of ritual purification it is in any case the symbolic gesture which is all-important. So what could be more appropriate than to attack that perennial scapegoat of society, so conveniently accessible and vulnerable—the prostitute? On 24 April 1946 France abolished her brothels.

They were allowed six months to wind up their affairs; during that time 190 famous French houses sold their furniture and fittings. An era ended, and Juliette Greco sang:

> While I was still a girl at school
> they closed the houses where I spent my days
> reading Baudelaire and Mallarmé . . .
> Where are they gone, the *maisons closes*
> where I passed such sweet days?

It was no accident that the prime instigator of the reform was Marthe Richard, councillor and also heroine of two world wars. How easy it was to see her as representing the true spirit of France, thrusting aside the corruption of the past and preparing the nation for the great new age that was about to commence! Under the laws which ever after were linked with her name, the prostitute was liberated as France herself had been liberated. Prostitution was not a criminal act, as it was in the United States; and though prostitutes continued—until 1960 when the United Nations condemned any kind of discrimination of the prostitute—to carry a card, it was a health card rather than a police card and steps were taken to ensure that all was confidential.

It seemed a great victory for those who had always maintained that the brothel was an archaic institution unworthy of a modern civilised nation. Unfortunately, within a few years, the number of prostitutes in France doubled, particularly in the amateur sector. Syphilis was rampant; 40 per cent of clandestine prostitutes were found to have VD compared with 1.5 per cent of brothel girls under the old régime. Moreover—no trivial consideration to the purse-conscious French—the clandestine prostitute could not be taxed since officially she did not exist.

Apart from closing the brothels, the Marthe Richard laws did not greatly change the prostitution scene. The same type of girl continued to

Prostitutes in a doorway in the rue St Denis, Paris

do the same kind of thing; now she was forbidden to loiter in the streets, but soon she had learnt to use the brightly illuminated entrance halls of hotels and apartment houses as a shop window for her wares. The typical French street girl of today is young and elegant, honest and clean, and thoroughly professional. A simple *passe* costs about 50 francs, with an additional 10 francs if she undresses completely, and other supplementary charges for additional services. In the sophisticated districts of Paris there are girls who could step out of the pages of *Vogue*; they charge upwards of 150 francs for a brief encounter, but the service will be professional, skilful and thoughtful.

Though the old-style brothel is dead, the new-style *clandé*, or clandestine brothel, has taken its place. It comprises a group of girls, supervised by a madame who makes the arrangements, and operates from an apartment for as long as they can avoid arousing the attentions of neighbours or the law; when that happens, as in the end it inevitably does, they pack their tents and silently steal away to a new address. In such a situation there can be no publicity; customers hear of it by word of mouth, and must be carefully vetted before being admitted. The costs are high—say, 500 francs for an hour with a girl—but she will be attractive, educated, good at her job, and the atmosphere will be friendly and discreet.

From the *bucolique*, who waits at bends of the road in the Bois de Boulogne to console the executive as he drives to or from his office, to the *marquise*, who offers more sophisticated delights amid the perfumed elegance of her Champs-Elysées apartment, the prostitutes of France have evidently found ways to fill the vacuum which Marthe Richard's well-intentioned reforms created. But beneath the surface the present system—or rather, the lack of it—is open to all kinds of abuse. Jacques Genthial, chief of France's Central Bureau for the Suppression of Traffic in Human Beings, declared his knowledge of at least fifty gangs operating in Western Europe, blackmailing girls or coercing them by providing/withholding drugs, allowing them a basic living wage and taking the rest of their very substantial earnings. The recruits are drawn from the amateur and clandestine prostitutes who, thanks to the new laws, are now so very much more vulnerable. In 1973 Marthe Richard herself admitted:

> I closed the brothels a quarter of a century ago, but I have reflected on the subject since then and today I would not be opposed to re-opening them, though only on the understanding that women were not slaves in them.

Remembering Maupassant's Maison Tellier, one feels it should not be impossible to permit brothels to operate while hedging them round with legislation to safeguard the interests of those who work in them. But among those opposed to a return to the state-recognised brothel are many of France's 300,000 prostitutes. Of all the great nations, France is supremely the home of the small trader, and most of her prostitutes want to retain their independence. The brothel would threaten their livelihood, they believe, as the supermarket threatens the street trader or the corner grocer. What the French prostitute wants is recognition as a responsible member of society, with a minimum of interference from the state.

Unfortunately the French state is uncertain how much it ought to interfere with the prostitute, blowing now hot, now cold, with unpredictable force. In the spring of 1975, for reasons still not completely explained, the police authorities of Lyons, using their discretionary powers, started so violent a campaign of harassing the city's prostitutes that the girls took sanctuary in the church of St Nizier; there, for more than a week, 200 prostitutes of Lyons, joined by sympathisers from other parts of France, staged a sit-in. 'It's the only place where the police can't touch us,' declared a girl called Carole, who revealed that her usual beat was the rue de Brest. Her faith was unfounded. The demonstration caused a national scandal; the girls' action was called blasphemous, while their defendants referred tellingly to Jesus of Nazareth. In Paris 5,000 prostitutes delivered a petition to the newspaper *Paris-Soir*, but the Lyons police, assisted by dogs, invaded the church and, with all the brutality of which police in France are capable, threw the girls back into the streets. Since then the controversy has continued to flow this way and that. The president, having regard to his public image, has promised to concern himself with the prostitute's case. The girls, no less concerned with their own image, have promised to conduct themselves in a more *sérieux* manner in future.

The brothels meanwhile remain closed:

> Now on the boulevard I meet the girls
> who worked there formerly.
> Now they are working on their own,
> their smiles are sad to see.
> I invite them for a drink
> at the corner café—
> they tell me their sorrows,
> the good days are so far away . . .
> (*Nos Chères Maisons*, sung by Juliette Greco)

For a top singer to record a sentimental lament for the brothels of yesteryear is not easy to imagine in Britain. But though public attitudes are apt to be either blinkered or hypocritical, and official positions two-faced, in practice the British have generally achieved a working arrangement between the prostitute and society which has largely avoided scandal and offence while giving the girls a kind of rough justice. Few would claim that the system is a good one, but most would concede that it works tolerably well.

The state of affairs during the years immediately following World War II was what it had been throughout the early part of the century. Prostitution as such was not illegal, nor was soliciting for custom; but any kind of disorderly, riotous or indecent behaviour was punishable. This gave the police a good deal of room to manoeuvre, and in practice—since virtually any prostitute when making contact with a customer could be described as behaving indecently—any prostitute could be arrested at any time. So what happened was that the police would bring in the girls in a more or less random order and charge them; they would plead guilty and pay a fine of between £2 and £5. It was a stupid arrangement and a waste of time—for the girls, the police, the magistrate—but it had the merit of preserving a measure of control. The girls themselves did not particularly resent it. They got to know the police on their beat and were not surprised to be told 'It's your turn tonight, Rosie'; once a week or once a month they would pay their fine as if it were an arbitrarily imposed tax. As one girl observed to a research worker, 'After all, they're only doing their duty.'

An anonymous researcher who, in the early 1950s, spoke to a number of London prostitutes found that Mayfair women—at that period charging £3 for a short time—were:

> . . .usually charming and sympathetic women, who dress well and reasonably tastefully; they have rooms, usually separate from their own homes, to which they take their customers, who are generally men of the upper and professional classes.
>
> (*Women of the Streets*)

In Soho, London's night-life area, she found the girls less elegant, more businesslike. They charged £1-£2; some had rooms, expensive but tasteless, while others used the walls of alleys. Around the main-line railway stations were girls who said they wouldn't go for less than ten shillings, but probably would; in the parks were those who would go with you into the bushes for ten shillings, or five if they used their hands only, and in the dock areas were women who would sleep with a man for the price of a bed. Most English prostitutes seemed to expect no more than a reasonable living. The author of *Women of the Streets* concluded:

> The economic side of prostitution is not the cause of any woman's becoming a prostitute, but there is no doubt that it is an important factor in influencing her behaviour, and might be classed as a 'precipitating' factor. I often heard stories of how a girl's first night as a professional prostitute came about, and always it was the opportunity to earn good money which tempted her to put her behaviour on a professional basis, and always it was the economics of the situation which confirmed her prostitution. Jenny made £14 on her first night 'and me only seventeen', and so it is with many

> women; however frightened they are at first, or however conscious of the critical glances of the 'nice ladies out walking with their dogs', they find that the financial rewards of the life cannot easily be given up.

The British, like the French, were looking for a brave new world after World War II, but they went about it in a less emotional, more practical way. In 1954 Parliament appointed the Wolfenden Committee to study the question of prostitution. The Street Offences Act of 1959, based on the committee's findings, represented as significant a change of heart for the phlegmatic British as Marthe Richard's law had for the excitable French. Under the new Act, soliciting and loitering for the purpose of prostitution were made punishable; for those aspects of prostitution which had always been illegal, such as procuring, managing a brothel, or living off the immoral earnings of a woman, the penalties were increased. Prostitution itself remained legal.

The immediate consequence was that the prostitute had to keep off the streets. Though this was deplored by those who saw the advantage of having the girls where the police could keep an eye on them, most people welcomed the change. The man in the street was no longer pestered; now, if he wanted sex, he had to go and look for it.

So far, so good. Less beneficial was the opportunity now created for greater exploitation of the prostitute. Operating clandestinely, from discreetly advertised apartments, the prostitute was vulnerable as never before to the greed of gangsters, blackmailers, extortionate landlords and other predators. It became all the more necessary to obtain the backing of a pimp or the protection of an organisation. Among experienced prostitutes, the dangers of exploitation are diminishing; if a professional girl chooses to attach herself to a pimp, that's her business, and she is unlikely to be forced to act against her will. But with younger or less experienced girls, particularly if they have made themselves additionally vulnerable by drug addiction or financial debt, it is a different matter. There is no doubt that what amounts to sex slavery, though it constitutes only a tiny part of the scene, does exist in spite of legal safeguards. Agents haunt the London termini for young girls arriving from other parts of the country, and offer them hospitality, sometimes posing as welfare officers. Then, after gaining their confidence over a week or two, they pass the girls over to pimps who proceed virtually to enslave them, forcing them to work for a bare subsistence wage while appropriating the greater part of their earnings. An anonymous investigator told the magazine *Time Out* in 1975:

> I know of one girl who has been a prostitute since she was twelve. This girl has tried to get out but each time she was beaten up. When she signed an affidavit alleging that she had been forced into prostitution, the pimps found out and slashed her all over her body with a razor blade.

These girls work in the seedier areas of big cities, not only in the evenings but doing a busy lunchtime trade with businessmen. They charge from £4 for a short time in the back of a car or in a shabby neighbourhood hotel; they are likely to keep 40p from each trick, the rest going to their pimp. Even more pathetic are the 'battery girls' of whom there are said to be hundreds in the Whitechapel neighbourhood of London's East End; drug addicts, they allow themselves to be prostituted as often as their managers require, simply in return for their drug supplies.

Like the French, the British are well aware that the present state of affairs leaves much to be desired. Their makeshift solution is patently not a final one and, though in general most European nations have followed Britain's lead, a few are seeking more positive solutions. Ironically, however, the prevailing permissive climate of thought is not in every way the one most favourable to finding a solution. For a paradox emerges: permissiveness is by no means the same thing as freedom from regulation. When a government takes steps to regulate prostitutes, its very action implies a recognition that they exist—and, by inference, that they have a right to exist. It was this paradox which so bedevilled the efforts of Josephine Butler and her fellow reformers, which has confused the thinking of sociologists everywhere, and which has resulted in such a divergence of practice between one European nation and its next-door neighbour, to say nothing of countries farther apart.

The dilemma has manifested itself in a bewildering variety of behaviour patterns, some of them distasteful to many people. The proliferation of porn shops, strip shows, sex cinemas and other such establishments has been accompanied by a growing freedom in what can be written on the printed page or shown on the cinema or television screen. This has caused considerable alarm among reactionaries, notably in Britain where the well-intentioned but sometimes ludicrous investigations of the Longford Commission highlighted the unreality of allowing one section of society to impose on another its own threshold of unshockability.

If the prostitute is winning through to a new and more respectable social status, it is certainly no thanks to the purveyors of pornography or the managers of blue cinemas. The correlation between those who welcome the appearance of nudity on the television screen or find it offensive, with those who take an enlightened or a reactionary view of the prostitution problem, is far from clear-cut. Fortunately, those who lump all sexual matters together, though vociferous, are a diminishing minority; in general, the growing freedom from sexual taboos is creating a state of mind in which the problems of prostitution can be seen in sociological and psychólogical terms, and their solutions sought in a climate of enlightened concern.

It will surprise nobody to discover that enlightenment tends to increase as one travels northwards through Europe. But, ironically, the Scandinavian nations exhibit today's confusion at its most puzzling. Renowned for their permissiveness in matters of sex, the Swedes and Danes—having cast themselves in the role of pacemakers—are finding it anything but easy to hit on a workable formula; in 1965 the *Dansk Kvinde Samfund*, a Danish feminist organisation, were actually requesting official re-opening of the brothels, under state protection!

Their German neighbours seem more sure of themselves. Regulation was abolished back in 1927, but has reappeared during the last few years in a form which could indicate the shape of things to come—a technical breakthrough in prostitution to match the invention of the autobahn. The Eros Centres of Hamburg and Düsseldorf seem to many people, however, only too characteristic of the nation which gave the world Fritz Lang's *Metropolis*. The Hamburg establishment—built with municipal approval though privately funded, at an estimated 2 million DM—is four floors high, with accommodation for 136 medically supervised girls who work as independent tenants. They meet their clients in a ground-level courtyard and take them up to their clean, neat, characterless rooms, where they service them for a standard 50DM—some £12. Though expressively described as 'a petrol station in reverse', the aseptic character of the Eros Centre does not seem to inhibit trade; even at a very high rental, there is keen competition among girls to obtain a room—so much so, that a girl needs influence, or an influential pimp, to get her into this establishment whose *raison d'être* is in part to free her from the necessity of a pimp or protector.

Düsseldorf has a comparable establishment, with 180 girls paying 40DM daily rent and said to average nightly earnings of 250DM; Bonn, Cologne and Stuttgart have similar facilities, and Munich, after banning brothels as recently as 1973, was so appalled at the resulting chaos that only a year later it decided to open a municipal brothel on the grounds, as the mayor expressed it, that 'We cannot wipe out prostitution, so we have decided to control it'. Devoid of charm and character, the Eros

Along the canals of Amsterdam, the girls sit in their windows waiting for custom

Centres are characteristic of their age—as convenient as supermarkets and as unlovable.

On balance, it would seem that the Dutch come closest to an approach which successfully balances practicality with humanity. Here, prostitution and brothels are legal, but both are subjected to strict safeguards aimed at protecting society on the one hand, the prostitute on the other. The brothel quarter of Amsterdam is surely the most picturesque red-light district in Europe. Girls sit in the windows of neat little rooms—generally two or three share a room on a shift basis—and, so long as there is no active soliciting and no indecency, there is no official interference. Rates are modest—between £5 and £10; the girls are healthy and as contented as any are likely to be in this line of business. A Dutch Salvation Army worker is quoted as saying:

> All Dutch girls, whether they are prostitutes or not, like to stay at home. Here, a prostitute knows where she stands. She likes to visit her family, and to run her life in her own way. If she has a boy-friend, he is more of a housekeeper than a business manager, doing her shopping, cleaning her flat, and getting the sack if he is unsatisfactory; the financial side of the business stays firmly in her own hands.

The brothel girls of Holland's big cities are complemented by apartment girls in smaller towns, and by an extensive call-girl system which includes a number of housewives, part-timers and downright amateurs. But while, even in Holland, prostitution has its seamy side, the general scene today is one of honest acceptance of realities and efficient organisation—just as it was in the eighteenth century when Bernard Mandeville praised the city fathers of Amsterdam for their good sense and discretion.

# 13
# *OUT OF IMPOVERISHMENT*

Polly Adler, the New York madam who knew more about the prostitute than the sociologists will ever know, describes in *A House is Not a Home* what motivates a girl to enter the profession:

> In my opinion the greatest single factor is poverty. It is true that, though many girls are poor, only a small percentage take to hustling. But there is more than one kind of poverty—there is emotional poverty and intellectual poverty and poverty of spirit. As well as material lacks, there can be a lack of love, a lack of education, a lack of hope. And out of such impoverishment the prostitute is bred.
>
> When a 15-year-old girl looks around her with the new awareness of adolescence and sees only poverty and ugliness, the groundwork is laid. She doesn't want to wind up like her mother, wornout from too much child-bearing, slopping around in an old ragged dress, beaten by a drunken stupid husband every Saturday night. She wants a chance at the kind of life she's seen in the movies . . . Then one day she meets a guy with a new convertible and a snap-brim hat and a fast, easy line. He tells her she's beautiful, and he can see she's got too many brains to stay in this little tank town, and how would she like to take a trip? So why not?
>
> He has told her he's a salesman, but she finds that his line is selling underwear and junk jewelry to girls who work in joints. When she's gotten used to that idea, she meets some of the girls and the madams, and it seems he's kind of in love with one of the girls in one joint. When she questions him, he tells her she's helping him get the money together to buy a shop. Soon she understands that he would love her more if she helped him too. He takes her to the madam and she goes to work. She stays there all week, and at the end of the week he comes and collects the money she's made. She gets a card, which she wears fastened inside her working dress (with a zipper down the front, easy to get out of, which is important since no man can

spend more than fifteen minutes with her according to house rules), and every time she takes a customer, she holds out her card so it can be punched. When it looks like a lace curtain, she's made her quota. At first she's a little offended that the men don't even take off their shoes, but pretty soon she stops noticing those things. She makes about £150 a week, at £2 a customer. She's glad when her period intervenes to keep her from working, and she can spend the time with her sweetheart. Only, after a while, he tells her he knows a way she can work that week, too. When she cries, he tells her to forget about it. But she learns that Dolores does it, so she agrees to work the full month, and then he loves her again. When they're raided and she's thrown in jail, he gets her out. When she has to move on because they're tired of her in that house, he gets her in another. When she gets pregnant, he pays the doctor who takes care of her. She can't do without him.

But one day she rebels. She screams and yells because suddenly she's gotten a vision of how it really is and what's really happening to her. He quiets her down with a needle. And then for the first time since she was a kid (now she's seventeen) she's happy. The time goes by and she almost forgets that there's any other way of living, and when she remembers, there's always the needle. But now he says she's got to work harder. On the dope, she costs him more, and he withholds the dose, tells her she's an old bag, that he can't sell her in the houses any more, and she can get out and walk the pavements for the money to pay for her stuff. So she hits the small hotels, the beer gardens, the street corners, learns how to stand in the shadows so the men won't see her too clearly. After a while she can't kid herself any more, she knows she's sick. One day she walks up a dirty stairway to the doctor's office, afraid all the time that her sweetheart will find out she's spending the money on this, or that the doctor will say she has something that will keep her from working. And the doctor does say that. He tells her she must have an operation or she'll die, and she says it's got to be some other way—she can't take the time. Only there's no other way.

She's almost calm when she stumbles down the wooden stairs. Now she doesn't have to worry any more because tomorrow (and she knows when she's charged it'll be easy to go through with it) she's going to step into the East River. She likes the idea of death by water. There won't be any blood or noise or pain, and the river will feel cool and it will be dark and solemn as death should be. But first there is tonight, and maybe tonight he'll be nice to her.

While Polly Adler's devastating picture of the prostitute's life relates specifically to the American scene it is important both for what it has in common with experience elsewhere and for its equally significant differences. The fundamental difference is that prostitution is illegal in all but one of the United States. Except for a few, all the call-girls, brothel girls, streetwalkers and hookers of America—there are somewhere between 250,000 and 500,000 of them—are working illegally. It is a ridiculous situation, and one which a great many Americans would like to change. As things are, the police and the authorities have to choose whether to actively implement the law or look the other way; in either case, substantial sums of bribe and protection money find their way into policemen's and other officials' pockets. Sordid and ignominious devices are used to entrap prostitutes; the police justify the use of decoys as the only sure way to secure evidence. And, like all other illegal trades in America, prostitution is largely in the hands of organised crime.

To understand why this situation is allowed to persist, one must first understand the Americans—and who can claim to do that? They are at once the most permissive and the most puritanical of peoples. The most explicit sex movies can be seen by anyone who can pass for an adult; yet, in 1975, a hundred-year-old engraving of Livingstone's explorations was banned from an educational textbook because it depicted native African women with bare breasts. Paradox pervades every aspect of the American's approach to sex:

> In sex-obsessed America, sex is still hard to get. Why are call girls getting $50 to $150 for one visit? If men have enough, why the hunger for pornography? If sated, why the boom in X-rated movies? If wives and girls give fellatio readily, why the excitement over *Deep Throat*? If sex is adequate, why is there such a demand for the infected prostitutes of the Times Squares of most cities? If men are still not hungering, why do the millions of married men, who have it available any night, go to Las Vegas and pay $50 to $100 for one episode? Why do some pay $1,000 for a showgirl? Why, at another level, is there so much rape?
>
> (Gabriel R. Vogliotti, *The Girls of Nevada*, 1975)

The closest thing to solid ground in the history of American sexography was provided between 1948 and 1957 by a team led by Dr Alfred Kinsey, who appropriately occupied the chair of zoology at Indiana University. Those researchers would be the first to admit that in so controversial a field there are many factors which defy the yardstick and the slide-rule; but, within their limitations, the Kinsey findings give the most trustworthy available account of the sexual behaviour of modern America.

To most readers, the Kinsey revelation that sexual activity in America was greater both in quantity and quality than had been hitherto suspected came as something of a cultural shock. Paradoxically, it was found that though the prostitute is a dominant symbol of sex, she plays a smaller part in actual sexual life than is generally supposed. Perhaps the most impressive single finding was that some 69 per cent of white American males had at one time or another had experience with prostitutes; but against this must be set the fact that the 'one time only' customer is no rarity, and fewer than one in five had sexual relations with prostitutes more frequently than 'a few times a year'. Of all sexual activity, less than 4 per cent was with prostitutes.

Kinsey's facts help to put Polly Adler's vivid account into perspective, but one further element must be taken into account if we are to answer Gabriel Vogliotti's rhetorical questions: what does the customer want from the prostitute? Murtagh and Harris, in *Cast the First Stone* (1958)—the most intelligent study of American prostitution to date—recognise what perceptive madams and prostitutes have known for years: that, except at the lowest level, the prostitute is providing much more than just a physical body to meet a physical need. They quote a sixty-two-year-old respectably married man:

> Why is it that a prostitute can make me feel like a man, while my own wife can't? Sometimes after I go with a woman, I look at myself and say, Martin, are you really the man your family thinks is so great? You're not great, you're disgusting. And yet those girls make me feel good while I am with them. I forget everything else. It's like a dream. I watch TV and I see myself being a wonderful lover to a beautiful young girl. So I go out and pick up a prostitute. A fine end to my beautiful dream! I never met any prostitute yet who was the kind of girl men dream about. But they do give me the illusion I'm young again—for a little while.
>
> (*Cast the First Stone*)

For the younger customer, going with a prostitute offers a different kind of experience, no less illusory but no less important to him. The same investigators quote a youthful client:

> What do you mean, what do I want with prostitutes? What do you think I am, a pansy or something? I'm a fellow who's got to have girls.

Both these customers could in theory have been satisfied without having to patronise professional prostitutes, but even in today's permissive climate circumstances are not always favourable. The old man might not have been attractive enough to find willing partners; girls of his own age might not have satisfied the youthful hero's need for self-projection.

Young and old continue to need the prostitute. How, despite the law, are their needs being met in contemporary America?

The clean-up associated with World War II just about finished off the brothel as previous decades had known it. The lament of one madam—'New York has the name but not the game'—could be echoed across the continent; recently a former Seattle brothel proprietor told an interviewer, 'Just before World War II there were more than a hundred houses here. Now I doubt there's one.'

Brothels do continue to exist, but they are not to be found except by those who know where to ask, and even then they may no longer be where they were last reported. For today's brothel operates in the knowledge that, protected or not, it will sooner or later be busted—the fines are built into its overheads. It operates in apartment houses, discreetly and quietly so as not to alert the neighbours. Its furniture is basic, for no proprietor wants to invest in expensive décor that may have to be abandoned at the warning ring of a telephone. The staff is liable to consist of no more than the proprietor, a maid, and three or four girls.

Xaviera Hollander—whose endearing book *The Happy Hooker* (1972) must have done more to improve the image of her profession than any sophisticated public relations campaign could have done—makes out a strong case for the brothel:

> If my business could be made legal, the way off-track betting is, I and women like me could make a big contribution to what Mayor Lindsay calls 'Fun City', and the city and state could derive the money in taxes and licensing fees that I pay off to crooked cops and political figures. Since the beginning of time no government has ever stopped prostitution, because men want it. The proof of this is that my best clients represent the highest echelon of government and business circles and keep me in business no matter how often I am harassed by the police and have to change addresses.

Well-groomed and wearing no make-up, she kept what was by any account a high-class, well-run establishment, where the girls were not permitted to wear 'flashy, whorish clothes' and were expected to put themselves out to satisfy their clients:

> A prostitute is a girl who knows how to give as well as take. She knows how to make a man feel good even if he is under-endowed, a lousy lover, four feet tall, and has a face only a mother could love. In that case, she should fake it and let him enjoy what he pays for.

Xaviera Hollander reckoned to lose 20 per cent of her potential take from debts which she could not recover because a brothel has no legal standing. At police raids, which occurred at least once a year despite the $1,000 plus that went every month in pay-offs to the police, she and her girls were fined; then came the cost of re-furnishing the new place, re-connecting the telephone. Clothes, laundry, servants and secretaries, drink, equipment for flagellation and other specialities, all had to be paid for along with the services of landlords, porters, lift operators, druggists and lawyers. Although she still managed to make a good living, it is hard not to sympathise with her when she writes:

> The coarse, thieving, aggressive street hookers are something else, I realise, but those of us who stay home quietly and merely take calls without soliciting on the street or in hotels should be allowed, even *encouraged*, to carry on our business in the delicate, hygienic, genteel manner in which I conduct mine.

Each of the fifty American states may decide for itself whether to permit prostitution. In 1978, forty-nine states said 'No'; one only, Nevada, said 'Yes'. And even in Nevada it's a very guarded 'yes'; in effect the buck is passed to the individual counties, who are at liberty to decide whether or not prostitutes constitute a 'nuisance' in their area. In Storey County the authorities have decided that a brothel need not be considered a nuisance until it has actually caused offence to other citizens; brothels may operate within the law provided they behave.

Nevada has a tradition of pragmatism with regard to prostitution, largely owing to the miners who constituted the most influential element in its population during the early years. Few restrictions were imposed; one of the few was that no brothel should operate within 300 yards of a church or schoolhouse. There is a story which has become part of American folklore: when it was pointed out to the inhabitants of Beatty, Nevada, that they had a brothel operating within the proscribed distance of the schoolhouse, they hastened to comply with the law—the schoolhouse was duly moved.

There are a good many brothels operating in Storey County, all hoping to catch their share of the tourist trade from Las Vegas and Reno where prostitution is still not legal. Probably the best-known brothel operating in contemporary America is Joe and Sally Conforte's Mustang Bridge Ranch, eight miles outside Reno on Route 80. The establishment was merely tolerated, on pain of good behaviour, until 1970, when the

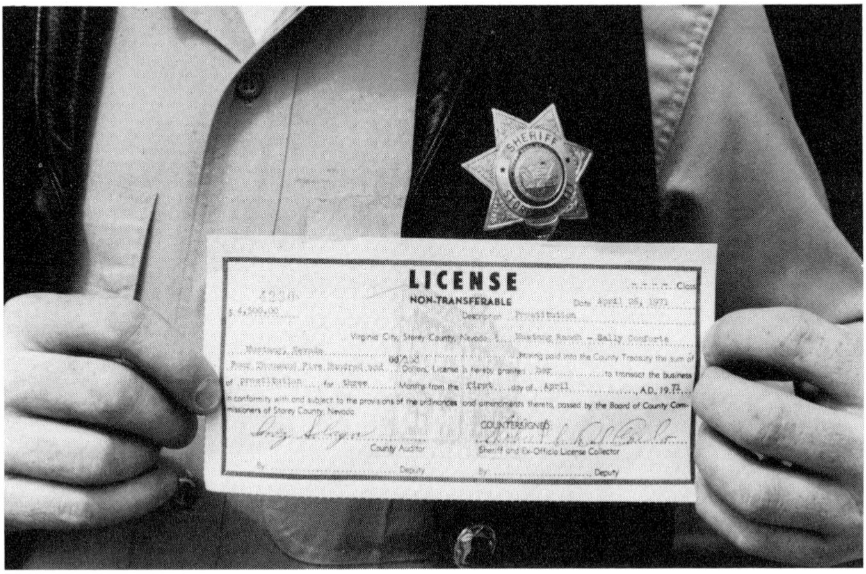


The licence for the Mustang Bridge Ranch, Nevada, America's only legitimate brothel

county agreed to grant an official licence—at a cost of $4,500 quarterly. The Confortes have about thirty girls working at any one time; each makes between $300 and $600 a week, of which nearly half goes to the management. Working conditions are excellent; the girls are allowed time off, and receive medical attention. The food too is said to be first class.

From the customer's point of view, the Mustang Bridge Ranch is hardly in 'the great tradition' of the brothel. It is clean and safe—but unimaginative. What is on sale is sex, with a minimum of trimmings. Charges start at $10, which is modest enough by any standards; even if a customer takes on two girls at once and asks to see a blue movie show first, it will set him back only $40. Yet many clients would probably prefer something a little less perfunctory than, immediately on arrival, to be shown into a room furnished no more attractively than a motel and confronted with a row of girls in bikinis. This is sex in the spirit of pioneer America, none of your fancy folderols from way back east.

However, these limitations aside, it is evident that Conforte and Hollander in their respective ways provide something a good deal better than the low cribs that typified the traditional American whorehouse at its worst—and they are providing what a good many Americans want. But at the same time a large proportion of people in the United States continue not to want brothels in any shape or form, nor do they want others to be allowed to have them. The brothel issue divides even those who believe that prostitution itself should not be a criminal offence. The champions of Women's Liberation, in particular, see the brothel as the most blatant symbol of man's exploitation of woman, even though the madam and all her staff happen to be women—and despite the persuasive argument that nowhere more than in a brothel is man exploited by women!

In 1971 a bill was brought before the California Assembly to legalise prostitution and bring it under some measure of control. Prostitutes were to be licensed ($100 annually) and also brothels ($4,000), the licences being revocable in case of disease or misconduct. Additional clauses protected the individual prostitute against exploitation by brothel proprietors. Despite its sensible and humane intent, the bill was not passed, and it is significant that opposition came not only from the traditional opponents of regulation, who believe that legislation is tantamount to approval, but also from feminists who saw the proposal as

> . . . suggested, written, and adopted by men who have a vested interest in turning prostitution into a legitimate and licensed 'business' that can better serve the needs of male customers.

Girls at the Mustang Bridge Ranch

Not all women are blind to the social benefits of brothels. In January 1975 Mrs Dean Hill, a forty-seven-year-old mother of three sons and herself a Washington Suburban Sanitary Commissioner, urged the county authorities to legalise prostitution and license brothels. Though conceding that her proposal was a political 'hot potato', she argued that it was the most effective way of combating the increase of suburban rape in America. Her proposal was not accepted, but the mere fact that a woman of her social standing could seriously put forward such a suggestion is an indication that Americans are moving towards a realistic discussion of how the problem of the prostitute may be solved.

Does the brothel represent more or less exploitation of women by men? Is a legalised brothel girl more or less independent than an illegal and police-harassed street girl? On these issues not only America but the entire world has been unable to make up its mind. But, if the abstract principles remain a matter for debate, the facts of the matter are undeniable. Joe Conforte is having to turn away girls who want to come and work at his Mustang Bridge Ranch, just as the girls of Hamburg need all the influence they can muster to get a room in the Eros Centre, and just as The Sphinx in Paris used to receive ten letters a week from would-be recruits.

Ladies were massaging gentlemen in ancient Rome, and the association of bathing with sex has been a continually recurring feature in the history of prostitution. So the recent proliferation of sex establishments masquerading as massage parlours is simply a fresh variation on a time-honoured theme. The massage industry is booming, particularly in the United States, because the illegality of prostitution makes it a convenient and attractive loophole. In city streets throughout America a man is liable to have trade cards thrust into his hand inviting him to patronise The Garden of Pleasure (Additional Feature: Knicks and Ranger Games on Closed Circuit TV); The Regency ('Beautiful Models for Private Sensitivity Session'); Relaxation Plus ('My Tender Touch guaranteed not to put you to sleep'), or Tahitia Spa ('The incredible Pleasure Island that begins where all the others leave off, where your most erotic daydreams become a reality . . . the most beautiful, most sensuous, most provocative girls completely and privately at your service. Major credit cards taken').

Though a few massage parlours are 'straight'—providing massage without sex—the majority of those which thrust themselves on the passer-by offer masturbation at the very least (average price $10); a good

Advertisement for a massage parlor, New York, 1976

many offer fellatio ($20), but only a few the full copulatory treatment ($30 to $50). None offers any subtler variations or specialities of the fetish kind, though some cater for homosexuals. The fees are in the form of tips to the individual masseuse, the customer having paid the manager $15 to $25 for the 'straight' services of the establishment. He selects his masseuse from the group of girls sitting in the waiting area and follows her to one of the half-dozen 'private suites'; these are in fact simply cubicles furnished chiefly with a massage couch, and as hygienic and functional as any health inspector could wish. In the room the masseuse asks the customer what he requires; if he wants something extra a tip is agreed. The girl generally strips to the waist; the customer undresses completely—this is obligatory for, ironically, the only way the establishment can convince an inspector that it is operating a genuine massage service is by requiring the client to strip down to a state which is also the most conducive to sexual acts. After a perfunctory massage of the back—few girls are trained masseuses—he turns over and the girl does whatever she has agreed to do.

Massage parlours have obvious attractions for the girls, who can make

$100-$150 a day without having to take more than a limited and not too demanding role unless they choose to do so. For the amateur, which most girls are, it is a relatively clean and not too degrading way of making a good deal of money at little cost beyond an aching wrist and a sense of *déjà vu* at the sight of the hundredth erection of the week. The attraction for the client is the efficiency, the cleanliness, the convenient location and relative security.

The legal position is unequivocal: if the parlours offer sexual services they are operating illegally. But it is next to impossible to prove that they are doing so. In an old-style brothel, if the police burst into a room and found a man with his trousers down and a half-naked girl in attendance, the conclusion was obvious; but in a massage parlour a perfectly innocuous explanation may be the true one—and it is up to the law to prove otherwise if it can. So it would seem that the massage parlour has successfully called the bluff of the die-hard opposition, without causing too much public resentment. James P. Sterba, of the *New York Times*, wrote in 1974:

> They appear to be widely tolerated by the public. Massage parlours that advertise sex blatantly but provide it discreetly seem to generate little of the community outrage that is often aroused by a few streetwalkers on a downtown corner.

Nevertheless the streetwalker—prostitution in its oldest and most traditional guise—continues to be very much part of the American scene despite the patent illegality of her activities. What she does and the way she does it follow time-honoured patterns; surely the street girls of ancient Rome had their own version of a contemporary New York street girl's patter, quoted by Murtagh and Harris:

> Why, it's jus' plain up to you, honey. You gimme five, you gimme ten, twenty, jus' as you like, it's all the same to me. Mind, I ain't sayin' it's all the same for you, honey, 'cause it ain't. You gimme a five spot, I'm just around, you do your own work. You gimme a ten spot, why, I helps you out some. But honey, you gimme twenty, and you don't have to do nothin' but hang on!

This is the open end of the prostitution market, where the customer can appraise the merchandise more objectively, where he doesn't have to commit himself by passing through doors or making an appointment, where he can hope to indulge his private tastes with the least danger of exposure. Murtagh and Harris, in *Cast the First Stone*, cite Marsha Green, a street girl who got herself pregnant and decided to let it ride:

> You wouldn't believe it, would you, but I been making more money than ever since this baby started in showing. Tricks who never gave me a tumble before think I'm something special now. Fools. I can name you plenty of times when I seen them turn down cute young chicks and take me instead.

No profound analysis is required to see that what is operating here is a basic feeling on the customer's part that pregnancy, being 'natural', somehow compensates for the 'wrongness' of going with a prostitute in the first place; going with her in this state is a tribute to femininity—and throws a revealing sidelight on customers' motivations.

Because of the hazards of working the streets, street girls are more likely than other kinds of prostitute to be tied to a pimp. The emotional link between a girl and her pimp is one that has always puzzled investigators, the wisest of whom admit they are baffled by girls who hand over all their earnings to their pimps, freely and gladly, and expect only a tiny fraction back for their living expenses. A girl will do this even though she knows her pimp spends the money on clothes for himself, on his Cadillac, on drinking and eating with his friends, even on other women.

Murtagh and Harris cite Anna, who gave her pimp $300 a week (in 1958) and was allowed $25 for her apartment, food and clothes. The rest—and what he got from his other girls—was for him to spend as he chose. Anna was twenty-two and not unattractive, yet:

> . . . her dearest wish is to earn more—not for herself, but for her pimp. It is a point of pride to earn more for him. And it would be absolutely the same however badly he treated her; and even if she knew that—as he almost certainly does—he has other girls, even may prefer one of them to her. In short, her pimp is her whole reason for living.
>
> How do the pimps do it? How do they manage to keep their stables? Nobody knows the answers; not judges, or police officials, or psychiatrists, or social workers. The mistake they make is to think they know. They talk to a minority of prostitutes who have become so disillusioned with their pimps that they are ready to talk to the authorities, and they accept the stories as the whole of the pimp-prostitute picture, when, in reality, it is the merest part. The result is that official sources tell us that pimps hold their girls through physical force and intimidation . . . It may be true that they

The prostitute and her pimp. Drawing by Heidbrinck, 1880

live in virtual bondage to their men, but the condition is a voluntary one, and its roots must be sought in the prostitute's background as well as in that of the man she keeps.

In 1972 Susan Hall and Bob Adelman did a round-the-year study of a New York negro pimp named Silky; more than any *a priori* analysis, this in-depth documentation gives authentic insight into this puzzling relationship. Here is Sandy speaking, at twenty-seven the oldest as well as the most reflective of Silky's girls:

> A woman's relationship with a pimp must be selfless. Most women are very self-centred. It's hard to care more about someone than yourself. It gives me great pleasure to give myself completely to my man . . . You might think I'd be jealous—me being in love with Silky and him having other women. I'm not. I accept the fact that he's a pimp. That automatically means he has other women. Sometimes it's hard when Silky cops a new girl. I'm proud of him, because he's pimping well, but I'm also a little bit afraid that she'll be nicer or prettier or younger than me and Silky will like her best. But I know that all men are promiscuous. If I were involved with a straight guy, he'd be playing around with other women behind my back. Our relationship would not be honest. With a pimp, you know who he's with and where and when and why. That's why you can have a beautiful and complete understanding.
>
> (*Gentleman of Leisure*)

If we could truly understand it, it may be that in the relationship between a prostitute and her pimp there is the kernel of the love-hate relationship between women and men. It might give us a unique insight not only into prostitutes but into women in general and their attitudes towards men in general, not only into pimps but into men in general and their attitude towards women in general. It could also be that the feminists and women's liberators, before they take it on themselves to speak out so trenchantly on behalf of their entire sex, should find out why Sandy, and Anna, and millions like them, are willing to give up, not just all they earn, but all their love and all their life, to that most universally abhorred of all social parasites, the pimp.

---

If the massage parlour is today's preferred equivalent to the brothel, the call-girl may be a supermarket version of the courtesan; she offers discretion, security, a reasonable level of good taste, a guarantee of health and hygiene. She may be no latter-day Phryne or Ninon de l'Enclos, but she is the sophisticated answer to a sophisticated problem. She meets the needs of the client who, though his basic sexual urge demands the same final solution, wants it packaged in an inoffensive way that does not leave him with an after-taste of self-reproach. If he is a business executive or professional man of some position in society, though sometimes the whim may come over him to consort with a blowsy floozie from the wrong side of the tracks, he is more likely to want what the modern call-girl gives him—an intelligent, entertaining companion, good looking and well-groomed, fun to be with, skilled but discreet in her professional capacity, living in a tasteful apartment in a respectable neighbourhood, avoiding giving offence to her neighbours, drawing attention to herself only by her attractive looks and personality.

When New York analyst Harold Greenwald conducted an investigation in 1958 he found that a typical call-girl could ask $10 for a short time, and often five times that sum. There is probably no other sphere of prostitution in which rates are so apt to vary, for here the prostitute is selling herself, her individual skills and talent and personality, over and above the temporary use of her body. So rates of $100 to $300 and even more are by no means unusual for an all-night session and, if special services are offered—and the majority of call-girls are ready to perform almost any act their clients can dream up—the fees can go a lot higher even than that.

But the call-girl's expenses, too, are high. She has to live well and dress well because that is part of the job. Like the brothel proprietor, she must expect to pay over the odds for every service—from landlords, cab drivers, porters, lift men, lawyers. All these and her pimp too. Though a minority of call-girls—perhaps a growing one—manage to be independent, the majority still choose the bondage of the pimp-prostitute relationship. It is often in the call-girl's best interests to have an influential protector; operating illegally, wholly dependent on being free to serve her clients, she is particularly vulnerable to predators of every kind, as well as to unscrupulous customers.

The call-girl's *modus operandi* is simple. She sits in her apartment waiting for the phone to ring. She seldom touts for business; her clients come to her, usually having been given her telephone number by another customer. She can check their references in her own records—an essential item in her equipment—and decide for herself whether or not she wants to take on the assignment. At the commencement of her career she may operate through a madam or some kind of agent, who will take 40-70 per cent of her earnings; but, once established, she will prefer to make her own contacts and rely on the grapevine among the class of customers with whom she feels most at home—businessmen, salesmen, tourists and so forth.

Most of her work will be performed in clients' apartments or in their hotel rooms. She may sometimes have to use her own apartment, but only reluctantly because it is vital not to offend her neighbours or the management of the building. For the most part she will prefer a larger number of short jobs to fewer long ones, even though the fees for the latter can run high. Long jobs and all-night stays mean harder physical effort, even if a lot of the paid-for time is spent sleeping, and prolonged encounters can involve greater emotional demands if the client tries to deepen the relationship. The call-girl will be skilled in the usual—and perhaps even some unusual—variations; but in general what she prefers is a simple uncomplicated session.

For the successful, intelligent call-girl, the life represents the best that prostitution has to offer. One of Dr Greenwald's interviewees, Diane, told him:

> I'm lazy, and hell, all a man wants is to get into you, so why not make it pay off? Instead of your boss and a lousy £60 a week, get yourself a lot of bosses, work when you want, and sleep till you want to get up.

It may not be every girl's idea of 'the good, the meaningful and fulfilled life', but it suits a good many. It can be argued that, from the customer's point of view or that of the girl herself, this is prostitution in its least offensive, most acceptable form.

# 14
# *MARGERIES AND DILLY BOYS*

In almost every society at every period, homosexuality has been a taboo subject. When that taboo is reinforced by the taboo on prostitution, the result is predictable: the male prostitute becomes just about the least mentionable thing on earth. Yet he has existed throughout history, and often in very great numbers; there is every reason to suppose that homosexuality has existed for as long as heterosexuality, and male prostitution as long as female prostitution.

Havelock Ellis suggested that 2-5 per cent of men have homosexual tendencies, and Kinsey raised the figure to 6 per cent; but other sexologists would argue that such estimates beg the question by assuming a firm division between homosexuality and heterosexuality. So perhaps a more useful starting point is another Kinsey finding: that two out of every five American males had at one time enjoyed homosexual experience to orgasm. This implies that being a homosexual is not at all the same thing as taking part in homosexual practices, and supports the suggestion, made most notably by Wainwright Churchill in *Homosexual Behaviour Among Males* (1967), that there is no such thing as 'being a homosexual'—it would be more accurate to describe a man as being more or less homosexually inclined.

This lends support to the opinion, generally voiced whenever historians and sexologists venture to speak on the subject at all, that male prostitution is, and always has been, hardly less widespread than its heterosexual equivalent. A man willing to sell his sexual companionship has, and always has had, as good a chance as his female opposite number of finding a market; and a male seeking such companionship has had as good a chance of finding what he sought, although his search had to be conducted more discreetly.

This being so, it is somewhat remarkable that any written reference to male prostitution should almost invariably adopt a tone of extreme virulence—to the extent that one is driven to suspect the setting up of a deliberate pretence. *The Yokel's Preceptor*, published at the time of the Great Exhibition of 1851, warned country cousins of the dangers they might encounter in the capital:

> A few words on Margeries, in order to become acquainted with the ways and hiding-places of these brutish beings. In the last few years the number of these brutes in human shape, generally called 'Margeries', 'Pooffs', etc, has increased in the capital to such an extent that for the sake of public safety an exact knowledge of them is necessary. The punishment for their abominable crimes is not nearly severe enough, and so long as the law will not treat them more drastically, there can be no hope of their suppression. The fellows are too well paid (mainly because they are—as is generally known—supported by their rich associates) to care a jot if they have to spend a few months in prison. Why was punishment in the pillory abolished? Would it not be very wholesome for such brutes? They cannot be sufficiently disgraced and humiliated.
>
> The reader must believe that it is a fact that these monsters walk the streets just like feminine prostitutes on the look out for opportunities. The Quadrant, Holborn, Fleet Street and the Strand are full of them. They are recognisable by their effeminate appearance, fashionable clothing etc. When they see anyone whom they think might be a good catch, they put their fingers in a curious way under their coat flap and move them about there; this is their way of offering their services.

One could be forgiven for suspecting the writer of deliberately steering his readers in the margeries' direction, under a protective smokescreen of disapproval. For the most part even the most scurrilous periodicals fought shy of the topic, except when a major scandal hit the headlines, as it did not infrequently throughout the Victorian period. In 1833 a member of the newly reformed parliament, named Bankes, was caught in a urinal adjacent to Westminster Abbey, together with a soldier, both of them having their breeches and braces unbuttoned; an unsavoury court case ensued. Another concerned the conduct of two young men of respectable family, Ernest Boulton and Frederick William Park, who in 1871 were charged with conspiring to commit an unnatural offence. They had a fondness for dressing up indiscriminately as male or female, and this confusion was reflected in almost every aspect of their case. At one stage an unhappy witness deposed: 'I kissed him, she, or it, believing at the time it was a woman.' But, while nobody had much doubt that homo-

Boulton and Park arrested. From *The Day's Doings*, 1870

sexuality was somehow involved, the jury was not convinced that a punishable offence had been committed and found the pair not guilty. Perhaps it was the comic aspects of this sexual confusion which encouraged the popular press to defy the usual taboo and enjoy an uninhibited field day with the story.

The press was more directly concerned in the more serious scandal which erupted in connection with a male brothel at 19 Cleveland Street, London. On 4 July 1889 a theft of a few shillings occurred at the General Post Office; a prime suspect was a telegraph boy named Charles Swinscow, who seemed to have more money in his pocket than a lad of his age could be expected to carry. Innocent of the theft, he could prove it only by revealing the source of the money: he had prostituted himself in the Cleveland Street house for 4 shillings a trick. The brothel was raided forthwith; the proprietor fled the country, others were arraigned and convicted. But it quickly became known that people in very high social positions were also involved, and a radical newspaper, the *North London Press*, accused the establishment of punishing the small fry while enabling more important offenders to escape; among those it named were Lord Arthur Somerset—son of the Duke of Beaufort and assistant equerry to the Prince of Wales—who made his escape to the Continent. It was further reported that one of the male prostitutes had said of the Earl of Euston, 'he went with me on one occasion . . . he is not an actual sodomite, he likes to play with you and then spend on your belly'. The Earl insisted that he visited the house only in hope of seeing some *poses plastiques*—the Victorian equivalent of a strip-show—and sued the editor of the *North London Press* for libel. Not sufficient evidence could be produced against Euston, and it was the editor who went to prison. But it was by no means a complete victory for the establishment; one of the defending lawyers, who had sought to spirit away the boys from Cleveland Street to prevent them giving evidence, also went to prison—though only for six weeks—and Lord Arthur Somerset remained in exile for the remaining thirty-six years of his life.

There were other noted male brothels in Victorian London. One was the house at 13 Little College Street which was to achieve a permanent place in history thanks to one of its most distinguished customers, Oscar Wilde. Another was Mrs Truman's, conveniently close to the Albany Street barracks, near Regent's Park. The soldiery were much inclined to sodomy; Havelock Ellis, writing about 1900, quotes an anonymous informant:

On summer evenings Hyde Park and the neighbourhood of Albert Gate is full of guardsmen and others plying a lively trade, and with little disguise, in uniform or out. In these cases it sometimes only amounts to a chat on a retired seat or a drink at a bar; sometimes recourse is had to a room in some known lodging-house, or to one or two hotels which lend themselves to this kind of business. In any case it means a covetable addition to Tommy Atkins' pocket money.

That a similar situation existed in other countries is the opinion of another of Ellis' informants, named Raffalovich, who claimed that the majority of French soldiers in the nineteenth century were given to homosexuality, largely no doubt because they were so poorly paid, but also partly as a result of lonely service in foreign stations, which gave them tastes that they did not necessarily relinquish when a wider choice again became available. The French General Lamoricière—referring to Marshal Changarnier in a letter which can hardly have been intended for the public eye—wrote: 'In Africa we were all that way inclined, but he stayed one of them.' In the Foreign Legion it was found that the French, the Spaniards and the Italians tended to be the lovers, while the Swiss and Germans were more likely to be the beloved—a distinction which could provide a field day for all who are fond of racial generalisations. In the larger garrison cities, brothels were kept for homosexually inclined soldiers, with a few female maids to give an appearance of 'normality'. In the Austrian army no such concessions were made and recruits were warned against the dangers of homosexual indulgence.

It is a regrettable fact that published accounts of male prostitution are even today based on a minimum of first-hand research and a maximum of unbridled imagination. As recently as 1955 the British Medical Association, in the course of making recommendations regarding the legal status of the homosexual, could speak of the subject in these astonishing terms:

Homosexuals are often charming and friendly people, and many of them are well known to be of artistic temperament . . . [but] effeminate men wearing make-up and using scent are objectionable to everyone.

Apart from the simple untruth of the latter statement, the patronising tone and sweeping generalisation indicate that those responsible for the report—though the BMA is the most prestigious medical authority in Britain, with access to the greatest diversity of documentation and research, and despite the fact that a good many doctors must themselves be homosexuals—either had no first-hand acquaintance with their subject or were too blinkered by prejudice to see it objectively.

Fortunately attitudes are changing with praiseworthy if belated rapidity. Legislation in Britain has removed a substantial part of the injustice from the official treatment of homosexuals, and a fair degree of tolerance has been achieved—even to the extent of seeing avowed male

French homosexual brothel

prostitutes treated sympathetically on television. Prostitution is now permitted between males in most European countries, though age limits vary: twenty-one in France; eighteen in Germany, Denmark and Sweden; sixteen in Italy and a surprising fourteen in Luxembourg. But a great deal of reticence still attaches to the subject with the result that facts are not easily obtained.

Fundamental differences between homosexual and heterosexual prostitution are notable on the sociological level, as well as in the psychological and emotional spheres. The interaction between prostitution and marriage, for example, is necessarily quite different, though the form such difference takes will depend on personal feelings and inclinations. Most heterosexual customers of prostitutes, while they may welcome love or the pretence of it, understanding and sympathy, do not in practice expect them, and are generally ready to settle for no more than the gratification of their physical needs. The homosexual client, on the other hand, is more liable to be seeking a genuine relationship, however fleeting, particularly if he is married or has heterosexual relationships. While there are a few customers of female prostitutes who simply want to sit with them and enjoy their company, the majority expect to experience orgasm—or, if they don't, it's not for want of trying. But the homosexual customer may actually prefer that his temporary companion should be the one, and often the only one, to experience orgasm, the client being content with the companionship and the excitement.

This has consequences which dictate the nature and character of the homosexual prostitution scene. One very evident effect is that certain parts of the world have come to be associated with homosexual activity: Amsterdam among European cities; Morocco and other cities in North Africa; Beirut and elsewhere in the Middle East—places where male prostitution is freely available without the subterfuge and pretence which are still generally imposed by society even where the law itself is tolerant and official attitudes lenient.

Male prostitution exists everywhere, of course. Hardly a city of any consequence lacks clubs or bars where homosexuals congregate and a customer can pick up a prostitute. Some places of rendezvous acquire a certain notoriety: public toilets, for example; underground stations, amusement arcades, specified parts of parks and public buildings also gain a reputation over the years.

Youths in their late teens who, at this stage of their development at any rate, are often more or less bisexual, frequently become prostitutes. They see prostitution as a convenient and not too arduous way of earning additional spending money, enabling them to live well at an age when their earning powers might otherwise be limited. The 'Dilly Boys' who ply their trade in London's Piccadilly area are typical of a category which has its equivalent in every major city in the world. Arriving in London from the provinces, without qualifications and with no sense of purpose or direction, they are out for what they can get; prostitution—at first an economic necessity—becomes a valuable support, sometimes adopted more or less permanently, sometimes only until something more satisfactory comes along.

From the prostitute's viewpoint, homosexual prostitution is not always as satisfactory a way of life as female prostitution can be. There are fewer rules and traditions and established procedures; it doesn't make for a settled, relaxed, easygoing existence such as can be enjoyed by the shrewd call-girl or a prostitute in a well-organised heterosexual brothel. Boys can be picked up in bars and streets easily enough—for anything between 20 and 200 francs in Paris, 20 to 200 guilders in Amsterdam, 30DM in Hamburg, £5-£10 in London—but the typical male prostitute is the equivalent not of the professional female prostitute but of the opportunist bar-girl who hangs round bars and cafés in the hope of a big break, though ready to settle for whatever offers, even if it's only bed and company for the night.

This 'amateur' approach is further expressed in the boys' attitude to the money they earn. They are not career-prostitutes, and the money they make isn't income—it's 'dirty-money', as one put it—money for spending, and spending fast. Indeed, the Dilly Boy is anxious not to be labelled as a homosexual—for, in his view, homosexuals are effeminate and contemptible. The Dilly Boy aims to keep his cool, letting the customer do what he wants, while he himself proves his masculinity by avoiding emotional involvement. It's a confused ethic, not easy for an outsider to understand; here is 'Jamie' trying to explain to a researcher:

> I did not look upon myself as being a homosexual prostitute. I did not understand many of the things that were happening. Boys come to the Dilly, and get mixed up in male prostitution because it is the only thing they know and in which you can earn a quick £5. But you don't see it in the light of being homosexual. You limit yourself in what you do. You do not have the hang-ups of a relationship . . . A lot of the boys who have relationships with homosexuals are really looking for security. You say to yourself that you are not homosexual but that it is just a thing you are doing to survive.
>
> (Mervyn Harris, *The Dilly Boys*, 1973)

The Dilly Boys, like the 'Midnight Cowboys' of New York and their opposite numbers in cities round the world, represent a transient form of a permanent institution. Only some of them are homosexual by nature; only a minority will continue to behave homosexually after they have lost their good looks and can no longer pick up those £5 customers whenever they like. For them, as for many young girls, prostitution is only a temporary solution, a means to a very immediate end—survival.

For the same practical reasons that female brothels have declined in number over the years, there are not many male brothels. In Paris the last house of any repute catering for homosexuals—in the rue du Dragon in St Germain—closed in the 1960s. Others no doubt exist but have to maintain a low profile even today, so that they are known only to those with access to the grapevine. The more usual place of contact is the gay bar or café, where assignations are made for transaction elsewhere. One way or another, the traffic is maintained, for prostitution is no less a necessity to the homosexual client than it is to the heterosexual. So the male streetwalker stands beside his sister on the sidewalk; the male massage parlour is across the street from its female counterpart; and, in gay bars as in straight bars, the boys and girls sit waiting.

Girls on a Berlin street

# *EPILOGUE*

If in spite of all the humiliations, risks, obstacles, atrocious punishments, ostracisms and fears of hell, prostitution has continued unabated up to the present time, it is fair to presume that it will continue to persist in the future. But it will persist not because it always has: it will persist because it satisfies a definite and important biologic need, and answers it in a way that no other present arrangement does.

But while it answers a definite need and is therefore to be considered as a pro-social agency, it is not an unmixed good. It carries some evils in its train, which must be eliminated. And they can be eliminated by an intelligent handling of the problem, and by a proper attention towards the prostitute. The profession of prostitution must be declared perfectly legal and legitimate; nay, it must be judged as an occupation of public utility. If the idea were not so shocking to those who have not freed their minds of the cobwebs of traditional dogma, we would say that it should be placed among the honourable occupations.

(Dr William J. Robinson, speaking to the 1929 Sexual Reform Congress in London)

# BIBLIOGRAPHY

In the course of researching this book I consulted many hundreds of books, magazines, pamphlets and periodicals. The following list includes only those to which I am most particularly indebted.


ACTON, WILLIAM. *Prostitution* (London, 1857; expanded edition 1869). An exemplary study, by a doctor, of prostitution in the nineteenth century, raising many issues of wider significance.

ADLER, POLLY. *A House is Not a Home* (New York, 1953). Reminiscences by a noted American madam, containing much perceptive comment as well as unique first-hand documentation.

ASBURY, HERBERT. *The Barbary Coast* (New York, 1933).

—— *The French Quarter* (New York, 1936). Profusely documented social histories of the underworlds of San Francisco and New Orleans respectively.

BARLAY, STEPHEN. *Sex Slavery* (London, 1968). The modern white slave traffic, somewhat sensationally treated.

BOOTH, CHARLES. *Life and Labour of the People of London* (London 1889-1903). Solid factual documentation based on first-hand reporting.

CHURCHILL, WAINWRIGHT. *Homosexual Behaviour among Males* (London, 1967). A perspective and penetrating study.

COMMITTEE FOR SOCIAL INVESTIGATION AND RESEARCH. *Rescue Work* (London, 1919). An illuminating document, commendably frank for the period.

COMMITTEE OF FIFTEEN. *The Social Evil: with special reference to conditions existing in the city of New York* (New York, 1902). A remarkably balanced and enlightened analysis of the situation then prevailing.

COUSINS, SHEILA. *To Beg I am Ashamed* (London, 1953). An excellent first-hand memoir by an English streetwalker.

DUFOUR. *Histoire de la prostitution* (Paris, *c* 1860). A monumental history of prostitution up to 1860, solid with documentation.

ELLIS, HAVELOCK. *Studies in the Psychology of Sex* (London, 1910). An epoch-making work by a pioneer of sexual reform.

FRAZER, SIR J. G. *The Golden Bough* (London, 1922). A landmark of anthropology, with vital documentation for the origins of prostitution.

GREENWALD, HAROLD. *The Callgirl* (New York, 1958). Valuable first-hand documentation.

HALL, SUSAN, and ADELMAN, BOB. *Gentleman of Leisure* (New York, 1972).

—— *Ladies of the Night* (New York, 1973). Two books based on taped interviews which give unique insight into the way pimps and prostitutes in contemporary New York think about themselves, one another and their work.

HARRIS, MERVYN. *The Dilly Boys* (London, 1973). A valuable study of male prostitution in contemporary London.

HENRIQUES, LOUIS FERNANDO. *Prostitution and Society* (3 vols, London, 1962-8). A definitive study of the sociological aspects of prostitution.

HIRSCHFELD, MAGNUS. *The Sexual History of the World War* (New York, nd, ?*c* 1930). Regrettably, nobody has attempted a similar work for World War II.

HOLLANDER, XAVIERA. *The Happy Hooker* (New York, 1972). A valuable chance to hear what a contemporary prostitute and madam has to say about her profession.

HYDE, HARFORD MONTGOMERY. *The Other Love* (London, 1970) An important study of homosexuality.

KINSEY, POMEROY, MARTIN. *Sexual Behavior in the Human Male* (Philadelphia, 1948).

—— and GEBHARD. *Sexual Behavior in the Human Female* (Philadelphia, 1957). Though limited to the American male and female, the books are basic to any research in the sexual field.

LECKY, W. E. H. *The History of European Morals* (London, 1869). An epic and important work.

LICHT, HANS. *Sexual Life in Ancient Greece* (1932). Not much insight, but invaluable information.

McCABE, JAMES, JNR. *Lights and Shadows of New York Life* (New York, 1872). Trenchant exposure of corruption and hypocrisy.

MANDEVILLE, BERNARD. *A Modern Defence of Publick Stews* (London, 1724). A shrewd and perceptive proposal from the age of enlightenment.

MANKOFF, ALLAN H. *Lusty Europe* (New York, 1975). An informative and entertaining guide to the sex life of Europe with a refreshingly unlubricious approach.

MARCHANT, JAMES. *The Master Problem* (1917). A little on the pompous side, but full of important documentation.

MARCUS, STEVEN. *The Other Victorians* (London, 1966). Sidelights on the Victorian underworld.

MARIE-THÉRÈSE. *Histoire d'une prostituée* (Paris, 1964). First-hand account of a French prostitute's life.

MAYHEW, HENRY. *London Labour and the London Poor* (London, *c* 1860). His fourth volume is largely concerned with prostitutes and contains a mass of magnificent first-hand documentation, unique for its time, unsurpassed even today: a landmark in the history of reportage.

MOORHEAD, ALAN. *The Fatal Impact* (London, 1966). The arrival of Europeans in the Pacific.

MURTAGH, JOHN M. and HARRIS, SARA. *Cast the First Stone* (New York, 1958). The most perceptive, sympathetic and informative study of prostitution in modern America, with much first-hand material set in a broader perspective—most of it still very valid even after two decades of change.

PEARL, CYRIL. *The Girl with the Swansdown Seat* (London, 1955). Informative account of sexual goings-on in Victorian England.

PEARSALL, RONALD. *The Worm in the Bud* (London, 1969). A thoroughly documented history of Victorian sexuality in all its aspects.

PETRIE, GLEN. *A Singular Iniquity* (London, 1971). This book about Josephine Butler is a lot more than that—a perceptive and well-researched contribution to the literature of prostitution.

PLOWDEN, ALISON. *The Case of Eliza Armstrong* (London, 1974).

POLO, MARCO. *Travels.*

RESTIF DE LA BRETONNE. *Nuits de Paris* (Paris, 1788).

SANDFORD, JEREMY. *Prostitutes* (London, 1975). A sympathetic and enlightened study of prostitutes in contemporary Britain.

SANGER, WILLIAM. *A History of Prostitution* (New York, 1858). The classic American history, intelligent if not always very perceptive, and with invaluable period documentation.

TAXIL, LEO. *La corruption fin-de-siècle* (Paris, 1894). Thoroughly untrustworthy account of the Paris underworld, whose very incredibility is a revealing insight into contemporary opinion.

VATSYAYANA. *The Kama Sutra* (trans. Burton and Arbuthnot) (London, 1963).

VOGLIOTTI, GABRIEL R. *The Girls of Nevada* (Secaucus, New Jersey, 1975).

'WALTER'. *My Secret Life* (*c* 1882) (reprinted New York, 1966). Memoirs of a sex addict. Indispensable documentation not only for its period, but for a customer's-eye-view of sex in any period.

# *INDEX*